Praise for *Litanies of the Heart*

"*Litanies of the Heart* provides innovative approaches linking Christian meditation and psychology that will help the broken find comfort, consolation, and healing for their wounds."

— **Matt Fradd**

Creator and host of the *Pints with Aquinas* podcast and author of multiple books, including *Does God Exist? A Socratic Dialogue on the Five Ways of Thomas Aquinas*

"In *Litanies of the Heart,* Dr. Gerry Crete offers us a treasure trove of wisdom and pathways of healing. He provides several books in one: an expert teaching on psychology; a deep reflection on Scripture through the lenses of psychology and Catholic theology; and a compassionate way of discovery, understanding, and healing for our hearts. I was repeatedly moved to tears while I read the poignant stories of suffering that also shone a light on my own heart. I was moved to hope for deeper healing and integration, and I kept thinking of various people with whom I am excited to share this book. It is not a quick read — it is an in-depth exploration, a real journey into our hearts. Dr. Crete is an expert guide for this journey. He has a rich integration of Catholic faith and complex psychological models gained through prayer, study, extensive personal experience, and extensive therapeutic experience. He generously shares that lifelong integration with us in this masterpiece."

— **Fr. Boniface Hicks, O.S.B.**

Monk of Saint Vincent Archabbey and director of Spiritual Formation and the Institute for Ministry Formation at Saint Vincent Seminary; co-author of *Spiritual Direction: A Guide for Sharing the Father's Love*

"*Litanies of the Heart* is an incredible integration of cutting-edge psychotherapeutic approaches with orthodox Catholic theology and practice. I especially enjoyed reading about the different conditions of our wounded and frightened hearts brought into the light of God's merciful love and following that by praying Litanies of the Wounded, Closed, and Fearful Hearts. This book will lead you on a lifelong journey of "re-collection" — gathering all the divided, sinful, and traumatized parts of your heart into wholeness and communion with God. I highly recommend it for everyone who desires to embark on this journey of healing and for those who assist in this journey."

— **Bob Schuchts, Ph.D.**

Founder of the John Paul II Healing Center in Tallahassee, Florida, and author of *Be Healed, Be Transformed, Be Devoted,* and *Be Restored*

"This beautiful book needs to be in the hands of every Christian on a journey of healing and those involved in trauma recovery work! Dr. Crete has written a book that has finally brought needed clarity to the Internal Family Systems model for Christians. As a wounded healer myself, I found that the Litanies of the Heart finally gave parts of me the language to call out to my Beloved Father in gentleness and trust."

—**Shannon Mullen, Ph.D., CSAT-S**
Licensed psychologist, level-2 trained IFS therapist,
and founder of Mosaic Psychological Services

"On a foundation of the Holy Trinity as three-in-one, Dr. Crete walks the reader through the human condition of parts of self at war with each other, in response to adversity or trauma. He guides us through self-state work, enlivened by an ever more intimate relationship with the Most High, to resolve these inner conflicts and to increase loving compassion for self. Why should we settle for merely secular parts work when divinely inspired parts work is so accessible?"

— **Sandra Paulsen, Ph.D.**
Clinical psychologist and author of *When There Are No Words: Repairing Early Trauma and Neglect in the Attachment Period* and *Looking Through the Eyes of Trauma and Dissociation: An Illustrated Guide for EMDR Therapists and Clients*

"St. Paul, St. Augustine, and many other profound spiritual doctors have vividly described the disordered state of the soul, with its parts in conflict. In this fascinating book, Gerry Crete draws from the insights of contemporary parts-work therapy, viewed in the light of Christian Scripture and Tradition, to show how the grace and power of Jesus Christ can bring the healing and wholeness we so desperately need."

— **Paul Thigpen, Ph.D.**
Best-selling author of more than sixty books, including *Manual for Spiritual Warfare*

"There's a powerful movement that's been brewing in the world of Catholic integration with secular psychology. In this book, Gerry emerges on the cutting edge of a profound development in our understanding of the person through the revealed and the observed. I've been waiting for a Catholic perspective on IFS to connect the deep dots, and Gerry does not disappoint. I'll be sharing this with clients and professionals alike for years to come."

— **Greg Bottaro, Psy.D.**
Executive director of the CatholicPsych Institute
and author of *The Mindful Catholic: Finding God One Moment at a Time*

"I wholeheartedly recommend *Litanies of the Heart* to therapists, counselors, and individuals seeking a parts approach, tailored to the Christian community, to healing trauma. Through this book, readers will discover innovative ways to integrate Ego State Therapy and Internal Family Systems concepts within a Christian framework, fostering opportunities for healing and transformation that respects the multiplicity of self. It is a testament to the author's expertise and compassion and undoubtedly a valuable resource for anyone navigating the complex terrain of trauma in the human mind and spirit."

— **Wendy Lemke**
Licensed psychologist and co-founder of Ego State Therapy International

"In *Litanies of the Heart*, Dr. Crete delivers a clear, relatable, and highly useful bridge between clinical approaches to trauma and the Catholic anthropological understanding of the human person. This book provides hope for both souls who have suffered trauma and those who accompany them in their goals of achieving authentic healing. This is a text that I will refer to in my practice for years to come."

— **Mark S. Glafke, Ph.D.**
Clinical psychologist, coordinator of counseling services,
Pontifical North American College, Vatican City

"As I read this book, with the turning of each page, there was a unified internal chorus that gleefully cried out: Triumphant! I was captivated as Dr. Crete wove a beautiful tapestry with Scripture, teachings of saints, and the tools of parts work. I discovered wounded parts of me that yearned for the love and warmth of Christ's sacred healing. This book creates a tangible pathway to unburden pains from the past — a path that will surely change the lives of many, from the inside out. 'Therefore my heart is glad' (Ps. 16:9)."

— **Elizabeth Galanti, M.B.A.**
Licensed mental health counselor and
certified Internal Family Systems therapist

"*Litanies of the Heart* resonates with the heart, mind, and spirit. Gerry Crete writes with a clear, authentic tone, and his words feel present and alive. This book walks the reader through the layers of the human experience in a compassionate, relatable way. It is a must-read for anyone interested in a Christian perspective of healing anxiety and trauma."

— **Deborah Kennard, M.S.**
Founder and EMDR trainer at the Personal Transformation Institute

"If you long for freedom and healing, you must read *Litanies of the Heart*. Dr. Gerry Crete masterfully integrates Internal Family Systems with the Christian faith. This book's combination of powerful storytelling, rich research, and practical advice is surprisingly satisfying."

— **Drew Boa, M.A., P.S.A.P.**
Author of *Redeemed Sexuality* and
founder of HusbandMaterial.com

"I have long awaited a Catholic Faith–integrated IFS book to recommend to clients and fellow clinicians that is neither Catholic-lite nor IFS-lite. It has arrived, and it is edifying for both head and heart!"

— **Peter Martin, Psy.D.**
Licensed psychologist and internship director of Integrated Training and
Formation at Immaculate Heart of Mary Counseling Center in Lincoln, Nebraska

"As both an executive coach and business owner, I find it helpful to coach the whole person, not only the parts of the person that desire growth. The hidden, stubborn, and self-sabotaging parts also need compassion and coaching. *Litanies of the Heart* is a gift to coaches and managers who aspire to coach the whole person as a pathway to human formation and flourishing for the glory of God."

— **Patrick Molyneaux**
Co-owner of Molyneaux Home and co-founder of Human Formation Coalition

"Catholics who long for greater healing and integration of the deepest parts of themselves have much to celebrate in this new work by Dr. Gerry Crete. Grounded powerfully in Scripture and Catholic truths, *Litanies of the Heart* is itself a masterpiece of integrated parts."

— **Lisa Mladinich, PCC**
ICF and Gallup-certified coach and award-winning
author of *True Radiance: Finding Grace in the Second Half of Life*

"*Litanies of the Heart* is brilliant, humble, and grounded. This beautiful weaving together of psychology, Scripture, and Catholic tradition will inspire and minister to your heart, soul, and mind. Professionals and pastoral ministers will find the appendices particularly enriching — they answered all of my questions!"

— **Jennifer Madere**
Licensed professional counselor supervisor, EMDRIA-approved consultant
and trainer, and co-founder of Intuitus Group

"Beautifully integrating Christian Scripture, tradition, and theology with brilliant psychological insights, helpful exercises, and healing prayers, *Litanies of the Heart* will accompany and woo your heart away from pain and suffering toward freedom and joy."

— **Kimberly Miller, M.Th., LMFT**
Author of *Boundaries for Your Soul*

"Gerry Crete provides readers with a fresh and extremely useful guide to understanding stress and anxiety in the context of faith. He not only provides fascinating information about a Catholic approach to Internal Family Systems, but he walks the reader through this powerful process to discover genuine hope and healing on the journey."

— **Greg Popcak, Ph.D.**
Founder and executive director of the Pastoral Solutions Institute
and radio and television host

"If you desire inner harmony and freedom, this book is for you! Dr. Gerry Crete will be your gentle and caring guide on an amazing journey into the heart, in which he will help you grow in self-knowledge, self-leadership, peace, and joy. In this amazing book, Dr. Gerry integrates cutting-edge parts psychology with the riches of the Catholic tradition. Great treasure lies within."

—**Andrew Sodergren, Psy.D.**
Clinical psychologist and director of psychological services at Ruah Woods Institute

"In *Litanies of the Heart,* Dr. Crete marvelously walks us through a process of healing that will untangle our inner world, develop a richer spiritual life, and bring restoration to those who still suffer. He integrates cutting-edge Internal Family System techniques with the heart of the Christian life."

— **Kathryn Wessling, Ph.D.**
Author and founder of the Catholic Story Groups

"I was a skeptic with questions on the compatibility of Internal Family Systems and the Catholic Faith. This book put those questions to rest. Dr. Crete eloquently grounds the work of IFS in a firm Christian anthropology, elevating the nobility of the 'self' to a 'self' with the potential to enter a divine union with God by grace. The ultimate integration Dr. Crete speaks of is one that surpasses the integration of internal parts or personalities to a redeemed reintegration of man through Jesus with himself, his Creator, and the Body of Christ."

— **Matt Ingold**
Co-founder, Metanoia Catholic Coaching

LITANIES OF THE HEART

Gerry Ken Crete, Ph.D.

LITANIES *of the* HEART

Relieving Post-Traumatic Stress and Calming Anxiety through Healing Our Parts

SOPHIA INSTITUTE PRESS
Manchester, New Hampshire

Cover design by Updatefordesign Studio.

On the cover: heart-shaped leaf (1905163813) © Zamurovic Brothers / Shutterstock; background (4593360) © Lifestyle_Graphic / Freepik.

Sophia Institute Press
Box 5284, Manchester, NH 03108
1-800-888-9344
www.SophiaInstitute.com

Sophia Institute Press is a registered trademark of Sophia Institute.

paperback ISBN 979-8-88911-060-6

ebook ISBN 979-8-88911-061-3

Library of Congress Control Number: 2023950283

Fifth printing

To my cloud of witnesses:
St. Michael the Archangel, St. Gabriel the Archangel,
Our Lady Untier of Knots, St. Joseph, St. John the Baptist,
St. John the Beloved Apostle, St. Anthony the Great,
St. John Chrysostom, St. Basil the Great, St. Gregory of Nazianzus,
St. Gregory of Nyssa, St. Mary of Egypt, St. Augustine of Hippo,
St. Benedict of Nursia, St. Gregory the Great,
St. Maximus the Confessor, St. Brendan the Navigator,
St. Dymphna, St. Catherine of Siena, St. Gregory of Palamas,
St. Francis of Assisi, St. Thomas Aquinas, St. Francis de Sales,
St. Ignatius of Loyola, St. Teresa of Ávila, St. John of the Cross,
St. Kateri Tekakwitha, St. Seraphim of Sarov,
St. Marie of the Incarnation, St. Damien of Molokai,
St. Elizabeth of the Trinity, St. John Henry Newman,
Servant of God Dorothy Day, St. Maria Goretti,
St. Teresa of Calcutta, St. John Paul II, Bl. Carlo Acutis

I bless the Lord who gives me counsel;
in the night also *my heart instructs me.*
I keep the Lord always before me;
because he is at my right hand, I shall not be moved.
Therefore, my *heart is glad,* and *my soul rejoices;*
my body also rests secure.
For you do not give me up to Sheol,
or let your faithful one see the Pit.
You show me the path of life.
In your presence there is fullness of joy;
in your right hand are pleasures forevermore.

— Psalm 16:7–11, emphasis mine

CONTENTS

Appendices

DISCLAIMER

This book is not meant to be a replacement for therapy. The information in this book is not meant to offer medical, psychological, or emotional advice or to diagnose or cure any psychological disorder. If you experience psychological or emotional problems, seek the help of a licensed mental health professional (such as a psychiatrist, a licensed psychologist, a professional counselor, a marriage and family therapist, or a clinical social worker).

Each story or vignette in this book is inspired by multiple real-life cases. Each character is a composite, however, and does not represent any one individual. Additionally, names, places, situations, and details have been changed to protect confidentiality.

FOREWORD

"Grace perfects nature," St. Thomas Aquinas tells us, "it does not destroy it." If grace perfects nature, then there must be a human nature to perfect. In other words, human nature is relevant. That's why Pope St. John Paul II, in his apostolic exhortation *Pastores Dabo Vobis*, described human formation as the basis of *all* formation — including spiritual formation, intellectual formation, and pastoral formation.

Gerry Crete understands this reality, the need for solid human formation, more deeply than almost anyone else. And his book is not only an invitation for you to explore deeply your human-formation needs, but it also provides guideposts and trail markers for you to follow to have those legitimate needs met in ordered ways. This is not just a book for your head — this is a book for your heart. Through stories, experiential exercises, and questions for deep reflection, Gerry invites you into your own heart, with a focus on healing and growing.

Why? So you can better love the Lord your God with your *whole* heart, with every part of you, with every fiber of your being, carrying out the two great commandments: to love God fully and to love your neighbor and yourself fully. St. Thomas Aquinas is very clear: you cannot love God or your neighbor if you do not love yourself in an ordered way. Practical guidance on how to love yourself properly has been sorely lacking, especially when trauma and its effects complicate matters. It is such practical guidance that this book addresses so well.

Don't just read this book with your mind. Engage this book with your heart. Experience this book in all your being. Take the exercises in this book to the parts of you that have not yet been seen, heard, known, and understood. Have the courage to go on the adventure this book offers you. If you do, you will "taste and see that the LORD is good" (Ps. 34:8).

— Peter Malinoski, Ph.D.
Clinical psychologist, level-3 trained IFS therapist,
host of the *Interior Integration for Catholics* podcast,
and co-founder and president of Souls and Hearts

ACKNOWLEDGMENTS

First, I want to thank my dear friend and colleague Dr. Peter Malinoski for his tireless dedication to the integration of Internal Family Systems and the Christian faith. Our partnership has been a source of vision, support, mutual challenge, and growth. His impressive work with the Resilient Catholics online community has been a great source of inspiration.

A very special thanks to my dear friends and professional support system, including Dr. Malinoski, Dr. John Cadwallader, Dr. Mark Glafke, Dr. Eric Gudan, Dr. Andrew Sodergren, and Dr. Peter Martin. I am blessed to count them as brothers. I am also very grateful for the invaluable feedback Dr. Martin and Dr. Malinoski provided on this manuscript.

To good friends who have inspired and encouraged me: Matt Fradd, Mac Barron, Danny Ryan, and Ruth O'Neil.

To Fr. John Hibbard of the Diocese of Kingston, Ontario, Canada, for being a mentor and friend during a formative time in my life.

To all my clients who have shared their stories with me and taught me so much about life, love, healing, and growth. I am honored to be a part of your journey.

Special thanks to my children, Ben, Kat, and Abby, and to my sister, Juliette, and my mother, Evelyn, for their unwavering support and encouragement.

Finally, I'm eternally grateful to my wife, Kasey, my soul mate, for believing in me, supporting me, and loving me.

PREFACE

I invite you to join me on an inward journey to discover your spiritual center, which connects you with God and reflects His love and grace. On this journey, we will learn that, with God's grace, we can be relieved of any burdens of shame, fear, and self-hatred, and we will learn how to love ourselves in a healthy, enriching way. We will join with St. Paul in saying, "I delight in the law of God in my inmost self" (Rom. 7:22).

In this book, we will learn how to connect with this inmost self through litanies and meditations that will also help us to experience connection with God in a way that is both safe and intimate. The Israelites understood the experience of pain, suffering, and great loss, and they turned to their God with open hearts, revealing their physical, emotional, and spiritual wounds. Their God — indeed, a loving parent — guided them to safety.

A litany is a form of prayer, usually with a repeating response, in which we give thanks to God or cry out for help. One of the first Judeo-Christian litanies is a song expressing gratitude for the way God loves us, rescues us, and leads us to salvation:

O give thanks to the Lord, for he is good,
  for his steadfast love endures forever.
O give thanks to the God of gods,
  for his steadfast love endures forever.
O give thanks to the Lord of lords,
  for his steadfast love endures forever; . . .

who divided the Red Sea in two,
  for his steadfast love endures forever;
and made Israel pass through the midst of it,
  for his steadfast love endures forever; . . .

It is he who remembered us in our low estate,
  for his steadfast love endures forever;
and rescued us from our foes,
  for his steadfast love endures forever;
he who gives food to all flesh,
  for his steadfast love endures forever.

O give thanks to the God of heaven,
  for his steadfast love endures forever.
(Ps. 136:1–3, 13–14, 23–26)

We also see examples of litanies of lamentation, such as Psalm 13:

How long, O Lord? Will you forget me for ever?
  How long will you hide your face from me?
How long must I bear pain in my soul,
  and have sorrow in my heart all day long?
How long shall my enemy be exalted over me?

Consider and answer me, O Lord my God!
  Give light to my eyes, or I will sleep the sleep of death,
and my enemy will say, "I have prevailed";
  my foes will rejoice because I am shaken.

But I trusted in your steadfast love;
  my heart shall rejoice in your salvation.
I will sing to the Lord,
  because he has dealt bountifully with me.

I realize that, for many people, God can be a frightening topic, and loved ones have not always been loving. We come with spiritual wounds and relational wounds, and as you work through this book, you may have negative reactions to some references to God. It takes time to untangle our negative images of God, based on our human relationships, from the truth of who God is and how He wants to be in relationship with us. But we all benefit from crying out to God in our pain, shame, or fear and letting Him work at a deep heart level to relieve our burdens and calm our anxieties. My prayer is that this book might help you in that untangling and that you might discover a new way of relating to God, if that is what you need.

My life's work as a counselor and therapist has been to help people recover from the difficult and painful experiences of the past. I have focused on how we relieve anxiety and live more fulfilling lives and enjoy more meaningful relationships. In this book, I offer you my knowledge, my insights, and my experience in the hope that you will experience not only relief from anxiety but inner harmony, greater life fulfillment, and a deeper, more intimate relationship with God.

I'm a wounded healer, a person who has experienced trauma and has needed to cry out to God as well. Sometimes those cries are tears filled with sadness, and sometimes they are tears of anger. Sometimes I have cried out in despair, and sometimes I have sung songs of thanksgiving. I recognize that I have many competing feelings, thoughts, desires, and impulses. Parts of me are pious, religious, and compliant. Parts of me are rebellious and self-sabotaging.[1] As you will see in this book, I have parts that want to explore the philosophy, the psychology, and the theology of our interior world. And so I want to journey with you as a fellow trauma survivor[2] as we explore what it means to heal, to grow, and to be transformed.

I recognize that you may be coming to this book with your own concerns, questions, and fears: Will the message of this book challenge my faith? Will

[1] I also like to relate to New Testament characters and associate them with parts of myself. I have within me an unworthy prostitute, a money-focused tax collector, a hypocritical Pharisee, a self-righteous Sadducee, an unclean leper, and a prodigal son. I also have within me an impetuous Peter, a fiery James, and a duplicitous Judas as well as a gentle John, a serving Martha, and a pious Mary. Christ came to heal and redeem all of me, my whole person. Each of my parts calls out to God in struggles, in sufferings, and in insecurities. And God will heal me, remove my burdens, and bring me comfort.

[2] As you continue reading, you will discover that we are all trauma survivors.

the message of this book challenge my understanding of psychology and the human person? Does the author understand just how bad I feel about myself? Does the author understand my level of anxiety?

I want to say yes, I understand. I not only rely on my life experiences, but I draw from my work with thousands of trauma survivors over many years. I know that every situation is unique, and I cannot promise that I would *fully* understand yours. I don't know your situation, but I can say that I have felt deep despair and intense consolation. I have been disconnected from my own body. I have been fiercely protective of my own wounds. I have been out of touch with my needs and my true identity. My own experience includes a deep and painful father wound, and I have resisted knowing and connecting with God while desperately longing for His love. I have sometimes been closed and sometimes fearful. I have been deeply in touch with my woundedness.

In the course of my own healing journey, I have been especially helped through spiritual direction and therapy. My faith in God and my relationship with Jesus have had a profound positive impact on my healing journey. My relationships with caring, loving, forgiving loved ones have also been impactful.

My work — really a lifetime of working with clients struggling with the question of sin and suffering, clients who have experienced the very worst kinds of trauma and betrayal — is a journey. I can't claim to have all the answers as I continue to learn and grow myself. But I can claim to have seen healing, and I can promise to be real and truthful about my experience and understanding.

Perhaps you are asking yourself, "Were my past hurts that bad?" Your trauma, no matter how seemingly small, is significant and worth attention and care. I want to invite you on this journey of self-discovery and healing. It is part of the human condition to experience trauma, and your trauma is just as important as anyone's trauma. We all experience the effects of being disconnected from God and from each other. We all suffer for living in a fallen world. And if you have experienced severe trauma — sexual abuse, military trauma, torture, the loss of a loved one, spiritual abuse, verbal humiliation, neglect, or emotional abandonment — then this book may provide a way to begin the healing process and grow in resilience as you also seek professional and spiritual counseling. I highly recommend that all trauma survivors receive professional counseling and spiritual direction. Although I pray that this book will be a source of growth and healing, we cannot do this alone.[3]

Each chapter in this book provides a brief explanation of the psychology behind parts work, a scriptural tie-in, reflection questions, and a prayerful meditation. You will also find in each chapter a short vignette — a snapshot, really — that speaks from the heart, whether a wounded heart, a closed heart, or a fearful heart. These hearts carry burdens not only of sin but of shame, pain, anger, and deep sadness. These burdens are the byproduct of unresolved trauma in our lives, trauma that causes us to cry out to God: "O Lord, God of my salvation, when, at night, I cry out in your presence, let my prayer come before you; incline your ear to my cry" (Ps. 88:1–2). The litanies of the heart, however, do not go unanswered as we turn to our God. He is our source of grace.

As you read this book, I invite you to notice your reactions. Let yourself be curious and nonjudgmental about your different feelings, whether they are positive or negative. As you work through each chapter, you will learn to bring compassion, curiosity, and calm to your inner world, and this, in turn, will help you form deeper connections with God and others.

I realize that I'm asking a big favor of you. I'm asking the protective parts of you to trust me on this journey. I promise to do my best to be honest, helpful, and nonjudgmental. And I invite you to join me in recovery.

[3] I'd like to remind you that this book is not meant to be a replacement for therapy. If you experience psychological or emotional problems, seek out the help of a licensed mental health professional, such as a psychiatrist, a licensed psychologist, a professional counselor, a marriage and family therapist, or a clinical social worker.

INTRODUCTION

The father of psychoanalysis, Sigmund Freud, popularized the idea of the unconscious mind. Our conscious mind has self-awareness, which includes mental processes, thoughts, feelings, and perceptions. The unconscious mind includes stored memories, feelings, thoughts, automatic skills, and subliminal perceptions. Much of Freudian analysis involved bringing unconscious and repressed material into conscious awareness. Freud conceived of the mind as having three constructs: an id (instincts and drives), an ego (conscious awareness and executive functioning), and a superego (conscience).

Whatever we may think of Freud's theories, he helped us understand the mind as involving complex inner dynamics. The mind is not a monolith but a rich interior world.

I will refer to this complex inner world as "the self-system." The self-system is made up of an inmost self and multiple parts.

The famous psychodynamic psychologist Carl Jung described complexes as "splinter psyches" or "little people." A complex, such as a hero complex, is really a part of the self-system, with emotions, thoughts, memories, and perceptions organized around saving others and gaining personal recognition. Another example, an inferiority complex, is really a part of the self-system burdened with a sense of inadequacy.

Systems theory is a discipline that examines how any group — such as a family, a community, a corporation, or a nation — works together as a system. This approach considers how human groups are made up of independent parts that form a complex whole. Like a factory or a hockey team, all the parts of human systems have interactive functions and roles. Even the Church is a system, as St. Paul says: "Just as the body is one and has many members, and all the members of the body, though many, are one body, so it is with Christ," and then later, "If one member suffers, all suffer together; if one member is honoured, all rejoice together." (1 Cor. 12:12, 26). When one part of the system is struggling in some way, the whole system is affected. When all the parts are working together collaboratively and cooperatively, there is harmony.

From the concept of systems, the psychiatrist Murray Bowen and others developed family systems therapy,[4] in which positive structural changes to the family system were shown to have positive effects on everyone in the family.

Internal Family Systems[5] and Ego State Therapy[6] teach that each person has an *internal* system, much like a family, with many independent "parts" working together in healthy or unhealthy ways. Our individual parts, or subpersonalities, have memories, feelings, beliefs, perspectives, and impulses that are unique to them. There are parts that hold negative beliefs and painful feelings associated with challenging and traumatic life experiences and that remain unintegrated. All the parts are naturally good and valuable, even if we currently experience them in a negative way. A "wounded" part of the self-system, often called an exile, for example, carries a burden from a past trauma.

Repressed memories can be understood as a traumatized part of the self-system holding painful memories and their associated negative feelings. Traumatized parts, exiles, are kept at a distance, perhaps in the unconscious mind, to protect the system from being overwhelmed. An exiled part may be stuck at a child's developmental stage and remains outside conscious awareness. Healing

[4] Family systems theory is a type of psychotherapy that considers the interactions and relational patterns of groups. Key developers of this model include Murray Bowen, Salvador Minuchin, Jay Haley, and Virginia Satir.

[5] Internal Family Systems is a parts-based therapeutic approach developed by Richard Schwartz in the 1980s. He applied a family systems approach to the individual's inner world. Schwartz developed the techniques known as unblending and unburdening.

[6] Ego State Therapy is a parts-based therapeutic approach developed by John and Helen Watkins in the 1970s. They applied elements from psychodynamic theory and clinical hypnosis to the individual's inner world.

happens when the inmost self, our spiritual center, guides and directs all the parts and invites the exiled parts into conscious awareness and offers them an emotionally corrective experience.

I'd like to invite you to encounter all the parts of your inner world and allow them to be seen, heard, known, and loved. As we get to know these parts, we will also discover our inmost self, our spiritual center, and we will learn that with God's grace, the inmost self can help relieve us of our burdens. The first step is to hear the cries of our parts, understand their pain, and listen to their stories.

THE SELF AND ITS PARTS

The basic premise of Internal Family Systems is that we have an inmost self and many parts of the self-system. These parts have their own distinct thoughts, feelings, perceptions, and memories. These parts often serve a variety of useful functions. I like to say that there's a "part of me" that shows up for social occasions and is capable of being friendly and polite. I have another part that shows up when I must negotiate a deal, buy a car, or handle a bad customer experience. I have yet another part that acts in the role of therapist with my clients and a part of me that relaxes when I hang out with my friends. I have a "part" that works tirelessly on projects and gets things done. I have another "part" that wants to do nothing but relax and binge-watch TV shows and read the news. My personality has complexity, and my mind is not a monolith. You might say that there are different sides to my personality or that I wear different masks, but this doesn't really get at the depth and reality of these parts. They are real subpersonalities with their own take on my life experiences, and they are not superficial or inconsequential. They are unique and filled with resources, skills, and important perspectives. Essentially, through our parts we have within us a rich diversity of perceptions, thoughts, and feelings.

Some of my parts have adopted roles that are professional or functional or useful. Some of my parts, however, are carrying wounds from the past and may be holding on to physical or emotional pain. Some are holding on to false beliefs about God, the world, and others. Some of my parts have experienced deep insecurities and have coped in ways that are not always healthy now. Internal conflicts and inner tensions arise when my parts are in conflict with each other. My parts have good intentions, but they may be burdened with distorted thinking and ways of adapting that are no longer helpful.

From a Christian perspective, we would not say that parts have an ontological existence, meaning that they do not have a separate substantial existence apart from the human person.[7] We say that they have a phenomenological existence, meaning that they provide a model, or analogy, for expressing a truth within our interior life. We truly experience various modes of experience or sides of our personalities, and we experience modes of desolation and consolation, but parts are not actual, objective entities.[8]

THE INMOST SELF

The inmost self is one's core self or true self, the spiritual center of one's being. It is inherently good and has compassion, creativity, and wisdom. It is kind, motivated by love, and desires healing and connection. It embodies confidence, calm, compassion, courage, creativity, clarity, curiosity, and connectedness, patience, persistence, perspective, playfulness, and presence.[9]

In the world of psychology, we might encounter terms such as *true self, inner self, best self,* or *core self*. I use the term *inmost self* because it is the term used by St. Paul: "I delight in the law of God, in my inmost self" (Rom. 7:22). This "inmost self" parallels the Greek word *nous* used in the Bible; *nous* connotes both the heart and the mind, perhaps a kind of "knowing" within the heart.[10]

7 In Thomistic terms, one might say parts have accidental, not substantial, form. They do not have their own will or intellect, even though phenomenologically it may *feel* as if they do.

8 Many of my clients have asked me, "Does this mean I have multiple personality disorder?" The answer is almost always a firm no. We all have an inmost self and many parts of the self-system.

9 These attributes, known in IFS as the "8 Cs" and the "5 Ps," will be explored in more depth in this book.

10 See, for example, Romans 7:23: "I see in my members another law at war with the law of my mind [nous], making me captive to the law of sin that dwells in my members."

The *Catechism of the Catholic Church* explains that "the spiritual tradition of the Church also emphasizes the *heart,* in the biblical sense of the depths of one's being, where the person decides for or against God" (*CCC* 368). If the inmost self can be seen as synonymous with the heart in this regard, then the inmost self also includes the conscience and can choose between good and evil.

When the inmost self engages with our parts and understands them, loves them, cares for them, and gives them what they need now, it is life-changing. Our insecure parts gain confidence. Our wounded parts heal. Our addictive parts learn to be present and enjoy life in new ways. When we allow our inmost self to interact positively with our parts, the entire internal system starts working in positive ways. We become more functional, more integrated, more present, and more relational. We find more joy and happiness. The "work" we do with our parts helps us live more fulfilling lives.

A DESCRIPTION OF PARTS

As we get to know our parts, we might have many questions: How many parts do I have? Do the parts come and go? Where do they come from?

There is no agreed-upon answer to these questions. There is no known set number of parts for each person. Parts can change, take on different roles, and function in new ways over time. The Internal Family Systems (IFS) model teaches that our parts are with us from birth. Some parts are very "handy" and help us with everyday tasks, while other parts seem more distant and may even exist outside normal conscious awareness. We may assign temporary names to our parts, but they prefer to name themselves. Our parts are unique and represent a rich diversity within the complex human mind.

The IFS model identifies several categories or types of parts, and these can be very helpful in identifying and understanding them. This list is not comprehensive, but it does provide helpful language to make sense of our parts. Let us look at exiled parts, manager parts, and firefighter parts.

Exiled parts: These parts are often "wounded" children, and they develop when we experience intense, unresolved emotions of shame, fear, and pain that are not yet integrated into the stories of our lives. Exiled parts often feel rejected and alone and carry burdens of self-hatred, fear, or pain. They often feel abandoned and worthless. Some carry a tremendous amount of repressed anger. Other parts are afraid that their strong emotions and intensity will flood the system and overwhelm us. By definition, exiled parts usually exist below conscious awareness, but when they are triggered, they may cause our protectors (either managers or firefighters) to react, and they may even cause a firefighter to leap into action. The reality is that these exiles need love, attention, care, and understanding. When we approach these exiles and allow them to feel their feelings and witness the origin of their burdens and when we provide them the care and understanding they always needed, we discover that they are, in fact, beautiful and lovable. When these children are allowed to play, we can delight in them and find a new place for them in our inner world. It is often difficult to approach and get to know exiles because they are guarded by fierce protectors. We need to obtain permission from the protectors before the inmost self can approach them. The exiles are often quiet and untrusting. They are isolated and living in pain. They may also be angry at being ignored and abandoned. It takes time to develop a trusting relationship with them. This can happen only when we see them as hurting children and when we bring genuine empathy and compassion to them. We must create a safe place for them to heal and be nurtured and loved. The most powerful emotion carried by the exiles is often shame, and they will need constant affirmation of their true worth.

Manager parts: These protector parts exist to help us function in daily life. We have parts that take on roles, such as worker, parent, spouse, professional, churchgoer, friend, and neighbor. The primary mission of managers is proactively to suppress and compartmentalize the intensity and pain of the exiles, keeping that intensity and pain in the unconscious. Managers are highly committed to preventing the exiles' distress from overwhelming our system.

Firefighter parts: These protector parts react in emergencies, when the exiles are jailbreaking and flooding us with the intensity of anxiety, grief, anger, or shame or are bringing up overwhelming desires or beliefs that could harm us or others. The firefighters leap in to distract us from the exiles, to try to insulate us from the pain the exiles are experiencing. Firefighters may urge us toward addictive or self-destructive behaviors with no thought for long-term consequences.

BURDENS

The parts of the self-system are not inherently bad; in fact, they are essentially good, part of our being, made in the image and likeness of God. Parts do carry burdens, however, and they have an agenda. They are often driven by some purpose, and they work together as a subsystem. For example, a people-pleasing firefighter part may protect a wounded exile part who carries the burden of being unlovable. Another wounded part may believe that he can't trust anyone, and a corresponding protector takes on the role of tough guy to protect him. These parts with their associated roles attempt to protect the exiles, the hurt and wounded parts, from further pain. They also try to protect the self-system from being overwhelmed by the strong emotions of pain, shame, or fear that the exiles are carrying. Manager and firefighter parts are burdened with extreme roles in order to protect the exiles or protect against the exiles. When the inmost self is eclipsed by a burdened, wounded, or "dysregulated" part,[11] then we behave in unhealthy ways. When the inmost self is in harmony with unburdened and regulated parts — that is, when the inmost self guides the parts — then we function in healthy ways in the natural realm.

UNBLENDING

Unblending involves separating the various parts from the inmost self. Sometimes our parts "blend" with the inmost self to the point at which we lose access to the inmost self and its qualities. A burdened part with its associated agenda dominates our conscious awareness. But as we identify our parts, we may be able to "picture"[12] them in the mind's eye or sense them nearby and recognize their

[11] Emotional *dysregulation* refers to an emotional reaction that is outside the normal range, given the current circumstances. It is often associated with early trauma and abuse. Examples of emotional dysregulation may include angry or violent outbursts, aggression toward others, suicidal threats, or excessive crying.

[12] Many people cannot visualize their parts, but they can sense their presence. The founder of IFS, Richard Schwartz, himself acknowledged that he does not "see" his own parts, and he estimates that about 30 percent of people cannot internally visualize their parts.

concerns. We become more objective about our parts, and clarity, compassion, and self-energy become available to them.

When a part is fully "blended" with the inmost self, it is like the moon totally eclipsing the sun. All you see is the moon. But as you notice the part, sense his presence, and connect with him, the part will come into "view." There will be a healthy distance between the inmost self and the part. The part is no longer running the show, and he is now available to the inmost self. This is called *unblending*. When unblending has occurred, no part overwhelms, and the inmost self can work with the part, understand his needs, help him work with other parts, and perhaps bring about healing. It is worth noting that unblending occurs on a continuum. Some parts are "partially" blended, and this is not necessarily a problem. A self-led part may be partially blended as he works with the inmost self, drawing on his own positive resources, to accomplish some purposeful goal.

UNBURDENING

Unburdening involves the inmost self helping the parts to let go of the burdens they are carrying. Exiles carry burdens of woundedness, and protectors carry burdens related to the extreme roles they have adopted. An unburdened part works in harmony with the self and can live up to his potential and function in healthy ways. A burdened part may believe lies and operate in rigid, avoidant, and anxious ways as he tries to compensate for his lack of a felt sense of safety and security. When an exile lets go of a burden, he generally feels tremendous relief. When a protector lets go of a burden, he also experiences tremendous relief and learns that he can take on new, rewarding roles. He can also typically integrate with the whole self in a complementary and collaborative way, with a sense of belonging and purpose.

INTERNAL FAMILY SYSTEMS AND CHRISTIAN ANTHROPOLOGY

Richard Schwartz, the founder of Internal Family Systems, saw IFS as a spiritual movement; to be clear, there are unmistakable elements of Eastern religions, such as Hinduism and Buddhism, evident in his later writings.[13] Because of this, I had growing questions and concerns about whether IFS is compatible with Christian anthropology, philosophy, and theology. On the surface, there is a great deal of compatibility. The process of unblending, for example, feels like an extension of the ministry of Christ, who understands people, heals their wounds, and relieves them of their sins and life burdens. Other aspects of IFS contradict certain Christian doctrines and need correcting. This book, therefore, is not a book on IFS per se but, rather, adapts IFS and other parts-based approaches, such as Ego State Therapy, to a Christian understanding of humanity; we recognize what is good and useful and reject what is problematic.

Christian anthropology recognizes that we are dependent on a personal God who created us, redeems us, and loves us. The human person is made up of an integrated body and soul (*CCC* 382), and the soul is "the innermost aspect of man, that which is of greatest value in him (cf. Mt 10:28; 26:38; Jn 12:27; 2 Macc 6:30) . . . by which he is most especially in God's image: 'soul' signifies the *spiritual principle* in man" (*CCC* 363). The soul, then, contains the core or inmost self and all the parts of the self.

The human person, which includes a physical body and a soul, is created in God's image. The inmost self, as the conscious spiritual center of the soul, reflects the *imago Dei* (the truth that we are created in the image of God) in its expression of freedom, creativity, and compassion. The inmost self and the parts are intrinsically good, but as a result of the Fall, described in Genesis 3, the inmost self is darkened, and the internal parts carry burdens. The human person is the principal agent in the commission of sins, but when our burdened parts blend with the inmost self (that is, when they take an "executive position" in our selves), they can influence our choice to sin: we see this influence most clearly in addiction, when a burdened part blends so severely with the inmost self that the human person no longer has full knowledge or gives deliberate consent to commit sin.[14]

[13] This is especially evident in his book, *No Bad Parts*, which I critique in appendix D.

[14] The Church teaches that there are two types of sin: venial and mortal. In terms of how these types of sin affect our selves, I would argue that venial sins contribute to the burdening of parts, decrease the internal communion between one's

Our entire human person, body and soul, including our inmost self and our internal parts, needs to be redeemed and regenerated in Christ, and we have been given the free will to choose good or evil (CCC 1730). Without the ability to choose evil, we would not be able to choose the good. Conversion and Baptism open us to receive divine and supernatural graces from God so that we may work toward our ultimate goal: complete union with God in Heaven. The goal of Christian parts work is purity of heart so that we may rid ourselves of burdens and pursue a life of holiness and sanctification.

We must remember that no therapy can replace our faith. While certain aspects of IFS can perhaps enhance some spiritual practices, we cannot create a utopia out of our fallen world by our own human efforts. As Christians, we recognize our complete dependence on God to save us from the evil in this world and from our own personal sin.

As you join me in this journey into the interior life, my prayer is that you will experience a measure of personal healing as well as a deepening relationship with God. As you read the vignette at the beginning of each chapter, I invite you to notice the movements within your heart. As you learn about parts and engage in the prayers and meditations, I invite you to encounter your own parts. Consider capturing these observations by taking notes in a journal. This "parts journal" can include drawings (stick people are just fine) that represent your parts as well as written descriptions that capture the roles, motivations, feelings, thoughts, and memories held by your various parts. A Christian parts-work approach may be the beginning of an entirely new and life-giving way to relate to yourself.

---

parts, and decrease one's ability to connect with other people. Mortal sin, on the other hand, the more serious kind of sin, occurs when the human person is separated from the light of God and loses connection with Him, and his heart is consequently darkened. Mortal sin requires a ritual return to communion with God through the sacrament of Penance and Reconciliation.

1

ORIGINAL TRAUMA

Alexandre's Story: The Boy Who Wasn't Good Enough

I used to joke that Canadians are born with skates on. My father was a rabid Montreal Canadiens fan, and you knew when he was watching a game because he would shout with glee when Guy Lafleur scored or curse like a sailor in French when the Bruins got through Montreal's defensive line. I remember some of my early excitement when it was decided that I would play hockey in first grade. I remember how important I felt when my dad took me to Zellers to buy the hockey equipment. When I unknowingly put the groin guard on my face and asked the saleslady what it was for, she said, "Ask your father." I turned red when it was explained to me that it was meant to protect my privates.

There were promises that my father would take me out to practice, but he never did. He complained about having to get up early and take me to the arena for early-morning practices. My team was sponsored by Smiley's TV Repair, and I was proud to wear my oversized shoulder pads, my sweaty helmet, and my wobbly skates. It turns out that, wobbly or not, I was a good skater and could glide forward and backward with ease. Nevertheless, I didn't really understand the mechanics of the game. I knew we were supposed to move forward with the puck and score, but I was easily overwhelmed by the overall strategy and the necessary teamwork involved in being part of an organic and effective team.

The truth is that, deep down, even then, I knew I was an imposter. I wasn't my father's beloved son but a lost boy, still full of energy and hope but pretending to be someone who was good enough. In first grade, I had no interest in hockey. I associated it with my father, who was loud, unpredictable, critical, angry, and condescending. And yet I soaked up his sudden interest in me as a future Maurice Richard or Doug Harvey. I did my best, and I fell short. I can honestly say I was a terrible hockey player. I knew it, and everyone on the team, if they paid any attention to me at all, knew it as well. My father said nothing, but he didn't have to. I was indeed a fraud. An unworthy mistake. I wasn't worth helping, fixing, guiding, or even consoling.

As you can imagine, by third grade I decided to quit hockey. I don't recall anyone begging me not to give it up. I knew my father was done with me. His unspoken body language was dismissive. His aspiration of living vicariously through my career as a future NHL draft pick was thrown into his pile of unfulfilled dreams.

Then, in fourth grade, one of my teachers noticed that I was always squinting to see the chalkboard. She reached out to my parents, and after having my eyesight tested, I received my first pair of glasses. I remember driving home with my new, extremely thick glasses and marveling at the detail and beauty of every tree branch. I didn't know how beautiful the world really was. No wonder I struggled to play hockey; the puck had always been a blur. It was too late, however, to go back to hockey because the damage was done. Every Saturday night, when *Hockey Night in Canada* played in our home, my father cheered or yelled profanities, but for me, it was only a reminder that I wasn't good enough and I didn't belong. I was an outsider.

There's a young, third-grade part of me who still lives mostly in the recesses of my unconscious mind. I may not be aware of him most of the time, but he still operates under the belief that he is not worth the time to teach, to mentor, or to encourage. In his mind, he is a failure in the eyes of his peers and his family. He is not good enough, not masculine enough, and a colossal disappointment. He carries a heavy burden of shame.

Shame is one of the most powerful and dreadful emotions, and no one wants to live perpetually under its heavy weight. To protect myself from this shame-inducing third grader, another part of me emerged. I began reading books and focusing on academic pursuits. I read the entire *Lord of the Rings* series in fifth grade and visited the local library weekly for more books. I wore out my library card! My father had never finished high school, and the only thing I ever saw him read was the *Journal de Montréal* for the hockey stats. If he wasn't going to include me in the masculinity club and affirm my worth, I would be better than him by being smarter. In this way, I developed an academic part of me, perhaps a book-nerd part, and it wasn't a bad thing. It opened me up to the world of literature and ideas and helped me pursue educational goals. The downside is that I often socially isolated and didn't relate very well to my peers. I became something of a loner as I retreated into a world of fantasy where I could feel safe.

THE PSYCHOLOGY OF THE INTERIOR WORLD[15]

In the story of Alexandre, we see how trauma can cause a part to be "exiled" or moved out of normal consciousness. Alexandre's third-grade or "child" part lives on, albeit covertly, and holds all the negative beliefs (e.g., I'm a failure or I'm not good enough) and all the negative feelings (e.g., shame).

We also see how a protector part of Alexandre shows up to prevent that feeling of shame from overwhelming his system. This part becomes a high academic achiever and escapes into books and learning.

Trauma causes us, and perhaps more specifically our "parts,"[16] to be burdened in some adaptive, protective way that can sometimes be helpful and sometimes harmful. In this case, Alexandre's achiever part offers some real benefits. He develops a lifelong love of reading and later pursues a degree in law. At this point, however, Alexandre hasn't addressed the real need of the exiled child part — the legitimate need to belong and to be affirmed and encouraged. Instead, that child part fears rejection and considers himself an outsider.

[15] In this section of each chapter, I'll lay out the psychological foundations for an understanding of the inmost self, the parts of the self-system, and how the process of healing works. I imagine that your rational and investigative parts will enjoy understanding the concepts and theories that inform a parts-therapy approach. Along the way, I'll provide resources so that you can explore further if you are interested.

[16] In the introduction, I outlined categories of parts (managers, firefighters, and exiles) in the IFS model. As we discover our parts, we can name them in different ways. Many people name them based on function (e.g., achiever part) or perceived age (e.g., five-year-old part) or how they appear (e.g., tired part). Typically, each part has a role in the self-system.

Attachment theory[17] is the psychological approach that best describes how we form attachments in childhood and how they impact us and our relationships later in life. Nonresponsive parenting and trauma cause our parts to develop insecure attachments that contribute to the experience of stress and anxiety.[18]

It is important to remember that we all experience trauma and that even though trauma takes many shapes and sizes, the patterns are similar. Complex trauma, interpersonal trauma, neglect, and emotional abuse affect the mind, body, and spirit. We carry trauma memories in our bodies,[19] and trauma even affects parts of our brains. We experience a threat to our sense of safety and connection to others. We see this when Alexandre realizes that his father isn't going to help him play hockey and that Alexandre isn't as good at the game as others. His natural and legitimate need to be affirmed as a good and worthwhile son is frustrated, and he adopts the belief that he is less than others. He fears further rejection, so he gives up. To avoid the pain of rejection and to manage his feelings of anger toward his father, he vows to be smarter than his father and to achieve in ways that he knows will keep his father at an emotional distance. In this vignette, we see how Alexandre's trauma establishes an exiled wounded child part and a protector achiever part.

Alexandre's child and achiever parts are both good, and both have good intentions for him. It is not our goal to get rid of these or any parts. Instead, we want to bring healing to their trauma by relieving the parts' burdens and helping them adopt healthier, less extreme roles. We do this, as we will see in later

[17] Attachment theory was originally developed by psychiatrist John Bowlby. Mary Ainsworth further developed this theory and introduced the idea of a secure base and various insecure attachment styles. Sue Johnson integrates attachment-theory, person-centered, and experiential approaches with couples to create emotionally focused couples therapy. Daniel Brown and David Elliott are key contributors in repairing adult attachment disturbances.

[18] In later chapters, we will see how God is the perfect attachment figure and how our inmost self, becoming more Christlike through God's grace, can relieve the burdens of shame, fear, and pain that our parts carry.

[19] Bessel van der Kolk's *The Body Keeps the Score* transformed our understanding of trauma and its relationship to the body. Other leading experts in body-based or somatic approaches include Pat Ogden, Peter Levine, Janina Fisher, and Robert Scaer.

chapters, by engaging these parts with the inmost self, who can bring healing, with God's help, to all the parts.

SCRIPTURE STUDY: FROM GENESIS TO EXODUS

The entire Old Testament tells the story of man's relationship with God and how God creates man and desires a relationship with him. In Genesis, we see the initial formation of a secure attachment between God and Adam and Eve. We then see how this relationship is ruptured and how man suffers due to this loss. But then the Exodus story shows us how God restores His attachment with His people. From Genesis to Exodus, we see how man loses his secure attachment with God, and with others, and then we see how man moves from insecure attachment in Egypt, which includes anxiety, shame, fear, and pain, to a renewed secure relationship with God and others based on faithfulness, connection, and love.

The Garden of Eden, the Fall of Man, and Sin

The pre-fallen Adam has a deep sense of connection with God, who literally breathed life into his nostrils (Gen. 2:7). We know, however, that despite his connection with God, Adam is lonely and has an intrinsic need for human connection (2:18). Adam is different from the other animals; none of them can be an appropriate partner for him because none of the other animals was created "in the image of God" (1:27). Adam is meant to care for the Garden: he has the special role of caring for creation, the earth, and its inhabitants (2:15, 20). God even gives Adam the job of naming the animals, which, in ancient times, means that he has authority over them.

Despite Adam's important role of caring for creation, God recognizes that there is a problem and sets out to solve it. The pre-fallen Adam undergoes the most amazing surgery of all time, and from his rib is created Eve, the first woman (2:21). The profound truth here is that man cannot be alone, and that man and woman are physically and intimately united, as she is "bone of my bones, and flesh of my flesh" (2:23). There is a deep connection now between man and woman that is different from the transcendent connection with God and the stewardly connection with animals. They share the same essence and purpose and can relate to each other in an equal and intimate manner. In marriage, they become "one body," which speaks not only to their union but to their primordial essential unity.

What do we have so far? Man's job is to take care of the earth and the animals. And he's meant to do that in communion with woman. Adam and Eve are naked and feel no shame (2:25). These are simple times. Animals also don't feel shame in being naked. There is an innocence to this "infancy" period for man and woman.[20]

The pre-fallen Adam was given life by God and warned that if he ate from the tree of good and evil, he would surely die (2:17). Later the serpent appears and tempts Eve by telling her that if she eats the fruit from the tree of the knowledge of good and evil, she will not die. This is a lie, of course. She is also told that by eating the fruit, she and her husband will become like gods. Eve sees that the fruit appears to be good and will give wisdom. So, the man and woman eat the fruit, and "the eyes of both of them [are] opened" (3:7). They immediately see they are naked and cover themselves up. They experience self-consciousness — and shame — for the first time.

This idea of their eyes being opened is fascinating — and tragic. They gain knowledge and insight, but they also experience shame! What could this mean? Perhaps they transcended their innocent nature and "saw" a greater moral landscape that involved both good — compassion, kindness, courage, and creativity — and evil — death, stealing, adultery, hatred, cowardice, and selfishness. Through their sin, our first parents proved that human beings, created in the image of God, have free will, which means that we are capable of choosing the greatest good and the cruelest evil. But this free will is necessary for us to be

[20] Sts. Irenaeus, Theophilus of Antioch, Clement of Alexandria and other Church Fathers considered Adam and Eve to be like children. Unlike God, who is uncreated, eternal, and perfect, Adam and Eve were full of unrealized potential. Despite being created in the image of God, Adam and Eve were childlike and vulnerable to temptation. God's purpose was to bring everything into fullness in Christ. If we enter a trusting relationship with God, we can become more and more like Him, whose plan was always for Christ to be the Savior of the world.

sons and daughters of God: you can't be a saint unless you at least have the option of being a devil.

Our capacity to make a genuine and free choice means that we can *truly* choose to love God and others. Without the ability to choose evil, we could never choose a higher good. Suffering, pain, and trauma exist in the world to give us more opportunities to choose kindness, goodness, and love.

> But *why did God not prevent the first man from sinning?* St. Leo the Great responds, "Christ's inexpressible grace gave us blessings better than those the demon's envy had taken away."[21] And St. Thomas Aquinas wrote, "There is nothing to prevent human nature's being raised up to something greater, even after sin; God permits evil in order to draw forth some greater good. Thus St. Paul says, 'Where sin increased, grace abounded all the more'; and the Exsultet sings, 'O happy fault . . . which gained for us so great a Redeemer!' "[22] (*CCC* 412)

Nevertheless, Adam and Eve know they have disobeyed God, and so they experience an existential and relational fear unlike anything they had ever experienced. I often tell my clients that fear and shame are the two strongest emotions. We know that fear and shame activate the amygdala, the primitive part of the brain that manages survival. This causes our blood pressure to rise, our heart rate to increase, our muscles to tense, and so forth. We go into a state of flight or fight. For the first time, Adam and Eve experience a fight-or-flight response with God. They experience trauma. For the first time, negative cognitions, such as "I'm bad" and "I'm unworthy," enter humanity. In response to this fear and shame, Adam and Eve choose to hide. This is the first time they adapt to their negative experience in an unhealthy, if understandable, way. *I'm overwhelmed by my experience and my emotions, so I'm going to hide rather than face them.* When questioned, the man blames the woman, and the woman blames the serpent (3:12–13). Likewise, humanity has learned to deflect blame rather than own it. We learn to manipulate the truth as a self-protective move. We are no longer honest with ourselves or with others.

[21] St. Leo the Great, Sermo 73,4: *PL* 54,396.

[22] St. Thomas Aquinas, *Summa Theologica* III,1,3, ad 3; cf. Rom. 5:20.

In this story of Genesis, we see all the same human responses that modern clinicians see today. We manage our fear and shame through deflection, blaming others, hiding, and dishonesty. We also see how this original sin created a disconnection between man and God and between man and woman. Man became isolated, defensive, self-protective, dishonest, and manipulative to cope with fear and shame and the enormous overwhelmingness of his experience. Here we have a cosmic "What have I done?"

The consequences of man's disobedience are very severe. God curses the serpent, tells the woman she will experience pain in childbirth and be ruled by her husband, and tells the man that he will have hard labor for the rest of his life (3:14–19). The greatest consequence of the Fall is death (3:19, 24). But it also involves pain, suffering, violence, inequality, and hard labor.[23]

We clearly have inherited original sin from our first parents, but I argue that we have also inherited *original trauma*. Since the Fall, man has had an inclination toward sin, known as concupiscence.[24] The *Catechism* is clear that original sin is "a deprivation of holiness and justice, but human nature has not been totally corrupted: it is wounded in the natural powers proper to it, subject to ignorance, suffering, and the dominion of death; and inclined to sin — an inclination to evil that is called concupiscence" (*CCC* 405). Fallen man is now capable of evil: he has tasted the fruit of the tree of the knowledge of good and evil, and he is capable of murder, as we see with Cain. Now man indeed has a tendency toward selfishness. But original trauma is the idea that original sin has caused an original experience of trauma that is also passed on generationally to all humankind. We all come into the world with an innate experience of the effects of trauma, such as anxiety and reactivity. Those effects are compounded

[23] Fourth-century Church Father St. Cyril of Alexandria describes Adam as living in pleasure and in tranquility and quiet. The Fall leads to the "law of the violent ... brought forth in our members" which disrupts his internal sense of unity. *Commentary on Romans* 5:18.

[24] Some theologians of the Protestant Reformation, such as John Calvin, expanded this idea into the problematic doctrine of total depravity, which teaches that man is completely enslaved to sin. In Calvin's view, man cannot choose God, refrain from evil, or accept salvation without the irresistible grace of God. Calvin believed that all human actions were displeasing to God and mixed with evil.

by further experiences of trauma as we interact with other people, who have their own responses to trauma.

This story of original sin — and original trauma — explains why we have pain and suffering today. We have a kind of collective post-traumatic stress that is intrinsic to being human. We can experience nightmares, worry, anxiety, irritability, restlessness, avoidance, isolation, rumination, self-blame, low self-esteem, and so forth as a result of the Fall and as a protective response to negative life events. The burdens caused by trauma perpetuate further unhealthy behaviors or sin.

The story of the Fall is powerfully the story of man's first experience with shame and fear. Haven't we all reached too far and been brought down to size? Like Alexandre at the beginning of this chapter, haven't we all felt the overwhelming feeling that we are not worth anything, that we failed, that we made a mistake so great that we will forever be rejected? Adam and Eve's mistake cost them dearly, as they were introduced to pain and suffering, inner conflicts, conflict with each other, and disconnection from God.

St. Augustine of Hippo, the fourth-century sinner who became one of the greatest Western Christian theologians and a Doctor of the Church, acknowledged the parts of his self-system that were burdened and disconnected from God when he wrote, "I will try now to give a coherent account of my disintegrated self, for when I turned away from you, the one God, and pursued a multitude of things, I went to pieces."[25] With trauma and compounded by our own mistakes, our parts are no longer integrated in a healthy way with our inmost self. One of Alexandre's coping strategies was to isolate himself from others; Adam and Eve likewise "hid themselves from the presence of the LORD God among the trees of the garden" (Gen. 3:8). We all find ways to survive, but these survival strategies can lead to an inner "disintegration" that leads to a further disconnection from God as well as unhealthy and insecure relationships.

This is the story of trauma. Our world is no longer safe, and we no longer trust others. Adam and Eve disobeyed God, fell from grace, and were expelled

[25] St. Augustine, *The Confessions*, bk. 2, sec. 1, cited in Bernard V. Brady, Christian Love: *How Christians through the Ages Have Understood Love* (Washington, DC: Georgetown University Press, 2003), Kinde, locations 1340–1341.

from Paradise. The Church teaches that this original sin is passed down to all men and women. "The whole human race is in Adam, 'as one body in one man.'[26] By this 'unity of the human race' all men are implicated in Adam's sin, as all are implicated in Christ's justice. Still, the transmission of original sin is a mystery that we cannot fully understand" (*CCC* 404). And so we all begin life separated from God and have an inclination toward sin, and we all experience trauma as a result of this sin.

But the story does not end here: as soon as He finished explaining the consequences of Adam and Eve's sin, God promised our redemption: the offspring who will crush the head of the serpent (Gen. 3:15). Indeed, Christ has redeemed us through His death on the Cross and has restored our union with God. Baptism erases the stain of original sin and turns us back to God, and we are justified by God's grace through this faith in Christ (Eph. 2:8). Now, with God's love and grace, we can begin the process of sanctification until we are ultimately brought into His holy presence for eternity.

Despite our utter failure, the Christian message, the point of the whole biblical narrative, is that we are called out of our exile into relationship with a loving God and with a community of forgiving and accepting people. This new world of true and safe intimacy is the calling to experience the kingdom of God.

This is indeed good news, but there are many challenges. We still live and struggle with sin in this world. We experience suffering and pain. We continually make mistakes, harm ourselves, damage our relationships, and feel disconnected from God. What does it mean to access this redemption and experience sanctification and healing in our lives?

As Catholic Christians, we have access to all the rich blessings and graces of the spiritual life: prayer, ascetical practices, and the sacraments, especially Confession and Communion. We can more fully embrace and internalize these practices when we help our parts unblend[27] from our inmost selves and release their burdens and thus bring harmony to our entire inner self-systems.

[26] St. Thomas Aquinas, *De Malo* 4, 1.

[27] Unblending is a process in the Internal Family Systems model, as discussed in the book's introduction.

Conversely, a life of prayer and the sacraments itself may also predispose us to willingly unblend and work with our parts toward greater healing.

Exodus

The story of the Exodus, in which Moses and the Israelites escape from captivity and slavery and are taken to the Promised Land, is an archetypal story of how God helps us reverse this traumatic situation. Over and over, we see in the Hebrew Scriptures (the Old Testament) how God brings the Israelites out of exile and into freedom. This same journey is offered to all humankind through the Person of Jesus, who reverses the curses of the Fall and restores man's relationship with God while bringing about the kingdom of God. This new order offers the potential for the restoration of the inner life of each person, as well as a new way of relating with others.

The story of the Israelites is also the story of each one of us. We have within us an inner world, a self-system made up of captives and slaves. Just as some of the Israelites supported Moses, some complained, and some questioned him, we have parts that are fearful, parts that are wounded, and parts that grumble. But the Israelites had a leader, Moses, and ultimately Moses cared for them and helped them. And so, in this analogy, Moses can help us understand the inmost self. Moses had to discover his true identity, which was not merely to be a prince of the world but to be one of God's beloveds, and he had to lead the people, despite all their flaws, out of slavery and to the Promised Land. In a similar way, we need to discover our identity in God and allow our inmost self to lead our parts to healing and union with God. As we work with our parts, we must see the process as a journey of self-discovery and healing, not a quick and sudden fix. We will sometimes struggle and encounter roadblocks in this fallen world, but we know God is with us.

The approach I propose here is an integrated healing of the whole person. In the spiritual realm, we seek a restoration of communion between the inmost self and God. This involves the supernatural experience of conversion and turning to God in faith, receiving sanctifying grace, and the process of ongoing sanctification. In the natural realm, we seek a transformed relationship between the inmost self and all the parts of the self-system. These two processes, although distinct, intersect and complement each other. Christian philosopher and theologian St. Thomas Aquinas famously said that grace does not destroy but perfects nature.[28] When the inmost self receives grace and extends it to the self-system, nature can be perfected.

IS THERE AN OLD TESTAMENT BASIS FOR PARTS?

Christians believe that God, although one, is also a Trinity — three Persons in one God: Father, Son, and Holy Spirit. We understand also that God *is* love (1 John 4:8) and that the Trinity expresses that love as an eternal communion between the three Persons. Although God is One, God is also a harmony of three divine Persons. God is both a unity and a multiplicity. And as created beings made in God's likeness, we share in some manner this inner multiplicity.

God reveals Himself in many ways in the Hebrew Scriptures. There are times when He is described as a Creator, a helper, a savior, a rock, a refuge, a consuming fire, a gracious and compassionate sovereign, a judge, a burning bush, and even a cloud. God is multidimensional, and in reality, He is truly indescribable. Nevertheless, God finds ways to express Himself in creation.

In Genesis, we are told that man was created in God's image, in the image of the Trinity, and so we can recognize that, in some way, we were created as a unity with a kind of multiplicity. St. Augustine of Hippo explains, "And so there is a kind of image of the Trinity in the mind itself, and the knowledge of it, which is its offspring and its word concerning itself, and love as a third, and these three are one, and one substance."[29] Therefore, I will posit that having parts is part of being a human being. Just as God expresses Himself in His creation, we express our personality — the inmost self and all the parts of the self-system — through our body.[30]

[28] St. Thomas Aquinas, *Summa Theologica*, I, 1, 8, ad 2.

[29] St. Augustine, *On the Trinity*, 9.12, 17–18.

[30] At a minimum, we are told that man has a heart and a mind, which should have an inner unity and be in union with God. "I will raise up for myself a faithful priest, who shall do according to what is in my heart and in my mind. I will build him a sure house, and he shall go in and out before my anointed one for ever" (1 Sam. 2:35). "And you, my son Solomon, know the God of your father,

The parts of the self-system express the multidimensional nature of who we are.[31] A Christian approach would not understand parts to be entities that are separate from us in any way but, rather, different states of mind that are intrinsic to us as created in the image of God.

In any case, parts are understood as having good intentions, and they often take on roles to fulfill tasks. Each part of the self-system has his own thoughts, feelings, perceptions, and attitudes. They often express unique strengths and qualities. The parts are ideally meant to work together as an internal system in harmony with the inmost self, but parts sometimes dominate or "eclipse" the inmost self, and this can lead the person to behave in problematic or extreme or sinful ways.

The Genesis story teaches us that the human race has "fallen" and that there are consequences to that Fall: we're out of connection with God, and we tend to sin. In a sense, we are in exile. We are like the Israelites held in slavery in Egypt, in need of the Exodus. And since we live in a world filled with people who have this inclination to sin, we are affected by one another's sins. I understand this tendency to sin, concupiscence, as a negative and unhealthy self-protective coping response. This response might take the form of isolation and withdrawal and even self-harm, or it can take the response of anxiety, reactivity, and harm to others.

We can reflect on this process and recognize that our God knows us and can break through all our shame, fear, and pain in order to love and redeem us. I invite you to read the psalm below. The psalmist's words are powerful and

---

and serve him with single mind and willing heart; for the LORD searches every mind, and understands every plan and thought" (1 Chron. 28:9).

31 IFS says that we have a set number of parts at birth. Ego State Therapy says it is unknown whether we begin with a set number of parts or whether some emerge later in life. Other psychological approaches understand parts as "modes of experience" or "self-states" that develop and change throughout our lifetime. Schema therapy, developed by Jeffrey Young, for example, refers to schema modes and modes of experience. A schema is an organized pattern of thought and behavior, and a mode is a way of being influenced by schemas and coping styles. Examples of schema modes include child modes, dysfunctional parent modes, and healthy adult modes. Professor of psychiatry Dan Siegel refers to self-states and "states of mind" made up of patterns of activation that include feelings, perceptions, attitudes, and memories.

deeply relational. In this psalm, God embodies the main ingredients of a secure attachment: He sees us, knows us, encourages us, and cherishes us. I recommend that you read the psalm slowly. My brief commentary is in brackets:

O Lord, you have searched me and known me.
You know when I sit down and when I rise up;
you discern my thoughts from far away.
You search out my path and my lying down,
and are acquainted with all my ways.
Even before a word is on my tongue,
O Lord, you know it completely.
You hem me in, behind and before,
and lay your hand upon me.
Such knowledge is too wonderful for me;
it is so high that I cannot attain it.

Where can I go from your spirit?
Or where can I flee from your presence?
If I ascend to heaven, you are there;
if I make my bed in Sheol, you are there.
If I take the wings of the morning

[God is always with us, and He truly sees us. He is present even in the most difficult experiences. He doesn't abandon us.]

and settle at the farthest limits of the sea,
even there your hand shall lead me,
and your right hand shall hold me fast.
If I say, 'Surely the darkness shall cover me,
and the light around me become night',
even the darkness is not dark to you;
the night is as bright as the day,
for darkness is as light to you.

For *it was you who formed my inward parts*;
you knit me together in my mother's womb.

I praise you, for I am fearfully and wonderfully made.
Wonderful are your works;
that I know very well.
My frame was not hidden from you,
when I was being made in secret,
intricately woven in the depths of the earth.
Your eyes beheld my unformed substance.
In your book were written
all the days that were formed for me,
when none of them as yet existed....

[We are created with an inner multiplicity. We were created lovingly. God truly knows us. He sees our goodness.]

Search me, O God, and know my heart;
test me and know my thoughts.
See if there is any wicked way in me,
and lead me in the way everlasting. (Ps. 139:1–16, 22–24, emphasis mine)

[God knows us at the deepest level. He sees our hearts, our inmost selves. He guides us away from evil and brings us toward Him.]

God knows all our ways and knows every part of us. He is not afraid to face and work with our burdened parts. He is not afraid of the darkness. Although it is unlikely that the psalmist understood "inward parts," as in the IFS conception of parts of the self-system, there is still the idea that God made every aspect of the human person. Seen through an IFS lens, this psalm supports the idea that God made, in our mother's womb, all the parts of the self-system. At the very least, our parts are not afterthoughts or merely projections of a traumatic mind. They are good, and along with the whole human person, they are made by God Himself.

God knows the depth and goodness of our hearts. He sees past the pain, the shame, and the fear that keeps us dysregulated and behaving badly. God invites our parts to be united and not divided when He says, "I will give them one heart, and put a new spirit within them; I will remove the heart of stone from their flesh and give them a heart of flesh" (Ezek. 11:19).[32]

St. Ignatius of Antioch, an early Church Father and a disciple of St. John, tells us to "love one another with an undivided heart."[33] We are called, then, to find an internal unity. We are invited to come to know our true inmost self and restore all the parts in communion with God through His grace.

LIFE APPLICATIONS FOR INNER TRANSFORMATION

Diaphragmatic Breathing

Diaphragmatic breathing means breathing from the abdomen, not the chest.[34] It is deep breathing. We take deep, slow breaths, and we can even watch our belly rise and drop. Breathe in deeply through your nose and release slowly through your mouth. This is a natural way to reduce anxiety.

Bilateral Stimulation and Tapping

Bilateral stimulation is a natural way to connect the "left" (logical, narrative, linear) part of our brains with the "right" (creative, affective, nonlinear) part. It is a very natural process. In fact, we often do natural forms of bilateral stimulation, such as walking. Have you ever noticed that a nice walk makes you feel better and "clears your head"? It is the same idea. Adding a mild form of bilateral stimulation when you pray, meditate, or relax will enhance the experience and "strengthen" the connections between both sides of your brain. It will assist with mental processing and allow negative thoughts and feelings to be processed safely and effectively.

32 "One" here is sometimes translated as "new" and sometimes as "undivided."

33 *The Epistle of Ignatius to the Trallians*, chap. 13.

34 For a demonstration of diaphragmatic breathing, see "Diaphragmatic Breathing Exercises," Physiopedia, https://www.physio-pedia.com/Diaphragmatic_Breathing_Exercises, or UCLA Health, "Diaphragmatic Breathing," YouTube video, 7:30, https://youtu.be/g2wo2Impnfg.

Tapping[35] is a very simple and easy form of bilateral stimulation. While seated, rest your hands against the outsides of your legs, as near as possible to your knees. Gently tap the sides of your legs with your fingers, one hand at a time. These taps are light, and the speed is up to you, but for this purpose, it is best to tap slowly and rhythmically.

You could also do a butterfly movement by crossing your arms over your chest and slowly and gently tapping on each side under your shoulders.

If, at any time, you feel as though you are overwhelmed or panicked, please stop the activity, and focus on breathing. If necessary, take a break. If you feel you have lost touch with the present moment (have become dissociated or "numb"), then please stop. Take a break and do something that will keep you connected with the present, such as drinking something cold, moving around, or talking with someone. Feeling agitated or feeling "numbed out" are natural body defenses when parts of the self-system feel overwhelmed. This is sometimes referred to as a "fight, flight, or freeze response." When our body perceives a threat, the sympathetic nervous system reacts by preparing the body for either combat or a quick escape. If neither seems possible, the body may respond by dissociating or numbing out. If this happens, I recommend that you discuss it with your counselor or therapist.

Meditation and Grounding Exercise

Find a quiet, peaceful place and invite yourself to have a moment of relaxation.

Invite the Holy Spirit to be present as you begin to experience a sense of peace and calm.

Notice what is going on in your body.

Notice that you are safe. We can begin to feel safe when we are safe.

Take full, deep breaths, and invite your muscles to relax as you exhale.

[35] To learn more about tapping, see Laurel Parnell's book *Tapping In*. Also, Eye Movement Desensitization and Reprocessing (EMDR) is a therapy developed by Francine Shapiro that incorporates bilateral stimulation. To learn more about EMDR, see the EMDR Institute at http://www.emdr.com, or the EMDR International Association website http://www.emdria.org.

Notice your heart rate come down as you connect with the present moment.

Notice how comfortable you are where you are sitting.

Take three deep diaphragmatic breaths.

Notice any bodily tension or muscle tightness.

Invite your muscles to relax, beginning with your feet, up your legs, through your pelvic floor, and up your spine, relaxing your arms, hands, neck, and face.

If you wish to use bilateral stimulation, begin tapping gently with your hands on each side of your leg near your knees. Do this in a slow, alternating, rhythmic movement.

Read the following Scripture passages slowly:

> Say therefore to the Israelites, "I am the Lord, and I will free you from the burdens of the Egyptians and deliver you from slavery to them. I will redeem you with an outstretched arm and with mighty acts of judgement. I will take you as my people, and I will be your God. You shall know that I am the Lord your God, who has freed you from the burdens of the Egyptians. I will bring you into the land that I swore to give to Abraham, Isaac, and Jacob; I will give it to you for a possession. I am the Lord." (Exod. 6:6–8)

Pause, take a deep breath, and relax your muscles as you exhale. Read:

> You shall be called by a new name
> that the mouth of the Lord will give.
> You shall be a crown of beauty in the hand of the Lord,
> and a royal diadem in the hand of your God.
> You shall no more be termed Forsaken,
> and your land shall no more be termed Desolate;
> but you shall be called My Delight Is in Her,
> and your land Married;
> for the Lord delights in you,
> and your land shall be married. (Isa. 62:2–4)

Pause, take a deep breath, and relax your muscles as you exhale.

Notice your body at rest.

Close by praying slowly: "Glory to the Father, and to the Son, and to the Holy Spirit, both now and ever, and unto the ages of ages. Amen."

Reflection Questions

The reflection questions here are designed to help you process what you have learned from this chapter. It is often helpful to write down in a journal your responses and any other thoughts and feelings you may have.

1. Recall an early experience in which you had your hopes dashed and faced disappointment. How old were you?

    a. What negative beliefs formed as a result of this experience?

    b. What negative emotions did you feel as a result of this experience?

2. As you recall this experience, what tension or sensation do you notice in your body? What message might this body sensation be trying to communicate to you?

3. How did you adapt to protect yourself from these negative emotions?

4. Try to identify a part of you that seems to protect you from strong emotions, such as fear and shame? Take a moment to thank that part of you for his good intentions and his efforts to protect you.

2

THE WOUNDED HEART

Alexandre's Story, Part 2: *The Burden of Shame*

In the eyes of my child self, my father was the very figure of masculinity. He was strong and good-looking and had a booming voice. He could curse out anyone. In his younger days, he rode a motorcycle, played hockey, and knew martial arts. He had a rifle in the closet and porn magazines in his dresser drawer. I was afraid of him because his demeanor always included an element of threat. No one messed with him.

The truth is that no one would have guessed that this paragon of masculinity was abusing me.

For many years, I carried that burden of shame. As a child, of course, I didn't know about sex, and I had no words for what was happening. My father was normally rough and loud and irritable, but then he would become playful and include me in his "secret." It was the only time I felt as if he wanted me around, but at the same time, I was scared and overwhelmed by the abuse. He made it clear that I could never say anything to anyone about it. This is when I learned that the world wasn't what it seemed and that I couldn't trust anyone. These were my first lessons in compartmentalization and dissociation. I put the abuse in a box and pretended it didn't happen. And when it did happen, I exited my body and disconnected from reality.

The sad truth is that I carried that burden through adolescence and into adulthood. I could behave on the outside as if everything was all right. I could achieve good things and be the poster boy for overcoming adversity. But deep inside, that little boy was still there, hurting, uncared for, fearful, and deeply ashamed. I wondered if I was gay. I didn't want to have sex with men, but I couldn't get the images of the abuse out of my head. I hated my father, but I wanted deeply to be loved by a father. I wanted to be affirmed by a father. I wanted to believe I was man enough.

I was working as a lawyer in the early nineties and heard that Sheldon Kennedy, an NHL hockey player, came forward as a victim of abuse by his former coach Graham James. In Canada, many young talented hockey players were sent out west to live with host families under the care of a coach who managed every aspect of their lives and prepared them to be drafted into the minor leagues and eventually into the NHL. Sheldon's witness had a profound impact on me because here was an NHL hockey player — in my mind, the epitome of manhood — revealing that he had been sexually abused as a child. *I learned from his courage that the shame I was carrying didn't truly belong to me; it belonged to my abuser*. Sheldon inspired Theo Fleury, another NHL player who had played with Wayne Gretzky for Team Canada in the Olympics, to come forward with the truth that Graham James had also abused him. Not only did Fleury unburden himself of the shame, but he also chose to advocate for abuse survivors across Canada.

Releasing shame begins when we tell our stories — not only of pain and suffering but of resilience and growth. My first disclosures occurred with close friends, including my future wife. In time, I learned that in telling my story, I was able to receive the love and care and empathy that I needed as a child. When Oprah interviewed abuse survivor Tyler Perry and invited two hundred male survivors on her show, she was giving those men a voice, affirming their worth, and allowing them to stand with pride. The courage that Tyler and those men shared inspired me. Eventually I developed the courage to talk about my story more openly and tell it to others.

THE PSYCHOLOGY OF THE INTERIOR WORLD

In both IFS[36] and Ego State Therapy,[37] two psychological therapeutic "parts work" approaches, parts are often understood as subpersonalities, as we've already discussed. In IFS, parts are often categorized as protectors or exiles.

Recall that exiles are wounded and traumatized parts that are holding grief, pain, and shame. These exiles are usually young parts. Charles Whitfield and John Bradshaw described healing the "inner child." Our protector parts are divided into managers and firefighters,[38] and they keep us from feeling the pain of the wounded parts. Manager parts are often good at completing tasks or functioning effectively in some role, such as a parent, a worker, or a helper, whereas firefighter parts leap into action during emergencies when an exile begins to overwhelm the self-system. The protectors can take many forms, such as a critical voice, a wall, an anxious "doer," or a tough Navy SEAL. We know from the previous chapter that Alexandre has an achiever manager part, a withdrawn firefighter part, and a third-grade exile part. We also know he carries a heavy burden of shame.

Exiles are parts that hold distressing and disturbing emotions, thoughts, and beliefs that we call burdens. We often refer to them as "wounded children" because they are frozen in the past. When we work with exiles, we need to understand that developmentally they are often very young. We therefore need to speak to them as we would to a child who has experienced something very distressing. They may feel abandoned and rejected. They may blame themselves for things that were out of their control. They may feel lost, sad, or fearful.

It is possible that as you read this description of exiles, or as you read the first two parts of Alexandre's story, you have protector parts showing up to protect

[36] Internal Family Systems or IFS is a therapeutic approach developed by Richard Schwartz in the 1980s. He applied a family systems approach to the individual's inner world. Schwartz developed the techniques known as unblending and unburdening.

[37] Ego State Therapy (EST) is a therapeutic approach developed by John and Helen Watkins in the 1970s. They applied elements from psychodynamic theory and clinical hypnosis to the individual's inner world.

[38] Richard Schwartz and Martha Sweezy, *Internal Family Systems*, 2nd ed. (New York: Guilford Press, 2020), 31.

your exiles. You may have a protector who wants to challenge the ideas and concepts behind parts work. You may have a protector who wants to disconnect from your feelings. If so, this is perfectly normal. Take a break whenever you need to as you read this book. Thank your protector parts for working hard to defend you.

Parts are not bad in and of themselves, but many parts appear dysfunctional. As a result of traumatic experiences, our parts carry burdens. Manager and firefighter parts adapt and find ways to cope during difficult life circumstances. Some of these parts learned to adapt in ways that are now causing problems. For example, in the previous chapter, we saw how Alexandre's intellectual achiever part developed to avoid emotions because his father was emotionally volatile. If he focused on being smart and rational, he could avoid negative emotions. Here we discover that his child part also experienced sexual abuse and carried a burden of shame. As a child, he was unprepared to make sense of what his father was doing. The child just wanted his father to love him and affirm him.

Other parts, perhaps the intellectual achiever part, or some other part with a critical voice, might blame the child for being needy or not standing up to his father. These critical parts may not fully realize just how young the child part is. Since intimacy and abuse were inappropriately conflated for the child part, he may not be able to trust people who appear to be friendly and loving. We must appreciate just how difficult it is for abuse survivors to experience safety. We need to recognize that, deep down, we are dealing with a hurt, frightened child.

Real healing begins when Alexandre thanks his protector parts, including the critical ones, and then asks them to ease back as he invites the exiled wounded-child part into his present consciousness. The wounded-child part may have learned that sharing one's feelings is selfish or that one's feelings are to blame for another's bad behavior. Whatever the case, the wounded-child part is invited to share once he begins to feel safe. It may take some time for the child part to feel comfortable and be willing to receive compassion, care, and nurturing.

Although this book will help anyone discover his or her parts, unblend from them, access his or her inmost self, and begin the process of unburdening, many survivors of trauma require the help of a therapist trained in parts work[39] before

[39] Examples of parts-work therapies include IFS and Ego State Therapy.

they can complete all the needed work with an exiled wounded-child part. Everyone's story is unique, and everyone's needs are different. This book may be the beginning of your healing journey, a helpful resource for ongoing healing, or an adjunct to therapy, but it is not meant to replace therapy. It is necessary but often difficult to gain the trust and assistance of our protector parts before we engage an exile. If we bypass the protector parts, they may try to sabotage our healing efforts. Also, exiles carry strong emotions, such as shame, fear, anger, and sorrow. A therapist can help us through this often painful but important process. The relief that comes as we unburden and reconnect with our exiles is life changing. Most people describe this process as liberating; they feel lighter and experience newfound joy. You will see examples of this as you continue to read about Alexandre and others throughout this book.

Dissociation and Compartmentalization

Trauma causes our parts to dissociate or disconnect from our core or inmost selves, from each other, and from God. We become a "divided self," which implies we are not cohesive. Many spiritual writers such as Thomas Merton refer to the "false self," which is really a dissociated blended and burdened "part" coping as best as he can. Carl Jung correctly calls us to "make the unconscious conscious"; this means that our dissociative and disconnected parts enter our conscious awareness and can interact with our inmost self and helpful resourceful parts to bring about healing. We must learn from these formerly dissociated parts and must relate to, engage, empathize with, understand, and support them.

This can be a difficult task because these parts may not always present themselves in a positive way. We must see past their reactive exteriors to discover the pain and hurt underneath. A dog caught in a trap in the forest for days may attack its rescuers until it learns that they are there to help. Our broken, hurting, dissociative parts need to learn that we are safe. We can assure those parts that we are safe only when we approach them from our inmost self with calm, compassion, and patience. In later chapters, we will learn ways to access this inmost self.

The grounding exercise in the previous chapter can help us notice that our bodies are, in fact, safe in the present moment. It may seem obvious, but we need to experience calm and safety before we can believe it. When we take deep breaths and relax our muscles, we signal to our brains that our bodies are safe. Then we can share our feelings and eventually bring truth to the lies we have learned.

SCRIPTURE STUDY: RELIEVING BURDENS

The unburdening process often begins by our mustering the courage to tell our story to someone we trust. In the 1990s, psychiatrist Judith Herman described three stages in recovery from the effects of trauma: establishing safety, telling your story, and reconnecting with others.[40] When Alexandre heard the stories of celebrity survivors, it gave him permission to start telling his own story. In this chapter's exercise, we will pray the Litany of the Wounded Heart so that we may bring our woundedness to Jesus and bring our burdens to the foot of His Cross.

John the Baptist reveals Jesus as "the Lamb of God who takes away the sin of the world!" (John 1:29). What is this sin? In the Hebrew Scriptures, we find many cases where the word *sin* is defined as something tangible: either something needing to be forgiven and physically wiped away or a physical weight or a burden.[41] We find Moses complaining to God, "Why have you treated your servant so badly? Why have I not found favour in your sight, that you lay the burden of all this people on me?" (Num. 11:11). Isaiah admonishes Judah with the following words: "Ah, sinful nation, people laden with iniquity" (1:4); he later describes sin as something to be taken away on a cart by oxen: "you who drag iniquity along with cords of falsehood, who drag sin along as with cart-ropes" (5:18).

As a result of their mistakes, sin produced a heavy physical consequence for the Israelites. Examples of sinful behavior included worshipping other gods,

[40] See Judith Herman's *Trauma and Recovery*, was which was originally published in 1992.

[41] In Psalm 38:3–4, for example, we see sin described as a burden with a physical manifestation: "There is no soundness in my flesh because of your indignation; there is no health in my bones because of my sin. For my iniquities have gone over my head; they weigh like a burden too heavy for me."

murder, stealing, and adultery. These sins literally weighed the people down. To ease these burdens, God provided a way for the people to be relieved through a communal ritual. On the day of Atonement[42] the Israelites brought two goats to the temple. One was sacrificed, and the other was set free to run into the wilderness, which the Israelites often associated with the underworld. This process allowed the Israelites to be relieved of their burdens and restored their relationship with God.

Jesus, the Lamb of God, is the Paschal Lamb who takes away our sins. He is the suffering servant who allows Himself to be killed for us (*CCC* 608). When John the Baptist calls Jesus the "Lamb of God," he could also be alluding to this second goat from the Day of Atonement who carried the burden of Israel's sins and essentially cast it into Hell.[43] Jesus has come to take our burdens and cast them into a place where they will cease to exist.

In the Gospels we see Jesus cast out unclean spirits and demons. We also see Him heal physical illnesses, such as fevers, leprosy, paralysis, a withered hand, dropsy, blindness, and deafness. He even heals people who are dead or near death. Jesus relieves spiritual and physical burdens so that people can be free of pain and suffering. They, in turn, typically express gratitude and reconnect with God.

These spiritual and physical burdens can correlate with the emotional and psychological burdens experienced in our inner world. We know that relieving psychological burdens (e.g., extreme beliefs and feelings) has a positive effect on our physical bodies and our ability to practice a healthy prayer life and grow spiritually. The human person is made up of a spirit, soul, and body[44] that are interrelated and affect one another.[45] When the inmost self helps the parts of

[42] See Lev. 16.

[43] A fuller treatment of the idea that sin is a burden can be found in Gary Anderson's chapter "A Burden to be Borne" in *Sin: A History*.

[44] The glossary of the *Catechism of the Catholic Church* defines the human person as "made in the image of God; not some thing but some one, a unity of spirit and matter, soul and body, capable of knowledge, self-possession, and freedom, who can enter into communion with other persons — and with God."

[45] Second-century Church Father Justin Martyr said, "For the body is the house of the soul; and the soul the house of the spirit." *On the Resurrection*, chap. 10.

the self-system remove their burdens, there is a positive effect on the whole person. In EMDR therapy,[46] when a client has a disturbing emotion, we often ask them, "Where do you feel that in your body?" We then ask the client to notice that body sensation, which is connected to emotions, negative thoughts, and memories, and to continue processing.

In parts work, the unburdening process often involves noticing how the emotional or psychological hold has a physical "weight" in the body. When the psychological burden is relieved, there is a corresponding lightness in the physical body. When we give up our burdens of sin, we feel so light that we can "run with perseverance" with Jesus as the "pioneer and perfector of our faith" (Heb. 12:1, 2). Alexandre felt this when he accepted that the shame he felt was not his own, and he could release it.

We also know that Jesus relieves personal sinful burdens through forgiveness and that we are called to confess our sins and forgive one another. Jesus forgives the Samaritan woman at the well and offers her "living water" (John 4:10). To the Jews of Jesus' time, it is remarkable not only that He forgives someone but that He forgives someone who is both a woman and an outcast. Samaritans were considered unclean by the Jews. The inmost self also seeks out parts of the self-system who are in conflict with or rejected by other parts of the self-system. We may have a part who views pornography and has "many husbands" (or "wives") like the Samaritan woman at the well. We may have a part that feels ugly or unwanted or unworthy. We may have a part that is angry and reactive and seems unlikable. We may have a part that is needy, clingy, and codependent. We may have a part that is proud, judgmental, and arrogant.

All these parts of the self-system are loved by the inmost self and by Christ. These parts may be in conflict with other parts, but the inmost self sees them with compassion and understanding. Like Christ, the inmost self will not leave them alone and burdened; the self will call them lovingly and offer them

[46] Eye Movement Desensitization and Reprocessing (EMDR), a treatment developed by Francine Shapiro in the 1980s that involves the use of bilateral stimulation to reduce anxiety and recover from past traumatic experiences, is an example of one type of trauma treatment that considers the body.

something new, something they always needed: living water. This living water can be understood in IFS as "self-energy," or it can be seen as grace. The inmost self becomes a channel through which God renews us and inspires us. We gain a zest for life, and we become motivated with a new purpose. When the burden of shame was lifted for hockey player Theo Fleury, he was inspired to advocate for other abuse survivors.

Jesus tells us not to be anxious: "Therefore I tell you, do not worry about your life, what you will eat or what you will drink, or about your body, what you will wear" (Matt. 6:25). He calls us to bring our heavy burdens to Him so we "may not grow weary or lose heart" (Heb. 12:3). He then asks us to take the light yoke He provides. "Come to me, all you that are weary and are carrying heavy burdens, and I will give you rest. Take my yoke upon you, and learn from me; for I am gentle and humble in heart, and you will find rest for your souls. For my yoke is easy, and my burden is light" (Matt. 11:28–30).

Jesus also promises to send the Holy Spirit, who will teach us everything, and so we must "not let [our] hearts be troubled, and do not let them be afraid" (John 14:26–27). Each and every part of the self-system can take on the yoke of Christ and find rest. And each and every part of the self-system can know that the Holy Spirit is present and working through the inmost self to bring a deep sense of peace and inner safety.

Let us begin the process of healing by bringing our wounded hearts to Christ in the Litany of the Wounded Heart.

LIFE APPLICATIONS FOR INNER TRANSFORMATION

The Litanies of the Heart and Attachment Theory

The Litanies of the Heart were informed, in part, by attachment theory, which is a psychological approach based on years of extensive research. This theory was first developed by John Bowlby, who studied the relationship between adults and infants and identified their developmental and attachment patterns. Mary Ainsworth further developed this research and introduced the idea of a "secure base." She also identified various insecure attachment styles. Later research explored how these insecure attachment styles expressed themselves in adult relationships. Sue Johnson and Les Greenberg's emotionally focused therapy (EFT), for example, uses the principles of attachment theory in working with couples. The research of Daniel Brown and David Elliott was also influential in understanding how to repair and resolve attachment disturbances in adults.

The three original Litanies of the Heart were based on the three insecure attachment styles in attachment theory. The Litany of the Closed Heart is for the person with a dismissing-avoidant style. This type tends to be independent and has difficulty being vulnerable and sharing emotions. The Litany of the Wounded Heart is for the person with an anxious-preoccupied style. Those with this style want approval and intimacy and often become dependent. They often worry and are prone to emotional outbursts. The Litany of the Fearful Heart is for the fearful-avoidant style. Those of this type want close relationships but do not trust others. They also tend to believe they are not worthy of love. Although most people have a primary insecure attachment style, we all exhibit characteristics of all three styles at one time or another. As you pray the Litanies of the Heart, you may find that one is your preferred prayer, but you may benefit from the other two from time to time as well.

These healing litanies are rooted in a long tradition of Christian prayer, are infused with established psychological science, and draw upon my observations in working with clients and my own spiritual journey. The goal of all three Litanies of the Heart is to gently work through one's insecurities to enter a safe, loving, secure relationship with Jesus. He is the secure attachment figure par excellence.

Guidance for Praying the Litanies

You can pray the litanies on a bus, on a park bench, on a walk, on an airplane — anywhere! Jesus is happy to meet with us whenever and wherever we can make time for Him. But if you are able to be intentional about when and where you pray, here are a few suggestions that can help enhance the experience.

- Prepare a time and a place to pray.
- If you are praying with others, send them the prayers in advance or print out copies of the prayer for them to read aloud.[47]
- Find a comfortable and private place to pray. Some of us have the luxury of a dedicated prayer space in our homes. For others, it might be a comfy chair in a corner or a spot outside under a favorite tree. It's nice to have a place away from the hustle and bustle of regular life. A church or an adoration chapel is also a great option.
- Set an icon, image, or prayer card of Jesus before you. Select an image that means something to you and helps you remember Jesus in a positive way.
- Light a candle or burn incense, or both. A candle represents the light of Christ. Incense is a sign that our prayers are ascending to Heaven. The scent can also be soothing.
- No matter what setting you have chosen, before you pray, spend a few moments taking a few deep breaths and gently inviting all your muscles to relax. This prepares your body to be receptive and relaxed.

As you are praying the litanies, you may have distracting thoughts. Sometimes the cares of the world intrude and your mind might wander. That is perfectly normal. If that happens, just notice that it happens and redirect your attention to the words of the litanies and the imagery they produce. If you are

[47] Printable PDF copies of the litanies are downloadable from the Souls and Hearts website, and you can stream audio versions as well: https://www.soulsandhearts.com/lit.

praying alone, you can even pause and repeat a line or a whole section, but it is also perfectly fine to continue from where you are when you notice the distraction.

Litanies have a repetitive component like waves of the sea. As we develop a deeper, more secure relationship with Christ, we may find meaning in revisiting the litanies many times as we allow the words of the prayers to flow into our souls.

The Litany of the Wounded Heart

I invite you to pray the first of the three litanies, the Litany of the Wounded Heart. In this powerful prayer, we bring all our negative thoughts and feelings to Christ, we see Him in relation to our woundedness, and we allow Him to hold us as we develop a more trusting relationship with Him.

LITANY OF THE WOUNDED HEART

In the name of the Father, and of the Son, and of the Holy Spirit. Amen.

Lord Jesus, You created me in love and for love. Bring me to a place of vulnerability within the safety of Your loving arms. Help me today by transforming my wounded heart into a heart that can love You, myself, and my neighbor as You intend.

Jesus, I offer You my heart with all its sufferings.
Jesus, I offer You my heart with all its doubts.
Jesus, I offer You my heart with all its hurts.
Jesus, I offer You my heart with all its fears.
Jesus, I offer You my heart with all its burdens.
Jesus, I offer You my heart with all its hope and all its lack of hope.
Jesus, I offer You my heart with all its joy and all its lack of joy.
Jesus, I offer You my heart with all its love and all its lack of love.
Jesus, Son of God, *have mercy on me.*

When I feel unseen, *Lord, have mercy.*
When I feel unheard, *Lord, have mercy.*
When I believe I'm not good enough, *Lord, have mercy.*
When I feel inferior, *Lord, have mercy.*
When I doubt my worth, *Lord, have mercy.*
When I feel devalued, *Lord, have mercy.*
When I feel exposed, *Lord, have mercy.*
When I feel humiliated, *Lord, have mercy.*
When I feel discouraged, *Lord, have mercy.*
When I feel lonely, *Lord, have mercy.*
When my feelings overwhelm me, *Lord, have mercy.*
When I feel I'm too much, *Lord, have mercy.*
When I feel unlovable, *Lord, have mercy.*
When I feel despair, *Lord, have mercy.*
Jesus, I know You love me in all my wounds; *Lord, have mercy.*

Jesus, consoler of my sorrow, *open my heart.*
Jesus, most tender, *open my heart.*
Jesus, my dignity, *open my heart.*
Jesus, my hope, *open my heart.*

Jesus, You created me in love; *hold me in Your arms.*
Jesus, You created me for love; *hold me in Your arms.*
Jesus, You created me to be loved; *hold me in Your arms.*
Jesus, You created my heart; *hold me in Your arms.*
Jesus, You see my heart; *hold me in Your arms.*
Jesus, You know my true heart; *hold me in Your arms.*
Jesus, You comfort my heart; *hold me in Your arms.*
Jesus, You treasure my heart; *hold me in Your arms.*
Jesus, You encourage my heart; *hold me in Your arms.*
Jesus, You created me as Your beloved; *hold me in Your arms.*

Jesus, soothe and comfort my weary heart; *I trust in You.*
Jesus, see my pain; *I trust in You.*
Jesus, dispel my despondency; *I trust in You.*
Jesus, hear my cries; *I trust in You.*
Jesus, draw close to me; *I trust in You.*
Jesus, calm my fears; *I trust in You..*
Jesus, help me see my true worth as a child of God; *I trust in You.*
Jesus, shine Your radiant light on me; *I trust in You.*
Jesus, hold me in Your loving arms; *I trust in You.*
Jesus, help me love with my whole heart; *I trust in You.*
Jesus, You created me to love and to be loved; *I trust in You.*
Jesus, I offer You my heart with all its love; *I trust in You.*

Lord, You are the healer of my soul and my heart. I ask that, through this prayer, You would transform me more and more into the likeness of Your precious and Sacred Heart. Let Your kindness and compassion transform my heart and bring me always into the security of Your loving embrace.

In the name of the Father, and of the Son, and of the Holy Spirit. Amen.

Reflection Questions

1. Have you ever shared a painful part of your story with someone you trust? What was that like, and how did you feel afterward? If you have not, what makes it hard for you to do so today? Is there someone in your life you can confide in — perhaps a friend, a pastor, a spiritual director, a coach, or a counselor?

2. Our burdens often include negative beliefs and painful emotions. Can you sense or visualize your burden as something you carry? If so, what does it feel or look like, and where do you carry it on your body?

3. How do you imagine that Jesus views your burden?

4. Alexandre carried shame for sins done to him. Reflect on times when you have felt shame for the ways others have unfairly treated you. Do you carry any burden of shame that is not properly your own? How would you like to release this burden? Examples might include bringing it to the Cross, releasing it into the air, or tossing it into the sea.

3

THE INMOST SELF

Alexandre's Story, Part 3: The Crucifix

Although I attended a Catholic school, my parents didn't attend church when I was growing up. My second-grade religion teacher, Mrs. Prahbu, told us that God gave us the whole week and He asks for only one hour on Sunday. I didn't know enough at the time to correct her — God actually asks for the whole day to be a day of rest — but the point nevertheless sank in. I observed other families get into their cars together on Sunday mornings and head off to church. As my father watched old westerns on television and my mother busied herself about the house, I decided, at the ripe old age of eight, to walk over to St. Michael's Church and attend Mass. I liked to sit up in the balcony in that upper front row and spy down on the congregation. I noticed one of my friends who sang in the choir with his father. This little choir belted "On Eagle's Wings," "Here I Am, Lord," and "Be Not Afraid" with everything they had. I was moved by their genuine enthusiasm and passion. The priests were kind and friendly.

While perched in my nearly private viewing box, I was most fascinated by the large crucifix that hung above the altar. It was realistic without being gory. Christ's eyes looked down in reverent agony. I knew in an instant that He understood my suffering. In a powerful moment of grace, my childlike inner self developed an immediate kinship with Christ. It was as if He knew my pain and He grieved for me. He wasn't going to take it away, but from that point on, I knew that He was by my side and that His suffering and death brought salvation to the world, and so my suffering united with His could have meaning. I feel that this profound insight at such a young age was a special grace from God.

Many years later, I attended a retreat for male survivors of abuse. This retreat, centered on the Stations of the Cross, was meant to help participants connect their abuse stories with the story of Christ's undeserved Passion and death.[48] One night during the retreat, the men sat in the chapel, and we wrote about our burdens in a letter to Jesus. Then we gathered around a firepit and placed the letters in the fire, added incense, and venerated the cross, usually with a kiss. The retreat leader played the song "At the Foot of the Cross (Ashes to Beauty)" by Kathryn Scott with these lyrics: "Trade these ashes in for beauty, / And wear forgiveness like a crown, / Coming to kiss the feet of mercy, / I lay every burden down, / At the foot of the cross." Each year I participate in this retreat, I add my own letter, and I tear up when I see young college guys as well as Vietnam vets and corporate executives — many with tears in their eyes — offer up years of pain, shame, and sadness during this powerful but simple ritual. I feel honored to witness what is, for many of these men, the first time they opened up about their pain in the presence of others.

Whether it was my child self [a wounded exile part] gazing at the crucifix or my inmost self venerating the cross, something in both my body and my spirit releases a heaviness each year as I continue to unite my sufferings with those of Christ. The lost and wounded part of me reengages with my inmost self. I feel seen, known, and cared for. I breathe deeply, and I am grateful to be reconnected with my own body and with a loving God.

THE PSYCHOLOGY OF THE INTERIOR WORLD

In the world of psychology, we encounter terms such as *true self, inner self, best self,* and *core self.* In IFS, Richard Schwartz coined the "8 Cs" and "5 Ps" to describe the qualities of the "Self":[49] confidence, calm, compassion, courage,

[48] These Stations of the Cross were written by Sue Stubbs of the Archdiocese of Atlanta. You can find them in the book *The Way: Stations of the Cross for Survivors of Abuse* on Amazon.

[49] I prefer the term used by St. Paul, *inmost self,* rather than Schwartz's *Self.* Capitalizing the word *self* could imply that the self has a divine essence or is to be equated with God. Instead, the inmost self is the faculty by which we connect with God. St. Athanasius refers to this as "the mirror of the soul" (*Against the Heathen,* 34) because it reflects the image of God. It can also be understood as

creativity, clarity, curiosity, and connectedness; patience, persistence, perspective, playfulness, and presence.

I would also add that the inmost self is the unifying principle[50] of all the virtues, including the capital or natural virtues (chastity, temperance, charity, diligence, kindness, patience, and humility), which are remedies for vice, as well as the cardinal virtues (prudence, justice, fortitude, and temperance), which aid us in fostering a virtuous life. [51] The inmost self, as it exercises these qualities and virtues, has the ability to heal, encourage, and bring greater harmony to all the parts.

The parts, such as Alexandre's achiever part and third-grade part, may carry burdens and have agendas, whereas the inmost self is more of a compassionate and loving presence. Our goal is to be "self-led"; this means that the inmost self is making decisions, as opposed to any individual part. The inmost self listens to the parts and connects with them and earns their trust. The parts become helpful resources for the inmost self, and they work together in a unified and purposeful manner. The inmost self is inspired by God and led by the Holy

---

the "eye of the heart," which is the innermost part of the person and the very center of conscious spiritual activity.

50 This relates to the concept of the "unity of the virtues," described by St. Gregory of Nyssa when he insisted that virginity was not only related to the physical body but influenced all aspects of the human person. St. Augustine, in his *Answer to the Pelagians*, III, said, "Zeno may not permit us to call justice the greatest virtue, for he maintains so great a connection and unity of the virtues that, where there is one, he says that all are present and that, where one is missing, he says that all are missing and that true virtue is that which is made up of the union of the four. In that case he will offer us much help when he teaches that one cannot possess prudence or fortitude or temperance without justice. In accord with that truth Ecclesiastes declares, *Whoever sins in one point loses many goods* (Eccl 9:18)." *The Works of Saint Augustine: A Translation for the 21st Century*, vol. 25, ed. John E. Rotelle, trans. Roland J. Teske (Hyde Park, NY: New City Press, 1999), 68. More recently, Pope Francis refers to the unity of the virtues in *The Joy of the Gospel.*

51 Virtues are essentially positive moral qualities that promote ethical behavior. A comprehensive exploration of the virtues is not possible in this book, but there are many excellent books that describe the virtues, such as Peter Kreeft's *Back to Virtue: Traditional Moral Wisdom for Modern Moral Confusion* and Rebecca Deyoung's *Glittering Vices: A New Look at the Seven Deadly Sins and Their Remedies.*

Spirit, who imparts His graces through the sacraments to give us "living water" and to energize the self. The more self-energy we have, the more we act with authenticity. With self-energy, we can be "in the zone" and feel a zest for life. And in the case of Alexandre, the inmost self can experience God's love and reconnect with his parts.

The goal of a parts-work approach is for all the parts to be securely attached to the inmost self. In this way, all the parts experience the inmost self as a secure attachment figure, a loving parent, a nurturing mother or an affirming father, a healing presence, and the very best of devoted friends.

Do not be at all surprised if you find it difficult to connect with your inmost self. It takes time to learn how to make enough space between your core, the inmost self, and your various parts. If you have parts that are eager, excited, and achievement driven, remind them that it takes time and practice, but it is definitely worth the trouble!

What Is the Difference between the Soul and the Inmost Self?

The difference between the soul and the inmost self is a complex topic because many terms, such as *soul* and *self*, get defined in many different ways in different times and in different cultures, but the Catholic Church teaches the following:

> The human person, created in the image of God, is a being at once corporeal and spiritual.... In Sacred Scripture the term "soul" often refers to human *life* or the entire human *person* (cf. Mt 16:25–26; Jn 15:13; Acts 2:4). But "soul" also refers to the innermost aspect of man, that which is of greatest value in him (Cf. Mt 10:28; 26:38; Jn 12:27; 2 Macc 6:30), that by which he is most especially in God's image: "soul" signifies the *spiritual principle* in man. (CCC 362–363)

The inmost self, in some sense, resides within the soul and communicates to the whole self-system, which includes all the parts.[52] It is not separate from the soul, as "spirit and matter, in man, are not two natures united, but rather

[52] IFS would say that the soul is the Self and that the Self is a small portion of the greater SELF that could be understood as God. This understanding cannot align with Christianity because it borders on pantheism (the belief that the universe

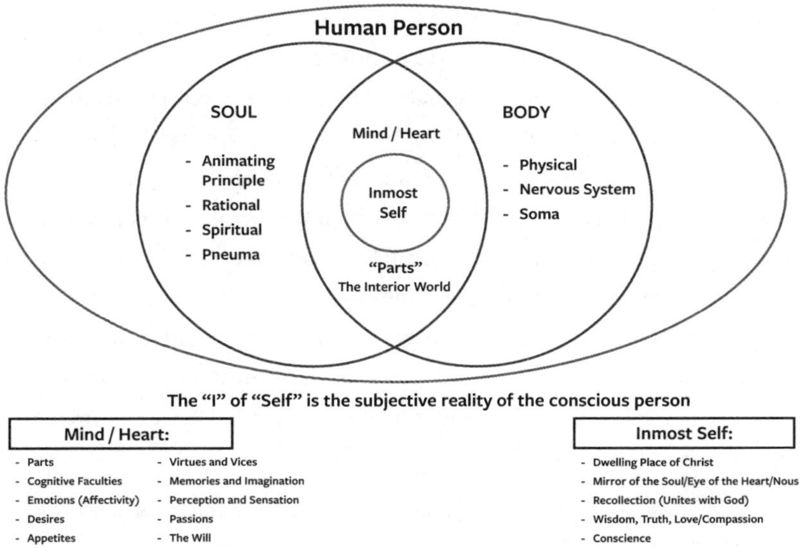

their union forms a single nature," or, more simply put, "man, though made of body and soul, is a unity (*GS* 14 § 1)" (*CCC* 365, 382). As we discussed in the introduction, the inmost self can be likened to the "heart," which the Church speaks of as "the depths of one's being, where the person decides for or against God" (*CCC* 368).

I created the diagram above, although it is imperfect,[53] to illustrate the relationship between the soul, the heart, the mind, the inmost self, the parts, and the body. Ideally, this would be three-dimensional and would show the immaterial soul and the material body as fully connected. The heart and mind make up the interior world, or the self-system, made up of the inmost self and all the parts. The interior world has access to cognitive faculties, emotions, memories, and the imagination. It is where the passions reside and therefore where we develop virtue or vice. The inmost self has a unique role within the self-system, as it

is a manifestation of God and identical to God). I address my concerns with this idea in greater detail in appendix D, "A Critique of *No Bad Parts*."

[53] This will continue to be a work in progress as we develop more common ground and common language for the intersection of philosophy, theology, and psychology within a Christian worldview. See a larger version of the diagram on page 299.

connects the heart and mind to God through contemplation. The inmost self can receive the infusion of grace, exercise compassion, and form the conscience.

Just as Christ serves as the supernatural mediator between God and man,[54] the inmost self serves as the natural mediator between God and all our parts.[55] God's grace can work through the inmost self to bring healing and energy to our parts. Our parts are valued components of the whole human person and have their own personalities, concerns, talents, and agendas, but they are part of a greater whole, the self-system, and they help to keep us motivated, engaged, protected, and balanced. When the parts are evangelized, unburdened, loved, supported, encouraged, and in connection with the inmost self and each other in a positive way, we can say there is inner harmony, a kind of "true rhythm."[56] The

54 "There is one God; there is also one mediator between God and mankind, Christ Jesus, himself human" (1 Tim. 2:5).

55 St. Maximus the Confessor describes man as a "most capacious workshop containing all things, naturally mediating through himself all the divided extremes, and who by design has been beneficially placed amid beings — is divided into male and female, manifestly possessing by nature the full potential to draw all the extremes into unity through their means, by virtue of his characteristic attribute of being related to the divided extreme through his own parts. Through this potential, consistent with the purpose behind the origination of divided beings, man was called to achieve within himself the mode of their completion, and so bring to light the great mystery of the divine plan, realizing in God the union of the extremes which exist among beings, by harmoniously advancing in an ascending sequence from the proximate to the remote and from the inferior to the superior." Maximos the Confessor, *On Difficulties in the Church Fathers: The Ambigua*, vol. 2, ed. and trans. Nicholas Constas, Dumbarton Oaks Medieval Library (Cambridge, MA: Harvard University Press, 2014). 105. These divided "extremes" can be understood as parts of the self-system that are meant to find inner unity and then union with God.

56 Patristics scholar Paul Blowers describes St. Maximus the Confessor's view this way: "Maximus's preeminent concern is the cosmic struggle of created beings (notably rational beings) to align their existential 'modes' (τρόποι) with the logoi of their nature and thereby find their true rhythm, orientation, and freedom." Paul M. Blowers, *Maximus the Confessor: Jesus Christ and the Transfiguration of the World: Christian Theology in Context* (Oxford, UK: Oxford University Press, 2018), 113–114. This view aligns well with the view that we must develop an inner harmony among our parts (modes) in order to love others and God more fully.

whole interior world, indeed the whole person, is alive, purposeful, authentic, and filled with positive energy.

God Image versus God Concept

If the inmost self is a mediator between God and our parts, then it is important that we have a proper understanding of who God is and how we perceive Him. We may have learned proper details about God (our God concept), but in our heart of hearts, we may have a distorted image of who God is based on our often-traumatic life experiences.[57]

We may *know* truths about God that we have learned from the Church's catechism, from creeds, or from Sunday school. These might include beliefs such as that God is love, that His love is unfailing, that He forgives, that He created us in love for love, that He is sovereign, that He is always with us, and that He redeems us. These more "left-brained" God *concepts* are things that we *intellectually believe, know,* or *understand* about God.

On the other hand, our God *image* refers to the things we *feel* about God. Our feelings about God are more "right-brained," and they happen unconsciously and are often based on personal experiences. For example, a person with an abusive father may have a God image that is cruel and uncaring. Even though they may say that God is loving, deep down they respond emotionally to God as if He is unjust and dictatorial.

As we get to know our self-system, which includes all our parts, we discover that individual parts have their own God images. One part may see God as nice but incompetent and weak. Another part may see Him as a divine cop demanding perfection. Yet another part may see Him as disapproving and joyless.

One of the goals of this book is to help bring our God concepts and our God images into alignment. We want our God concept to be based on biblical truth and Church teaching. And we want those truths to sink into our hearts so that we experience them in a deeper way.

The Litanies of the Heart prayers were designed to do just that.

[57] Glendon Moriarty and Louis Hoffman are two of many experts in God-image research and literature.

In the next section, we will explore Jesus as a model for the inmost self, based on the Gospel accounts. Even though these characteristics of Jesus may be received as God concepts, I hope that you will pause with each one and allow perhaps one or two of them to be received in your heart. This may take more than one read-through. The meditation at the end of this chapter may also facilitate the movement of healthy, loving God images from the head to the heart.

SCRIPTURE STUDY: JESUS AS THE MODEL FOR THE REDEEMED INMOST SELF

What does it mean to have a redeemed or regenerated inmost self? We know that the effects of the Fall remain, and despite Baptism and a conversion of heart, we continue to wrestle with sin. Although the inmost self is enlightened with sanctifying grace and able to commune with God in blissful surrender, we often fail to live up to this potential. We continue, however, to rely on God's grace and strive to bring all the parts of the self-system into an unburdened communion with the inmost self and with God. We seek this inner harmony, a simple and unified focus, a dependence on a loving God, and a free expression of all the unique and beautiful qualities or strengths of the soul.

A tall order, right? It is indeed a journey to get there, something we strive for. It is also something God is calling us toward. Let's take the first steps with Jesus by our side.

In Jesus, we see the person whose inmost human self is not deformed by sin and whose suffering has not burdened His parts with lies or wrong beliefs. His inmost self remains in perfect communion with God. Not only is Jesus our Redeemer, whose death and Resurrection offer us reconciliation with God and life after death, but He is also our role model for this life.

Jesus as Model — Eight Characteristics of the Redeemed Inmost Self

Paul writes in his Letter to the Galatians, "I have been crucified with Christ; and it is no longer I who live, but it is Christ who lives in me. And the life I now live in the flesh I live by faith in the Son of God, who loved me and gave himself for me" (2:19–20).

When Christ "lives in me" the inmost self is regenerated and capable of connecting with God and capable of mediating grace to all the parts of the self-system. When Christ is *born* in the inmost self, the qualities and characteristics of Christ become available to the whole person.

In my doctoral work, I was attracted to qualitative research because of its emphasis on understanding people's stories. I was especially fascinated by phenomenology, which is the study of lived experience. In this approach, one discovers the core elements of that experience through a process of coding and theme identification.

As I considered the belief that the inmost self was created in the image of God and that Jesus Christ, although divine, was the perfect man, I speculated that Jesus Christ would possess all the qualities of the inmost self in communion with God. I decided then to "code" the Gospel accounts using a phenomenological approach to understand how Jesus expresses Himself to others. It seemed to me that this should inform us of how the inmost self would relate both to others and to the parts of the self-system. I hoped that I might discover a biblical roadmap for working with one's interior world.

What I discovered was indeed profound and beautiful, and it became clear that Jesus was indeed the exemplar for the inmost self. The goal of us Christians is to grow in holiness and to become more Christlike. We are to become saints, and Christ is the perfect role model. As we access the inmost self in communion with Christ, we can bring Christ's love to all the parts of the self-system and eventually to others as well. The results of my research revealed the following eight characteristics of the inmost self, based on how Christ interacted with others. Jesus calls and enables the inmost self to be:

- *the Lover,* who loves the parts with gentleness and humility
- *the Seeker,* who seeks the lost parts with confidence and attuned to the will of God
- *the Protector,* who empathizes, rejoices, and prepares a safe place for the parts
- *the True Friend,* who knows and affirms the parts
- *the Healer,* who relieves burdens

- *the Pathfinder*, who calls parts to righteousness and holiness
- *the Bridge Builder*, who calls parts to communion with each other, with God, and with others
- *the Nurturer*, who feeds, nourishes, and calls the parts to alertness and action

Let us explore the biblical foundation for these characteristics and explore how they apply to parts work and to healing and transforming our inner world.

The Lover

The story of the prodigal son is one of the best known and impactful parables of Jesus (Luke 15:11–32). Here we have a son who abandons his family and wastes his fortune on dissolute living in a foreign land. The son's "firefighter part"[58] was in full steam as he spent money on food and women. But now we see him as an exile, living in a distant land and full of shame and self-contempt. He chooses to return home in humility.

The father, who is normally understood to represent God, also can represent the inmost self as it receives a burdened, exiled part. The father runs to greet his lost son with joy, and he relieves him of his burden of shame and guilt. "But while he was still far off, his father saw him and was filled with compassion, he ran and put his arms around him and kissed him" (v. 20).

We may imagine the inmost self as a parent who is waiting and hoping for the return of all the lost parts of the self-system. The inmost self loves with a gentle and humble love, and he demonstrates sacrificial love. The inmost self has great affection for each part, no matter how lost, burdened, sinful, or difficult a part may appear to be.

When a reluctant, shame-filled part appears, perhaps for the first time in a long time, he is greeted, even from a distance, with great joy and delight. The father's humility is never clearer than when he runs to greet his son. Notice also that the father greets his son with genuine physical affection that flows from his

[58] Recall that a firefighter part is a protector part who takes on an extreme role to avoid or numb negative feelings.

joy, "for this son of mine was dead and is alive again; he was lost and is found! And they began to celebrate" (v. 24).

It may be that other parts of the self-system, like the older brother in the parable, begrudge the reappearance of this lost part. The good father, the inmost self, must also attend to these other parts who are burdened with resentment and must provide an affirmation: "You're always with me, and all that is mine is yours" (v. 31). This parable is a powerful example of the self's loving and working with multiple parts in a spirit of gentle and humble love.

The Seeker

Christ describes Himself as the Good Shepherd who "lays down his life for the sheep"; He says of His sheep, "I know my own and my own know me" and "they will listen to my voice" (John 10:11, 14, 16). The sheep are dependent on their Shepherd and trust Him. His authority rests in the fact that He truly cares for them and is willing to do anything for their good, including accepting death.

In the story of the prodigal son, we see the son coming back home and being well received by his father. But in the parable of the lost sheep, Jesus goes even further and seeks out the lost sheep at the risk of losing His whole flock (Luke 15:4). The point is not that the Shepherd doesn't care for the other sheep; it is that He loves the lost in a way that defies all logic and convention. His love breaks through all our shame, insecurities, and self-doubt. Likewise, the inmost self seeks after lost, exiled, and wounded parts of the self-system. Even though these parts may be far from our conscious mind, the self has a natural desire to find, heal, and bring them back into communion with himself.

The inmost self has authority in one's inner world and seeks out the lost and burdened parts. The inmost self draws strength from God, is attuned to His will, and acts with confidence.

When the parts of the self-system encounter the inmost self, there is a natural mutual recognition, and the goodwill of the inmost self is genuine and transparent. The parts can experience comfort in knowing that they are taken care of by a loving parent. And this loving inner good shepherd is, in turn, connected with, attuned to, and strengthened by a loving God.

The Protector

In the Gospel of Matthew, Jesus prefaces the story of the lost sheep with an admonishment not to despise "one of these little ones" (18:10). God cares about us when we are lost and sees us as little children. Children are the most vulnerable in society; they are dependent on others for their care and protection. When children are lost or abused, they suffer greatly, and the wounds can be devastating. God shows us that He is delighted when His children are returned to Him. In the same way, the inmost self is particularly loving toward exiled child parts. I have seen this joy over and over again when a client discovers and really sees and connects with an inner child part.

Jesus says that children are "the greatest in the kingdom of heaven," that "unless you change and become like children, you will never enter the kingdom," and that "whoever welcomes one such child in my name welcomes me" (Matt. 18:3, 4, 5). Jesus specifically has the children brought to Him so that He can lay His hands on them and pray over them (Matt. 19:13–15).

Just as Jesus calls and loves children, the inmost self empathizes with and rejoices in finding, healing, and restoring parts of the self-system. The inmost self particularly calls and loves the exiled child parts, grieves for lost and burdened parts, and prepares a safe place within for each part.

We also know from St. Paul that God provides our parts with spiritual means to protect and defend ourselves. God is faithful and "will strengthen you and guard you from the evil one" (2 Thess. 3:3). God provides a "shield of faith," "a "helmet of protection," and a "sword of the Spirit" (Eph. 6:16–17). Our inner world is often under attack by cognitive distortions (lies) and false beliefs. Our distorted God images and our low self-worth cause us to experience high levels of anxiety. One of the ways God protects us from this is to reveal His true nature and affirm our true identity as His children. He does this by empathizing with us and then lifting us up so that we no longer need to live in fear.

We must look to Jesus as our guide. He shows us that He is not only our protector but also our empathizer. After the death of His friend Lazarus, He was "greatly disturbed in spirit and deeply moved" to find Lazarus's sister Mary weeping, and when He reached the tomb, He "began to weep" (John 11:33, 35). In an act not only of protection but of compassion and restoration, Jesus then raised Lazarus back to life.

Jesus also experienced strong emotion and even anxiety. We read that in the Garden of Gethsemane, "in his anguish he prayed more earnestly, and his sweat became like great drops of blood" (Luke 22:44). Despite Christ's enduring the pain and suffering of the Cross, God ultimately reveals through Him the real plan, which is to destroy death and restore the relationship between Himself and humanity — to protect us from eternal death and bring us into an everlasting intimacy with Him.

The inmost self also empathizes with others, grieves, and experiences the pain and suffering of the parts. Like Christ, we must learn to surrender to God from our deepest heart, to receive renewed strength. We might have protector parts (managers and firefighters) that get in the way and try to prevent us from being fully human and fully capable of a range of healthy emotions, especially the painful ones, but the process of unblending and unburdening those parts is essential if we want to be Christlike and live a spirit-filled life. And since Jesus gave us the commandment to "love one another as I have loved you" (John 15:12), we must remember that the inmost self and all the parts of the self-system are meant to have a supportive relationship with each other based on love. Empathy, grieving, and experiencing pain and suffering are all forms of vulnerability, which can be a challenge for many of us. The idea here is that God promises to protect us as we choose to open our hearts and become more vulnerable.

Jesus was concerned that His followers, whom He calls "little children," would look for Him after He had gone (John 13:33). Jesus described the "Father's house" as a place with "many dwelling-places"; He promised His disciples that He would "prepare a place" for them with Him (John 14:2–3). Although Jesus was referring to a future perfect state of glorification in Heaven, we also know that the example of Heaven can provide both a prototype for building a kingdom of Heaven on earth and a vision for ordering our own internal world.

The True Friend

The Holy Spirit abides with the inmost self and is the source of friendship, connection, relationship, grace, and love for all the parts of the self-system. Jesus promises that the Holy Spirit will be with us forever as our true friend:

"I will ask the Father, and he will give you another Advocate, to be with you for ever. This is the Spirit of truth, whom the world cannot receive, because it neither sees him nor knows him. You know him, because he abides with you, and he will be in you. I will not leave you orphaned; I am coming to you" (John 14:16–18).

Jesus tells His followers, "I do not call you servants[59] any longer, because the servant does not know what the master is doing; *but I have called you friends*, because I have made known to you everything that I have heard from my Father. You did not choose me but I chose you" (John 15:15–16, emphasis mine). Jesus radically changes His relationship with His followers from one of servitude to one of friendship. This friendship involves intimacy as Jesus shares what He knows from the Father. We are included in His mission. He chooses us to be with Him. This passage is in the context of loving one another. Jesus invites us to participate in His mission of love, in which He builds a kingdom that is characterized by healing, freedom, compassion, and communion.

This love that Jesus has for us, and this love He calls us to have for others, can also be exercised within the self-system. The inmost self chooses to befriend all the parts and share with them his mission, which, like Christ's mission, is to bring healing, freedom, compassion, and communion. Jesus seeks the ultimate good for each of us, and He desires intimacy with each of us. Similarly, the inmost self sees the good intentions of each part of the self-system and guides them out of extreme roles and into healthy, meaningful roles. The inmost self chooses to call on the parts, empathizes with them, delights in them, and desires union with them.

God so loves us that He promises to be with us eternally. As with Abraham, it is through our faith in Him that we are called a "friend of God" (James 2:23). We have a life-giving, intimate, and mutual connection with Jesus. We can depend on Him to stay with us through any difficulty.

Likewise, the inmost self knows and affirms the worth of each part. The inmost self sees the inner dignity of each part aside from achievements or failures and teaches true humility, which is neither pride nor self-abasement. The

[59] Some translations say "slaves," which only underlines the radical nature of the change in relationship to include the concept of freedom and liberation.

inmost self practices true self-love, true self-friendship,[60] when it seeks healing and restoration for each part of the self-system. Its goal is unity, union, and harmony while always respecting and valuing the unique resources of each part.

The Healer

Jesus' ministry is characterized by physical healings: He heals lepers, paralytics, the blind, the deaf, the mute, a woman with a hemorrhage — anyone who is sick.[61]

Jesus also heals the heart. He heals our emotional wounds and our fears and anxieties (Matt. 6:25–34). He calms the storm (Luke 8:22–25). He forgives sins (e.g., Luke 7:49). He brings outsiders back into community.[62] He cares about each person by showing love and mercy and seeks his or her ultimate good.[63]

Jesus' healing miracles and profound moments of radical acceptance reveal His great love for humanity. His goal, however, is not simply to bring about healing in the short-term but ultimately to restore all things in relationship with God. The following passage perhaps provides some insight:

> Now before the festival of the Passover, Jesus knew that his hour had come to depart from this world and go to the Father. Having loved his own who were in the world, he loved them to the end. The devil had already put it into the heart of Judas son of Simon Iscariot to betray him. And during supper Jesus, knowing that the Father had given all things into his hands, and that he had come from God and was going to God, got up from the table, took off his outer robe, and tied a towel around himself. Then he poured water into a basin and began to wash

[60] For more on self-love and self-friendship see Anthony Flood's *The Metaphysical Foundations of Love: Aquinas on Participation, Unity, and Union.*

[61] An example of this is in Matthew 11:5: "The blind receive their sight, the lame walk, the lepers are cleansed, the deaf hear, the dead are raised, and the poor have good news brought to them."

[62] An example of this is in Luke 17:11–19, where Jesus heals ten lepers. Lepers were considered unclean and had to live away from the community.

[63] Examples of this include Christ's encounters with the Samaritan woman at the well (John 4) and the woman about to be stoned for adultery (John 8:1–11).

> the disciples' feet and to wipe them with the towel that was tied around him. He came to Simon Peter, who said to him, "Lord, are you going to wash my feet?" Jesus answered, "You do not know now what I am doing, but later you will understand." Peter said to him, "You will never wash my feet." Jesus answered, "Unless I wash you, you have no share with me." Simon Peter said to him, "Lord, not my feet only but also my hands and my head!" Jesus said to him, "One who has bathed does not need to wash, except for the feet, but is entirely clean. And you are clean, though not all of you." For he knew who was to betray him; for this reason he said, "Not all of you are clean." (John 13:1–11)

Although there is no physical healing in this passage, Jesus seeks to impart a spiritual healing, or an inner sanctification, through the washing of the apostles' feet. Notice that He approaches the task with love, and Peter must learn to receive this divine love. Jesus offers Himself fully to His friends — ultimately to the whole world — in self-sacrificial love.

The inmost self relieves the burdens of all the parts. He relieves anxieties and worries. He calms the parts. The inmost self is also in the role of healer for all the parts of the self-system. In the natural realm, the inmost self can approach each part with curiosity and exercise compassion as he helps each part let go of heavy burdens. In the redeemed Christian, Christ dwells in the inmost self (Eph. 3:17) so that, with His help, the inmost self can also be a channel of God's grace. Through the sacrament of Penance, the inmost self channels God's forgiveness to all the parts. Through the Anointing of the Sick, the inmost self channels God's healing to all the parts. Through the Eucharist, all the parts are nourished, forgiven, healed, and united with Christ.

In this way, the inmost self can be experienced as directing the parts into a loving relationship with God. The inmost self can also be experienced as providing love and care for the parts in a Christlike manner. In a certain sense, the inmost self reflects Christ's presence to all the parts in the same way that the Christian is called to embody Christ to others. Christ dwells in us, and we dwell in Him. The Incarnation is played out within our interior world just as it is meant to be played out in the Church, the Body of Christ. In other words, Christ is made present within us, and we are also Christ to others.

The inmost self seeks out and endeavors to heal all our burdened parts with a heart that beats in tandem with Christ's. "When the righteous cry for help, the LORD hears, and rescues them from all their troubles. The LORD is near to the broken-hearted, and saves the crushed in spirit" (Ps. 34:17–18).

The Pathfinder

A pathfinder is someone who shows others the way. In a Christian context, a pathfinder helps show us the way to union with God. The original pathfinder in the New Testament is St. John the Baptist, who paves the way for the coming of Jesus. John cries out, " 'Repent, for the kingdom of heaven has come near.' This is the one of whom the prophet Isaiah spoke when he said, 'The voice of one crying out in the wilderness: "Prepare the way of the Lord, make his paths straight" ' " (Matt. 3:2–4).

Jesus shows us the way to a deep and intimate relationship with God. He says, "I am the light of the world. Whoever follows me will never walk in darkness but will have the light of life" (John 8:12). Jesus doesn't fear going to places where there is danger. When the disciples are afraid of the reaction of the Jews, He reminds them, "Are there not twelve hours of daylight? Those who walk during the day do not stumble, because they see the light of this world. But those who walk at night stumble, because the light is not in them" (John 11:9–10).

As the Good Shepherd, Jesus is the ultimate pathfinder. He guides us through even our darkest moments. "Even though I walk through the darkest valley, I fear no evil; for you are with me; your rod and your staff— they comfort me" (Ps. 23:4). The Good Shepherd has an intimate relationship with His sheep. They know His voice, and they trust in Him completely. "The gatekeeper opens the gate for him, and the sheep hear his voice. He calls his own sheep by name and leads them out" (John 10:3). The Good Shepherd is willing to die for His sheep, that is how much He loves them (John 10:11).

The inmost self is also called to be a pathfinder for the parts of the self-system. This is expressed in IFS language as self-leadership. The more the inmost self leads with compassion and wisdom and truth, the more that the parts will trust. The parts discover that the inmost self wants only their ultimate good; this includes healthy roles within the system and a loving relationship with God and others. Sometimes the inmost self has to call out a part and provide direction. He is a loving but firm guide. When parts blend with the self, then the inmost self cannot provide leadership or self-governance. The process of unblending allows access to the inmost self, who can then work with and guide the parts to greater internal integration.

The Bridge Builder

A bridge builder is someone who creates or restores relationships that are damaged by conflict and broken trust. Jesus is the ultimate mediator or bridge builder because He restores the relationship between God and humanity. He also seeks to unite humanity into a community of love, the Church.

Jesus builds bridges between Himself and sinners. He meets the woman at the well and offers her living water. He meets with prostitutes and tax collectors. He heals the outcast, including lepers. He finds a way for them all to come to Him. Bridges allow access, and Jesus becomes the new access point between people and God. Jesus says, "I am the way, and the truth, and the life. No one comes to the Father except through me" (John 14:6).

Jesus builds the ultimate bridge through His death and Resurrection. St. Paul says that God "desires everyone to be saved and to come to the knowledge of the truth. For there is one God; there is also one mediator between God and humankind, Christ Jesus, himself human, who gave himself a ransom for all" (1 Tim. 2:4–6). Jesus finds a way to bring us into communion with God the Father. He takes the burden of sin onto Himself so that we can be liberated. He restores our dignity, and we become children of God. Jesus builds a bridge to God the Father and a bridge to loving relationships with each other.

In the same way, the inmost self is a bridge builder. The role of the inmost self is to help all the parts connect with God the Father and with each other. As we do this, we are also able to connect with others in more meaningful ways. Our exiled parts especially live in the deep recesses of our unconscious minds. We keep them away because they may hold painful memories, negative beliefs, and terrifying emotions. The inmost self, with the mind of Christ (1 Cor. 2:16), wants to reach those parts and bring them back into communion in order to love and heal them.

Parts work is not just about inner peace and harmony but also about connection with others. There is a real joy in worshipping with others who have also been freed of their burdens and who are living a life of recollection and are "in self." The inmost self can also act through the human person to build relationships and help others. This is the community that Jesus promised us when He told us about His "true worshippers [who] will worship the Father in spirit and truth" (John 4:23).

The Nurturer

A nurturer is someone who provides care for, encourages, and fosters growth in others. Christ nurtures the whole of us: body and soul. Jesus describes Himself as "the bread of life" (John 6:35), offering eternal life, and He implores Peter, if He truly loves Him, to "feed my lambs" (see John 21:15–17). Christ claims that His food is "to do the will of him who sent me and to complete his work" (John 4:34). Jesus feeds the hungry crowd with five loaves and two fish (Matt. 14:19–20). He says, "Let anyone who is thirsty come to me" (John 7:37). He promises that "out of the believer's heart" — the inmost self — "shall flow rivers of living water" (John 7:38). This living water is grace.

The ultimate example of Christ's nurturing us is in the Eucharist, which celebrates Christ's death and Resurrection and unites us to Him both physically and spiritually. His very person becomes part of us in order for us to be encouraged and transformed. He feeds us with Himself. He loves us completely.

We hear more about how Jesus calls the inmost self to nourish our self-system in the parable of the good Samaritan (Luke 10:25–37). A man who has been robbed and beaten lies on the road, and a priest and a Levite walk by and ignore his needs, but a Samaritan notices him and goes out of his way to make sure he is cared for, treated, and fed: "He went to him and bandaged his wounds, having poured oil and wine on them. Then he put him on his own animal, brought him to an inn, and took care of him" (v. 34). Just as the Samaritan cared for the injured man, the inmost self must love and care for hurting parts, even when there are other parts who ignore them, as the priest and the Levite ignored the injured man. This story calls us to care for our own wounded parts. As our own inner wounds are healed, we will also develop the capacity to serve and help others in need.

LIFE APPLICATIONS FOR INNER TRANSFORMATION

Meditation — God as a Secure Presence

I invite you to walk with me through an exercise to experience God as a loving and secure presence. As we do this, we can begin the process of healing past wounds and also give strength and grace to our inmost self. We recognize that others, even loved ones, will sometimes fail us, but the inmost self, inspired and strengthened by God's grace, can bring harmony to our inner world. Our basic needs are to feel safe, seen, known, comforted, valued, and encouraged.[64]

First, I ask you to become very comfortable. You might be sitting on a chair or a couch or even on the floor; just make sure that your body is in a state of rest, at least as much as you can. I ask you to take a little time and really notice your body. Notice anywhere that you might be feeling tension; notice your breathing; bring attention to how your breathing impacts your chest; notice your chest rising as you take in air and releasing as you breathe out. Also notice that it takes no effort at all to be at rest; if you're in a chair, it takes no effort at all to be supported there. Let the chair or the floor or the sofa do all the work, and allow your muscles to notice that they don't have to make any effort at all; they can just relax.

I invite you to notice that as your body relaxes, your breathing is deeper and slower and you feel a sense of calm. And if any tension should show up, just take a deep breath, hold it for a moment, and as you exhale, allow that tension to release on its own.

I invite you to take a few long breaths, and as you take in each breath, open your eyes fully, and as you exhale gently, close your eyes fully. Take a moment to notice your eyes as they open on the inhale and as they close on the exhale; just notice that several times. Inhale — open your eyes; exhale — close your eyes.

Reflect for a moment on your image of God. If possible, distinguish between the images of God that come from your own experiences of being hurt by others and the concept of God that you have learned from a healthy spirituality.

[64] See Daniel P. Brown and David S. Elliott, *Attachment Disturbances in Adults: Treatment for Comprehensive Repair* (New York: W. W. Norton, 2016).

In the Gospel of Matthew, Jesus compares Himself to a mother bird, or hen, who gathers her babies under her wings when times are rough (Matt. 23:37). In Hosea, God is described as tender and loving, "Yet it was I who taught Ephraim to walk, I took them up in my arms. . . . I led them with cords of human kindness, with bands of love. I was to them like those who lift infants to their cheeks. I bent down to them and fed them" (Hos. 11:3–4).

God is protective and loving, even when humans are not.

There are many possible examples of healthy, positive concepts of God.[65] These might include:

A dove

A good shepherd

A forgiving father

A light in the darkness

A nurturing mother

A suffering servant

A gentle, healing presence

A loving parent

We want to take our time and invite a healthy truthful concept of God to move from our thinking minds to our hearts.

Imagine yourself connecting with God as a loving parent, a forgiving father, a nurturing and protective mother, or another image that feels right to you.

In the Gospel of Luke, we read:

> Now when all the people were baptized, and when Jesus also had been baptized and was praying, the heaven was opened, and the Holy Spirit descended upon him in bodily form, as a dove, and a voice came from

[65] You will notice that I suggest images for God that are related to both mothers and fathers. I want to clarify that God is revealed as Father and Jesus is a man, but, strictly speaking, God is neither male nor female since He is pure spirit (CCC 370). The Bible contains several passages that describe the love of God in terms of maternal language, such as Deuteronomy 32:11 (which compares God to a mother eagle protecting her young), Hosea 13:8 (which compares God to a mother bear robbed of her cubs), and Matthew 23:37 and Luke 13:34 (which describe God as a hen gathering her chicks).

> heaven, "*Thou art my beloved Son; with whom I am well pleased.*" (3:21–22, emphasis mine)

God the Father manifested Himself and expressed affirmation and love for Jesus. As we sit with our image of God, think of how we are also affirmed in love:

God sees me with gentle love.
God knows my heart.
God sees my woundedness.
God relieves my burdens.
God comforts me.
God values me.
God encourages me.
I can feel safe with God.
God delights in me.
God knows exactly what I need right now.

What happens in your body when you experience God's love? How do you feel?

In the story of the Exodus, God notices the heavy burden of the enslaved Israelites; He takes care of them and helps them escape and find a home.

God says:

> I am the Lord, and I will free you from the burdens of the Egyptians and deliver you from slavery to them. I will redeem you with an outstretched arm and with mighty acts of judgement. *I will take you as my people, and I will be your God.* You shall know that I am the Lord your God, who has freed you from the burdens of the Egyptians. (Exod. 6:6–7, emphasis mine)

Even though others have hurt us and betrayed us, our loving God loves us and is with us. He wants to relieve us of our burdens and take us to safety. We can ask God for His peace and allow His love to sit with us a bit today.

Notice what happens in your body as you allow God to take your burden.

We know from the Gospel of John that God the Son, as the Good Shepherd, loves us and truly knows us, recognizes us, and protects us:

> My sheep hear my voice. I know them, and they follow me. I give them eternal life, and they shall never perish. No one will snatch them out of my hand. (10:27–28)

We know that in God's embrace we can find safety and that God can heal all of our wounds with loving care. He truly knows us, sees us, and wants the very best for us. And He delights in watching us discover our true selves.

Reflection Questions

1. How do you relate to God as an attachment figure? How do your parts' negative God images get in the way?

2. Which characteristics of Jesus speak to you the most today?

3. Recall a time in your life when you experienced Christ in the role of lover, seeker, protector, true friend, healer, pathfinder, bridge builder, or nurturer. What images of God reflect that experience? What happens in your body when you recall those images? What emotions do you feel?

4. Reflect on a time in your life when you were in the role of lover, seeker, protector, true friend, healer, pathfinder, bridge builder, or nurturer with your own parts or with someone else. What happens in your body when you recall being in that role? What emotions do you feel?

5. Do you have a part that needs a lover, seeker, protector, true friend, healer, pathfinder, bridge builder, or nurturer today? What happens when you invite your inmost self to be present with that part? What happens in your body? What happens to your emotions?

4

OPENING OUR EYES

Tom's Story: The Navy SEAL

My older brothers were all extroverted and popular. One played college football for the Aztecs, another one was a Rhodes Scholar, and one later became a successful neurosurgeon. I was the awkward, largely ignored younger brother. My parents, although generally kind and well-intentioned, were busy with their political careers. My father was a congressman, and my mother was an elected school board member. It was assumed, since I was quiet, that I preferred to be a loner. I wasn't good at sports, and I was a bit small for my age.

I had no meaningful friendships at school, my father was too busy to spend time with me, and I felt unwanted by my older brothers. It was the perfect setup for what happened next. I was only twelve when my father's youngest brother, my uncle Tony, who was nineteen years old, took an interest in me. He invited me to the movies, took me swimming, and played video games with me. I so looked forward to his visits, as I was starving for attention and affirmation.

I was completely taken by surprise when he began showing me pornography. I was both terrified and curious. When he began masturbating in front of me, I was frightened at first but concluded that he was including me in a masculine ritual. He invited me into a very personal and private space. I felt special. In time, he introduced me to more sexual behaviors that culminated in a moment of feeling completely overwhelmed. I remember going into the shower afterward and shamefully washing away the semen and blood. Soon after, my uncle went to a college in another state.

Throughout middle school and high school, I continued to isolate and became so withdrawn that my parents took me to see a counselor. I was so afraid of sharing what had happened to me with Tony that I said nothing about it. I was put on an antidepressant.

I spent my days in a state of constant anxiety. When I was in high school, I began binging on pornography to relieve myself of all the tension in my body from all that anxiety. I gravitated toward watching videos depicting men being physically and sexually degraded by larger, stronger men. I couldn't understand why, after the abuse I had experienced, I would look at that disgusting and perverted material. I thought this meant that I had wanted my uncle to abuse me and that there was something deeply wrong with me.

I used my fear to get through the engineering program at Caltech. I used my sharp focus to get a high-paying job in the cybersecurity world, where I was rewarded for my extreme diligence. I used my drive to push myself and stay physically fit. Once I had children, I used my hypervigilance to make sure they were always safe and all their needs were met. To the outside world, I was a superman, but inside I was this small, awkward, unwanted, abused child.

When my marriage was in trouble and my anxiety became unmanageable, I began therapy with a trauma-informed counselor. I finally confessed the painful truth of what Tony had done to me and my subsequent use of pornography. When my therapist asked how I felt toward the twelve-year-old part who had been abused by Tony, my answer was, "I hate him. He's weak and disgusting and needs to be punished." My therapist turned his attention to this voice, and we discovered that it represented a strong, buff, masculine part of me. When I looked closer to observe him, I pictured him as a Navy SEAL. His job was to shame and "beat up" this twelve-year-old part of me.

In time, I learned that the Navy SEAL was "beating up" my wounded-child part in a misguided attempt to protect him. My therapist referred to the SEAL as a manager part who was trying to prevent the shame-filled exile from overwhelming my system. When we spent more time with this SEAL, we learned that he was young himself, maybe fourteen or fifteen. In other words, this Navy SEAL was my fifteen-year-old attempt to manage and cope with the shame and overwhelmingness of having been abused by my uncle. In time, I was able to access my core or inner self, which was able to listen to and understand the SEAL. I helped the SEAL to realize that repressing and shaming the twelve-year-old part was no longer helpful or even needed. My therapist helped me show this manager part that a good SEAL would rescue, protect, and encourage a wounded twelve-year-old. He wouldn't hurt him. Real men transform pain; they don't transmit it.

Once the SEAL adopted his new role, we could spend time bringing love and healing to the twelve-year-old part. The young part was then able to express and feel his pain without overwhelming all of me. This young part was finally able to receive the attention and affirmation he always needed. With the Navy SEAL working to love and protect the young part, my need for self-harming pornography disappeared. When I have a slip, I know how to reconnect with my parts, soften the SEAL, and care for the twelve-year-old.

THE PSYCHOLOGY OF THE INTERIOR WORLD

As we get to know our parts, we may discover that some of our parts are cooperative, and some are not. We may discover that some parts appear unfriendly, difficult, or even frightening, like Tom's Navy SEAL. It is important to remember that the parts are essentially good but may be burdened because of both their experiences and their response to trauma.

We have wounded or exiled parts burdened by trauma that carry the weight of overwhelming emotions, such as pain, shame, and fear. We also have protector parts whose job it is to prevent the wounded parts from being seen or exposed. Some protectors are proactive managers who help us successfully function in life. Other protectors are reactive firefighters who seek out either comfort or a distraction from disturbing emotions.

Examples of common protector parts include workaholics, bullies, perfectionists, and critics. Some parts are furious and carry a great deal of anger. Other parts may be sarcastic, agitated, people pleasing, or controlling. In the case of Tom, the manager showed up as an abusive Navy SEAL, an idealized but toxic form of masculinity. When the SEAL beat the young part, it was an expression of his own internalized self-hatred. The SEAL's job was to distract Tom from the painful feelings of shame, loneliness, and rejection of his wounded child part.

We must remember that the SEAL's intention is good. Our protectors mean well.

Many therapies instinctively want to help the obvious victim and therefore bypass the protector part. Instead, we want to work with and heal protectors in anticipation of working with exiles. If we don't, there is often a backlash, which can take the form of a relapse into addiction or depression or even an increase in anxiety. When we work with protectors, and they become self-led, we gain in them a valuable resource and create more harmony within our interior world.

It is important to remind ourselves that protectors have good intentions. We see this in the case of Tom, in whom the Navy SEAL is a young part trying to make sense of the sexual abuse experience. Once the SEAL is truly seen and understood, the inmost self can reorient him to the present and help him to see new options.

Connecting with a Protector

As we reflect on our own protector parts, let's take a moment to see if we notice any tension in our bodies. If you can connect a physical sensation to a part, see if you can either picture that part or sense its presence.

We can look past any unpleasant veneer and really *see* or *sense* the protector part. Acknowledge the part and invite him to give some space so that the inmost self can notice him and get to know him.

Take time to really notice this part, and when you feel ready, ask yourself, "How do I feel toward this part?" Other parts will likely show up. If necessary, ask them to wait nearby. Return your attention to the first part and how you feel toward him. What does the part need? If he is anxious, would he be willing to relax with you? If he is angry, would he be willing to turn down the intensity and share his concerns?

Continue to really notice the part. Try to understand why he is doing what he is doing. Listen to his story. Is he a workaholic because he believes that if he doesn't achieve, he will be seen as worthless? Is he a bully, like the Navy SEAL, because he wants to prevent anyone from ever hurting him again? Is he a perfectionist because he fears that any mistake would be overwhelming? Is he a critic because he is afraid that a mistake might cost him attention, love, and security? Is he angry because he doesn't believe he will be heard any other way? There are so many possibilities, but when we pause, ask, and listen from the heart, the part will tell us.

As you access and approach the part with the "eyes" of the inmost self, you can bring love and compassion to this protector part, no matter how he presents himself. Even if you don't approve of the way the part has behaved, when you express empathy for him, when you show that you understand how he got there, the part will almost always experience a measure of calm. This part may have been trapped in a rather thankless role. You can tell this part, "Thank you for working hard for so long to protect us." Don't be surprised if you have tears when you thank an overburdened, long-suffering protector part. When you express compassion for the protector part, ask yourself if the part can feel it. What is it like for the part to feel compassion from your inmost self?

The key here is to remember that the part is operating from a place of fear. The protector part has a good intention, but he is afraid that if he doesn't do what he is doing, something bad will happen. It's important to connect with the protector by asking, "Why are you doing what you do?" and "What are you afraid will happen if you don't?" A protector may need to be reminded that you are not blaming him or trying to get rid of him. You are there to help. You may also bring in other parts or spiritual resources to help.[66]

In listening to the part as he tells his story, the goal is for the inmost self to become a trusted leader and ally with this protector part. We honor this part when we show we listen, understand, and express empathy. The part will naturally begin the process of trusting us and will reveal more about itself. Sometimes this part has only a partial understanding of the core inmost self. Sometimes the part doesn't know how old *we* are! We can invite the part to look at us now and see that we're adults. Just as it was important for the inmost self to truly *see* the part, it is now important for the part to *see* the inmost self.

We will explore below the importance of *seeing* or *sensing* in both the Genesis story and the Emmaus story. When the part starts to feel safe, you can ask it, "What part are you protecting?" and "If you didn't have to do this role, is there another role that you would prefer?" Eventually you can ask, "Would you like us to help you and the part you're protecting so that things can be better?" The protector will eventually allow you to see and encounter the part that is exiled, typically a wounded child part.

[66] In a spirit of prayer, we can invite Jesus or a favorite saint or angel to be present with us as we work with our parts. See chapter 8, on spiritual confidants, for more information on spiritual resources.

SCRIPTURE STUDY: THE ROAD TO EMMAUS AND THE BANQUET

We know from human biology and attachment theory that babies connect with their mothers or caregivers nonverbally and through the eyes. The "maternal gaze," as it's called, is a beautiful moment of intimacy and profound connection. Unspoken love is communicated through the eyes, and it is a powerful *knowing*. The intimacy of seeing and being seen is so powerful that it can sometimes be overwhelming and cause us, as adults, to have trouble with eye contact, especially prolonged eye contact.

We have parts that carry shame and self-protective parts that manage how much vulnerability we can handle. We turn away and fill the space with meaningless words and excuses. Deep inside, however, when unblended from our parts, with their false beliefs and their defense mechanisms, the inmost self longs for that gaze; it longs to be seen and to see into another.

If we return to the Genesis story, we may notice that the serpent tells Eve that if she eats the fruit, she will not die, but her eyes will be opened, she will be wise, and she will be like God. When she and Adam eat of the fruit, "then *the eyes of both were opened* and they knew that they were naked; and they sewed fig leaves together and made loincloths for themselves" (3:7, emphasis mine). The opening of their eyes signifies the beginning of the burden of shame as well as the burdens of childbirth pain, toil, and physical labor. The fact that the man will now "rule over" the woman means that this is also the beginning of power dynamics and imposing one's will on another. This represents the beginning of parts' taking on extreme roles. Notice also that God says, "By the sweat of your face *you shall eat bread* until you return to the ground, for out of it you were taken; you are dust, and to dust you shall return" (3:19, emphasis mine).

We also read about the opening of the eyes in the story of the road to Emmaus (Luke 24:13–35), which occurs after Jesus' Resurrection from the dead. An unknown figure encounters two of Jesus' disciples, disappointed and possibly disillusioned, on their walk to the village of Emmaus a couple of days after the Crucifixion. They had been looking forward to the coming of the Messiah. They had been told that Jesus' tomb was empty and that Jesus could not be found.

The stranger then tells them about the Messiah and the necessity that He suffer before entering His glory.

The stranger interprets the Scriptures for these disciples, beginning with the story of Moses, signifying to these disciples that a new Exodus has been inaugurated. Just as Moses led the Hebrew people from slavery to freedom, Jesus leads all of us from exile to restoration, from captivity to new life. Moses did not lead a bloody war against the Egyptians, but he did bring about their liberation from the military oppression. The Israelites had to walk through a path in the Red Sea that would have seemed like certain death, but it is through the dangerous waters that freedom is discovered, and it is through Christ's death on the Cross, not around it, that redemption is achieved. The kingdom of God will not come about by a bloody war against the Romans or any other worldly power. It will come about when we embrace love, even a love that is willing to die.

It isn't until that evening, when they reached the village, that the disciples were able to recognize this stranger as Jesus Himself. The key line here is the following: "When he was at the table with them, *he took bread, blessed and broke it,* and gave it to them. Then *their eyes were opened,* and they recognized him" (vv. 30–31, emphasis mine). When we juxtapose these passages with the passages from Genesis 3, it becomes clear that Jesus reverses the curse of Adam and Eve through His death and Resurrection. The breaking of the bread reveals this truth, and now their eyes are opened to see Jesus.

How does this relate to our parts? The inmost self must encounter the burdened parts of the self-system and *see* the Pharisees, the zealots, and the slaves as the protector parts or exiles that they are. This is also true of the parts who are bullies, perfectionists, critics, and Navy SEALs. All the parts of the self-system need redemption.

The inmost self, like Jesus, then must show our parts a radical new way of relating with love. The inmost self meets our inner prostitutes, our inner tax collectors, our inner pompous chief priests, and our inner rebels. The inmost self meets the passive-aggressive parts, the sarcastic parts, the isolated parts, and the defensive parts. These are all burdened protectors. And when we sit and eat with them, as Jesus did with His disciples in Emmaus, we discover that they are, in fact, protecting our inner lepers, our inner blind men, our inner sick and dying children.

After Jesus heals the leper and the paralytic, He calls Levi, who hosts a banquet with tax collectors and others who are considered outcasts. The Pharisees accuse Jesus, "Why do you eat and drink with tax collectors and sinners?" (see Matt. 9:11). All these parts, sinners and outcasts, filled with pain, shame, fear, and sadness, can be healed by Jesus' loving words and healing actions. Our inner prodigal can come home to the Father. Our inner woman at the well can reform her life and receive living water. Our inner critical parts can realize that they cannot cast the first stone. We gather our messed-up, bedraggled, sinful, hurting, and wounded parts and allow them to be in the presence of our inmost self, which is itself ideally in communion with a loving God.

All these parts are invited to the great feast, the great wedding banquet, where the last will be first. This is a prefiguring of the Eucharist, the heavenly banquet, where all these broken and burdened and protector parts will be honored and welcomed and healed. They will abandon their extreme roles and release their painful burdens. We bring both Navy SEAL and abused twelve-year-old parts. We bring the anxious overachiever and the porn-addicted and isolating parts. They are still appreciated and understood, but they are also beginning the process to be unburdened; this means they will no longer need to cling to old defense mechanisms, old maladaptive patterns of behavior, or old unhealthy extreme roles. They no longer need to cling to their former ways of coping that rely on control, worry, manipulation, ignoring pain, and overwork to survive. Our inner banquet is hosted by our inmost self, who is filled with compassion and invites all our parts with kindness, listens with curiosity, and offers food and rest to the weary heart.

LIFE APPLICATIONS FOR INNER TRANSFORMATION

Meditation — Connecting with a Protector Part

Find a quiet, peaceful place and invite yourself to have a moment of relaxation.

Begin with a simple Jesus prayer: *Lord Jesus Christ, Son of the living God, have mercy on me, a sinner.*

Notice what is going on in your body.

Slow things down and take a deep, cleansing breath.

As you slow your breathing down, see if your heart can become bigger, a little more open, a little more receptive, more caring, kinder, and curious.

Draw your attention inward.

What do you notice?

See if you can draw attention inward to body sensations.

What's happening inside could be thoughts or words, beliefs, assumptions, memories, or images.

The things that happen inside us are usually connected to parts.

If you notice something going on inside, you've noticed something related to a part.

If you can, with a big, open heart and with some curiosity, focus on whatever is drawing you in.

If you recognize a part, I invite you to be with that part.

Just notice what you're experiencing.

Parts have a reason for the things they do, but they have limited vision; they have only a slice of our experience. They don't always fully know what will be the consequences if their desires or impulses are enacted.

Does your part have a concern or a question? If so, let yourself get curious about that.

I invite you to ask God for His grace to be with this part in a gentle way. Allow any feelings of fear or self-condemnation to dissipate, and feel God's loving presence.

You may experience those graces as light or warmth. You can be open to this part in a way that's compassionate and connected.

It might be helpful to write it down in a journal or to draw what you see.

Just catch the messages, anything that a part might want to share with you.

All the parts have good intentions for us; they are trying to help.

Thank your part for letting you get to know him a bit more.
Let your parts know that you'll be back to check in on them.
We close with these words of Scripture:

> O Most High, when I am afraid,
> I put my trust in you.
> In God, whose word I praise,
> in God I trust; I am not afraid;
> what can flesh do to me? (Ps. 56:2–4)

Reflection Questions

1. Try to locate a protector part in your body. It might be a busy manager or a reactive firefighter. Can you visualize or sense this protector? What is his good intention? Does his behavior or desires or impulses cause any problems now? Does he need a new, less extreme role?

2. Consider how God has a plan for all your protector parts to go from extreme roles to new, life-giving ones led by confidence, calm, compassion, courage, creativity, clarity, curiosity, and connectedness. Invite a protector part to adopt a new role. How does your manager part feel about the new role? Is he resistant? Accepting? Delighted? Doubtful? Are you able to accept, but not necessarily endorse, that part's experiences without immediately judging them?

3. What does it mean for you to "open your eyes" and see God's plan for you and all your parts? Can you see them in a new way with curiosity and compassion?

4. How is the story of salvation, the Exodus, your own?

5

THE EVIL I DO NOT WANT

Bela's Story: The Wall, the Peacemaker, the People Pleaser, and the Critic

For a long time, my memories were lost behind "the Wall," where my eight-year-old part and her emotions used to live. As I began the healing process, a few key memories began to resurface. They became trailheads in my journey of self-discovery.

My older brother, Josef, held me while we huddled at the top of the stairs. The sound of our mother's voice, pushed to its limits, her screams, punctuated by sobs, caused me to clutch my brother's arm tighter. This was the third fight in one week. At least he didn't hit her; instead, he pounded his fist into the wall, again and again. The fighting might have been about his job, about his friends, or about his drinking or gambling, but this time, it was about another woman. He had been drinking, and his voice, sharp and toxic, was loud. Always loud like thunder. My brother whispered, "It'll be okay," but we both knew it wasn't true.

Later I went downstairs to find my mother weeping in a heap of tears and lost dreams. I tried to comfort her, and she cried for hours in my eight-year-old lap.

Josef, then five years older, could do no wrong. Over the years, I watched as my mother fawned over him, promoted his interest in writing, applauded when he became editor of the school newspaper, and celebrated when he became class president. I was in the background, chastised and corrected, an inconvenience and an annoyance.

My father was always barking. He barked at me to move out of the way or to fetch him a beer or to be quiet. I learned to be careful around him, quiet and invisible, as I predicted his needs and preemptively attempted to meet them. We all walked on eggshells around his unpredictable changes in mood. He could be funny and playful one moment, but in a sudden turn, he could cut you down to size. *"Who the hell do you think you are?"*

One time, I had two friends over for a sleepover. We were giggling and playing when he showed up and barked at us to be quiet. The other girls were terrified, and I was mortified. My mother intervened, and my parents began to fight, hurling insults until a fist went through the top of our wood-encased television. My mother broke down in tears. My father, in a drunken rage, continued yelling at no one. The two girls stealthily escaped out the back door and ran back to their homes. *"Look what you did!"* My father pointed to my mother crying on the sofa. He threw one of my dolls on the floor, breaking its head. *"How do you like them apples!"*

It was in moments like this that the Wall came to be. I survived by stoically repressing all my feelings of anger, pain, hurt, fear, and shame. With them went happiness, calm, playfulness, and joy.

On this side of the Wall, twin parts emerged; they appeared happy, gracious, and sometimes even funny, but they weren't, not truly. They were the peacemaker and the people pleaser. They believed that if they could be smarter, prettier, happier, quieter, and more helpful, I could keep my parents together, prevent my mother from crying, and keep my father from yelling.

And whenever the old feelings of anger, pain, or shame sneaked past the Wall, or when the peacemaker and the people pleaser weren't effectively managing everyone else's emotions, the critic was prepared to hurl accusations: *It's all your fault. You're in the way. You're not good enough. You're not lovable. You're a burden.* These accusations kept the peacemaker and the people pleaser whipped into submission and kept the overwhelming negative emotions behind the Wall. Homeostasis must be maintained.

I didn't learn about any of these parts and how they worked together until many years later. I was in counseling because I had been in one failed relationship after another. Each boyfriend was fun and charming at the beginning, but each turned out to be an alcoholic or an addict; each was dismissive and abusive. Each one eventually abandoned me, just as my father left my mother when I was nine years old. It is no wonder I developed a drinking problem of my own.

THE PSYCHOLOGY OF THE INTERIOR WORLD

Our manager parts typically care about social conventions and often try to be polite, worry about others, and want their hard work to pay off. Managers want us to look good, and they are often great planners. Bela's people-pleaser part wants everyone to have all their needs met. Her peacemaker part wants to make sure that everyone gets along and no one is fighting or crying. Her critic part criticizes the way she does it when it doesn't work. These managers become burdened with the roles of pleasing others, making sure everyone gets along, and being the internal taskmaster.

Meanwhile, the firefighter parts care about finding either relief or distraction from pain. In this case, Bela has a relationship part who turns to abusive men to distract her from her feelings of loneliness and abandonment. She also has a drinking part that turns to alcohol to experience relief when the relationships fail, and she has a Wall part to keep out overwhelming emotions.

When a manager and a firefighter have opposing goals, we have an inner conflict[67] or, as St. James says, "a war within you."[68] In this case, Bela has several inner conflicts. The critic may take issue with the relationship part when she is rejected by a man. The people pleaser may take issue with the Wall when she can't access her own feelings to comfort someone else. The peacemaker may take issue with the drinking part when, in a drunken stupor, she says something hurtful to someone.

We can resolve inner conflicts when our inmost self approaches each firefighter and manager part with empathy and understanding. Bela's manager parts, for example, learned early on that they must ignore their own needs to pacify someone else. Bela will need to connect with the people pleaser and let her know that she understands that the people pleaser took on this role to survive an inappropriate situation. She can help this part see that she no longer needs to parent others in order to stay safe. Her peacemaker part can learn that she no longer needs to sacrifice her needs to make others get along. Her critic can

[67] In IFS, this is sometimes called a polarization.

[68] "Those conflicts and disputes among you, where do they come from? Do they not come from your cravings that are at war within you?" (James 4:1). Here St. James identifies how external disputes stem from internal conflicts.

discover that she can be comforted when relationships fail and that she can choose healthier relationships in the future. The inmost self can take all these needs into account and lead from a place of understanding.

Ideally, the manager relaxes its inner criticism, and the firefighter relaxes its extreme coping at the same time. We approach both managers and firefighters with empathy and understanding, and eventually they may allow us to work with the exile. The exile, in this case, is the frightened little girl at the top of the stairs, the little girl who didn't want her mother to cry or her father to yell so much.

It is important to remember that the purpose of resolving inner conflicts is to help the parts work together in harmony. When the parts are self-led,[69] experience proper love from the inmost self, and function well with each other, the inner world of the human person experiences integration.[70] When the rich and beautiful diversity of each part is respected and functioning as a valuable piece in the greater whole, one experiences a sense of purpose and fulfillment. As we will explore in St. Paul's letter to the Romans, sin disrupts this inner unity, but a new life in the Spirit, which involves healing and unburdening, restores balance, freedom, and harmony.

[69] In IFS, when self-leadership occurs, the self leads the system, and the parts let go of their extreme roles. In the end, parts no longer fall into rigid categories of manager, firefighter, and exile.

[70] Philosopher Anthony Flood notes, "The lack of interior integration, having disordered self-love, prevents a person from loving others with a true love of friendship." Anthony T. Flood, *The Metaphysical Foundations of Love: Aquinas on Participation, Unity, and Union* (Washington, DC: Catholic University of American Press, 2018), 23. Benedictine priests Thomas Acklin and Boniface Hicks suggest that "in a certain sense, all of spiritual direction is a means by which the director helps the directee to come to a place of full interior integration, 'to mature manhood, to the measure of the stature of the fulness of Christ' (Eph 4:13). This involves an awareness of what is happening in the outer circle of our imagination, reason, and memory as well as learning how to bring our passions under the direction of reason." Thomas Acklin and Boniface Hicks, *Spiritual Direction: A Guide for Sharing the Father's Love* (Steubenville, OH: Emmaus Road Publishing, 2018), 32–33.

SCRIPTURE STUDY: ORIGINAL SIN AND ST. PAUL'S LETTER TO THE ROMANS

In his Letter to the Romans, St. Paul writes about our tendency to sin. Because of original sin, we experience concupiscence, the inclination or predisposition toward sin. We can never remove this inclination in this life, but its power over us can be greatly reduced.

St. Paul struggles with this inclination toward sin and famously said the following, which represents an essential passage for understanding a Christian approach to parts work:

> For we know that the law is spiritual; but I am of the flesh, sold into slavery under sin. I do not understand my own actions. For I do not do what I want, but I do the very thing I hate. Now if I do what I do not want, I agree that the law is good. But in fact it is no longer I that do it, but sin that dwells within me. For I know that nothing good dwells within me, that is, in my flesh. I can will what is right, but I cannot do it. *For I do not do the good I want, but the evil I do not want is what I do.* Now if I do what I do not want, it is no longer I that do it, but sin that dwells within me.
>
> So I find it to be a law that when I want to do what is good, evil lies close at hand. *For I delight in the law of God in my inmost self, but I see in my members another law at war with the law of my mind, making me captive to the law of sin that dwells in my members.* Wretched man that I am! Who will rescue me from this body of death? Thanks be to God through Jesus Christ our Lord! (Rom. 7:14–25, emphasis mine)

There is clearly a conflict happening within St. Paul. He speaks of doing things that he does not want to do. He speaks of delighting in his "inmost self," having within it the law of God. St. Paul teaches here that the inmost self is connected to God in a unique way. But apart from this inmost self, there are "members" who have "another law" at war with the mind.[71]

[71] It is unclear whether the members who make St. Paul captive are influenced by original sin, sinful social structures, personal sin, or some combination thereof. Personal sin is a deliberate defective choice. The effects of this choice

St. Paul feels that he is captive to the "law of sin" in his members. The word "members" could be interpreted exclusively as body parts, but here the context seems to imply more than that. These members are in conflict with the mind.

Even if St. Paul merely means "the flesh" when he refers to "members," "the flesh" in this case represents the fallen human person and "the world" and all its ideas, beliefs, and burdens, so I feel that these "members" are analogous to the "parts" of the self-system. They struggle with false or conflicting beliefs, negative thoughts, and sinful behaviors.

Elsewhere in this chapter of Romans, St. Paul says, "While we were living in the flesh, our sinful passions, aroused by the law, were at work in our members to bear fruit for death. But now we are discharged from the law, dead to that which held us captive, so that we are slaves not under the old written code but in the new life of the Spirit" (7:5–7). These "members" again can be understood as parts of the self-system, and they are affected by passions that influence them to act in harmful or unhealthy ways.[72] The new life in the Spirit occurs when the inmost self, through the grace of the Holy Spirit, unburdens and heals the

---

can lead to internal conflicts, negative and false beliefs about oneself, and burdens. Sinful social structures can lead to maladaptive behaviors, or sinful reactions to abusive, neglectful, or traumatic environments. The *Catechism of the Catholic Church* states, "Sin creates a proclivity to sin; it engenders vice by repetition of the same acts. This results in perverse inclinations which cloud conscience and corrupt the concrete judgment of good and evil. Thus sin tends to reproduce itself and reinforce itself, but it cannot destroy the moral sense at its root" (1865).

[72] The human person is the moral agent who is responsible for his or her sinful actions when there is sufficient knowledge and consent. Guilt may be mitigated when one understands the behavior through the lens of a blended and burdened part. The *Catechism* states, "*Unintentional ignorance* can diminish or even remove the imputability of a grave offense. But no one is deemed to be ignorant of the principles of the moral law, which are written in the conscience of every man. The promptings of feelings and passions can also diminish the voluntary and free character of the offense, as can external pressures or pathological disorders" (1860).

parts, and the whole self-system experiences a newfound interior unity, an inner harmony and freedom.[73]

Despite Baptism and personal conversion, there are parts of the self-system that are still attached to sin and are still carrying burdens. St. Paul says, "The mind that is set on the flesh is hostile to God; it does not submit to God's law — indeed it cannot" (Rom. 8:7). We may have parts hostile to God. This is the conflict expressed above by St. Paul: we have an inmost self in love with God, and we may have parts that act independently of that love.

It is the goal of Christian parts work to meet and unburden all the parts and bring them all into right relationship with God. Even though we may have encountered Christ and offered our lives to Him, we still struggle and are still in need of more sanctification. St. Paul says, "So then, brothers and sisters, we are debtors, not to the flesh, to live according to the flesh — for if you live according to the flesh, you will die; but if by the Spirit you put to death the deeds of the body, you will live. For all who are led by the Spirit of God are children of God" (Rom. 8:12–14). St. Paul calls all of us Christians to choose to be led by the Holy Spirit, who dwells in the inmost self and heals all the parts. It is in this way that we fully embrace our new identity as children of God.

As children of God, we allow ourselves to be relieved of the burdens that can lead to extreme roles, and we receive the love and comfort that we need. With the grace of the sacraments and a life of prayer, we turn away from vice, which keeps us in a perpetual inner conflict, and we cultivate virtue, which leads to inner harmony. We enter a relationship in which we receive compassion, and we feel connected and cared for. We no longer huddle in fear like Josef and Bela at the top of the stairs.

[73] The *Catechism* cites St. Augustine in his *Confessions*: "Indeed it is through chastity that we are gathered together and led back to the unity from which we were fragmented into multiplicity" (2340, citing St. Augustine, *Conf.* 10, 29, 40:*PL* 32, 796). Here we see how growth in virtue correlates with internal unity.

LIFE APPLICATIONS FOR INNER TRANSFORMATION

Dietrich von Hildebrand and True Consciousness

Catholic philosopher Dietrich von Hildebrand refers to the experience of "true consciousness," which aligns well with the idea of having self-energy and being "in self" but further includes the Christian idea of recollection. Von Hildebrand describes this true consciousness as an "actualization of the free and conscious center of his soul that a person comes of age morally and acquires the ability to utter that 'yes' in the face of God which He demands of us."[74] When we possess true consciousness, we are wakeful and alert, and we see every moment in light of our relationship with God and the meaning He gives to our lives.

The *Catholic Encyclopedia* defines *recollection* as "attention to the presence of God in the soul. It includes the withdrawal of the mind from external and earthly affairs in order to attend to God and Divine things. It is the same as interior solitude in which the soul is alone with God."[75] Von Hildebrand describes recollection further as a process of integration and unification. From a parts-work perspective, this means that the parts are in harmony with the inmost self, which, in turn, is in harmony with God.

In a state of recollection, we remain mindful rather than distracted. We do not lose sight of our focus, which is God Himself. Deep within our souls we experience a kind of unity, a communion between our inmost selves and the transcendent God. When this happens, our muscles relax, and we release all our current tensions.

When we connect with God in this way, we become aware of a deeper purpose to our lives. We gain a divine perspective. Von Hildebrand says, "To that end we should remember the last thing; and, from the whirlpool of the great and the small things of life, emerge towards God, the Cause and the Goal of all being. We return to what is truly and unchangingly omnipresent; the ultimate meaning of our life, our eternal destiny, our supreme goal."[76]

[74] Dietrich von Hildebrand, *Transformation in Christ: On the Christian Attitude* (San Francisco: Ignatius Press, 2001), 63.

[75] Arthur Devine, "Recollection," *The Catholic Encyclopedia*, vol. 12 (New York: Robert Appleton, 1911), New Advent http://www.newadvent.org/cathen/12676b.htm.

[76] Von Hildebrand, *Transformation in Christ*, 108.

St. Gregory the Great, citing St. Benedict of Nursia, used the term *habitare secum*, which means being or dwelling with oneself.[77] Von Hildebrand describes the importance of first looking inward to be fully human: "We must proceed to the depth in order to gain a full and adequate awareness of things, hearkening the depths of our being, *and bringing our most intimate selves to full actuality*."[78] Here is a description of how we find the inmost self, inspired by the presence of God and brought into action. The recollected inmost self is fully alive and engaged with the parts of the self-system. The parts are acting in healthy and productive ways. The more we stay "in self" and the more we are recollected, the more we can follow St. Paul's call to "Rejoice always, pray constantly, give thanks in all circumstances; for this is the will of God in Christ Jesus for you" (1 Thess. 5:16–18).

Meditation — Getting to Know Your Parts

Here are a few introductory steps you can take to identify and discover your inmost self and your parts.

Ideally, find a comfortable place, in a room or outside, with few distractions. Take a moment to invite the Holy Spirit to be present during this exercise. Perhaps begin with a passage of Scripture:

> "O Lord, you have searched me and known me.
> You know when I sit down and when I rise up;
> you discern my thoughts from far away.
> You search out my path and my lying down,
> and are acquainted with all my ways.
> Even before a word is on my tongue,
> O Lord, you know it completely.
> You hem me in, behind and before,
> and lay your hand upon me." (Ps. 139:1–5)

77 *The Dialogues of St. Gregory the Great*, bk. 3.

78 Von Hildebrand, *Transformation in Christ*, 108.

Now take a moment to connect with your body. Notice how the chair or sofa you are sitting on is cradling you. Notice your feet on the ground. Most of us live in a world that is moving at a fast pace, and we are both physically busy and mentally distracted. Almost all modern therapies and meditative practices agree that focusing on deep breathing can help bring about an initial grounding and relaxation. When we stop and breathe from our diaphragm, the world can seem to slow down, and we can gain access to more parts of the mind. Past trauma and current anxiety teach us to breathe shallow, rapid breaths, and that keeps our nervous system on high alert. We may not even notice how little oxygen we are taking in. When we breathe in deeply, we can really notice the air filling up every part of our lungs. We signal to the brain that there is no threat, and we open up access to the reflective, analytical, conceptual, and emotional parts of the brain.

The next step is to notice any tension in the body. We can hold tension anywhere in the body, but most people feel it in their shoulders, their face, their chest, their gut, and their pelvic floor. One way to relieve tension is actually to tighten the tense part, hold it, and then release slowly while breathing out. If you do that several times, you may find the muscle relaxes on its own. You can't "will" a muscle to relax; you can only invite it. In time, muscles will relax on their own as you breathe in deeply and breathe out the tension. When we relax the muscles of the pelvic floor, we send a relaxing message up the spine to the amygdala and other parts of the brain that it is okay to relax because we are safe at the moment.

Now I invite you to draw your attention inward and go inside with a big, open heart. Do this with gentleness, kindness, and a lot of patience. Allow yourself to be curious about whatever you may experience.

I invite you to close your eyes and imagine an interior living room or space. You may picture this comfortable space with chairs and sofas and lamps, a fireplace, a piano, and so forth. You can imagine this interior space any way you like. Some people like campfires, and others like conference rooms.

Just picture this interior space and notice how safe and comfortable it is there.

Next, invite a part to join you in that space. Notice whatever body sensations might be associated with that part.

Notice any images or visualizations that that part might be showing you or sharing with you.

Notice any impulses or desires that the part may have.

Notice any thoughts, beliefs, assumptions, positions, or attitudes coming up as you pay attention.

You might notice an inner voice with a message for you. Really pay attention. As you notice any internal experience, focus on it, and know that it is connected to a part.

Once you have some sense of the presence of a part, I invite you to ask that part how he would like to be addressed by you: What is your name? What would you like me to call you? Let the part tell you his name.

If it seems okay, ask the part what he would like to share about himself. What would he like you to understand about his experience?

Ask the part, "What is your job or your role in my system?"

Perhaps this part has a role of protecting you from something. See if there's an openness to talk about that:

- What is your good intention? What good are you seeking? How are you trying to help?
- If you didn't do that job, what are you concerned would happen?
- How long have you been doing this job for us? How old were you when you took on this job? How did it start?
- How do you feel about your role? How do you feel about this job you have?

Really let yourself extend compassion to this part.

How do you feel toward this part?

If you have parts who do not feel compassion or are resistant in some way, ask them to soften and give some space so that you can be with this part.

If you have a protector part who is not willing to give space, you can always shift your attention to that protector part. There's a reason he is protecting you against being with the other part.

If you can extend compassion to the part, what is that like for the part?

What emotions are you feeling right now? Sadness, anger, hopefulness, shame, compassion, guilt, pain, joy, disgust, or fear? Ask yourself again, "How do I feel toward this part?"

If the feeling is something like anger, shame, disgust, or fear, then you've identified another part. Welcome this new part into the interior living space.

Take a moment now and notice this new part who is holding the negative emotion. Pay attention to his thoughts, words, beliefs, assumptions, and memories. You can spend a bit of time and listen to the new part and try to understand his role, his feelings, and his thoughts.

If any other new parts show up, give each part permission to say or feel what he needs to.

As you continue to notice different parts, picture them in that interior space. Invite each new part to take his spot in one of the chairs. You can also draw them on a sketchpad or just imagine them standing. You may have identified only one or perhaps two or more. There's no right or wrong here, and it will likely change in the future.

Take time to notice and listen to each part and ask yourself, "How do I feel toward this part?"

If you feel compassionate, or joyful, or happy, or if you feel a sense of clarity, peace, a kind sadness, or love, then it is likely that your inmost self is responding to the part. Take a moment to notice that positive, calming, and loving feeling. See if the part can feel that compassion. Take as much time as you need.

You will find that you have many parts with a diversity of opinions and moods.

If any part begins to feel overwhelming, ask him to soften or turn down his intensity. Let him know that you can check in with him later.

The inmost self can be a real source of guidance and of leadership, extending compassion, clarity, kindness, courage, connection, and creativity to all the parts.

Is there anything else any part would like to share?

I invite you to express your gratitude to all the parts who showed up. Thank them for their good intentions and their efforts to keep you safe.

As we close, we thank the Holy Spirit for guiding and inspiring us, and we unite our hearts with the psalmist in the following Scripture:

> Praise the Lord!
> I will give thanks to the Lord with my whole heart,
> in the company of the upright, in the congregation.
> Great are the works of the Lord,
> studied by all who delight in them.
> Full of honour and majesty is his work,
> and his righteousness endures for ever.

He has gained renown by his wonderful deeds;
the LORD is gracious and merciful. (Ps. 111:1–4)

Reflection Questions

1. Identify a manager part whose focus is to manage life and relationships effectively. What is this manager's main concern? What firefighter parts do they most often butt heads with? How are they handling this conflict? What do those polarized parts not understand about each other? Does each part realize the other parts have good intentions for you as well?

2. Take a moment to express to the manager part that you understand his concerns and what motivates him. What do you notice when you bring clarity, compassion, confidence, and curiosity to this part? What would the manager part like you to know about himself and his role?

3. Take a moment to identify the firefighter part engaged in a conflict with the manager. What is his main concern? What do you notice when you bring clarity, compassion, confidence, and curiosity to this part? Would this part be willing to soften so that you can engage either the manager part or the exiled part? If so, what happens when the tension caused by the inner conflict is lessened?

4. Are you aware of the exile that the manager or firefighter is shielding? If so, let him know that you are aware of him and interested in learning more. Is there anything the exile wants you to know?

6

THE UNENDING MELODY

Camila's Story: My Anxieties Have Anxiety

There's a *Peanuts* comic strip in which Charlie Brown lies in bed and says, "My anxieties have anxieties!" That's me.

My father was a high-ranking government official in El Salvador who was assassinated by guerillas when I was seven years old. My mother arranged for safe passage to the United States for me, my younger brother, and her mother, my *abuela*. We experienced the poverty and humiliation of being refugees, all our wealth and status left behind. Then, in another cruel twist of fate, after only one year in the United States, my mother died of pneumonia. From that point on, my brother and I were raised by my *abuela*, who took cleaning jobs to make ends meet. She was a good woman and a loving caregiver but was a woman of very few words. I remember she often said, "*Lo que sea*," which basically means "whatever." It was her way of handling hardship. A few times, when she was really pushed to her limit, she would say, "*Estoy que exploto*," which meant that she was about to explode, and we knew to stay away.

It was a hard life, but I learned English, worked hard in school, and met the man of my dreams. We have six children, ages four to twenty-one, and I'm constantly in a state that ranges from worry to panic. I live in continual fear that one of my children will get sick and die, or that my husband will lose his job, or that I'll be incapacitated and my children will suffer, or that the economy will fall apart, or a nuclear war will erupt. I could go on.

I teach high school Spanish at a private Christian school. Despite the fact that I come in early and stay late, that my lesson plans are perfect, and that I get rave reviews from students and parents, I worry that the principal doesn't like me or that he'll think I'm a slacker or incompetent. If a student fails a test, I worry that the parents will be mad at me. I'm a complete nervous wreck waiting for standardized-test results to come back. I constantly worry that I'll fail my students and they won't learn what they need to or that I'll be fired because of budget cuts, enrollment changes, or a shift in administration. I'm afraid that I'll be revealed to be a fraud — that I'm not supposed to be there.

I know there's a connection between my childhood trauma and my current anxiety, but I don't know why I'm not past it. My husband is a good man, a kind father, a loving husband, and an excellent provider. My children are well adjusted and happy. We live in a nice home in a quiet subdivision. I have everything I could have wanted in life, and yet I'm always in a state of anxiety.

THE PSYCHOLOGY OF THE INTERIOR WORLD

Internalized Voices

Children internalize the voices and speech heard from adult caregivers. In most cases, these are the thoughts and feelings of the mother or the father. But children also absorb the thoughts and feelings of other family members, friends, teachers, coaches, and even the voices and thoughts and feelings of characters in books, in movies, or on television. Children internalize these voices as inner speech, and they are integrated into the children's own thoughts. Children "try on" these voices in their own speech, both internally and with others.

When a negative belief comes from someone else and is passed on to a child, IFS calls this a "legacy burden." Camila has likely absorbed her mother's and her grandmother's feelings of fear and loss. She also internalized the dismissive words to mean that feelings were not important and that we express them only when we have reached our limit.

All this absorption comes from a fallen world — a world scarred by original trauma and filled with people carrying burdens. The child is naturally going to have to make sense of competing thoughts and feelings, often unhealthy or sinful. For example, a child may learn from her mother that she is a "good girl" because she helped take care of her sister but then later hear from that same mother that she was "stupid" for letting her friend take her toy. She may learn from the Bible that God loves her and that she should be generous, and she may learn from a television show that she must stand up for herself.

That's a lot of complicated messaging for a child to sort through. The child's parts adopt roles to manage all the inner tensions and contradictions. As a result, a part may adopt a "generous and loving" helper role who cares for those in need. Another part may develop a "tough, no-nonsense" fighter or advocate role that can put others in their place and stand up for herself. Parts adapt to sort through and make sense of the complexity of life and human relationships. The generous part may then get rewarded in certain contexts, such as in church and school, whereas the tough part may get rewarded in friendships if she generates respect.

Adaptive Roles

In addition to the messages we hear and absorb from others, "life" can also offer real setbacks, devastating losses, and painful suffering. Capital-*T* trauma for children may include such things as the loss of a parent, a divorce, physical violence, sexual exploitation, bullying, and emotional abuse. Camila lost both her parents — a capital-*T* trauma. Children learn to cope with these more damaging experiences through adaptation.

As children, we find an "answer" that works to manage these problems and all the complex feelings that come with them. In response to trauma, a part of the self-system takes on a role and adopts a solution that works at the time. Camila adapted by learning to repress her feelings and focus on working hard and finding safe, stable relationships.

I learned about character types and mapping from EMDR consultant and trainer Deb Kennard,[79] who had adapted the work of Ron Kurtz and Hector Prestera[80] in identifying multiple "character types" that might emerge as a result of the experience of trauma. The idea here is that we overdevelop some skill or quality and underdevelop some other skill or quality to survive or cope.

[79] Deb Kennard offers EMDR training with the Personal Transformation Institute at www.emdr-training.net.

[80] See Ron Kurtz and Hector Prestera, *The Body Reveals: An Illustrated Guide to the Psychology of the Body* (New York: Harper and Row, 1976); Ron Kurtz, *Body-Centered Psychotherapy: The Hakomi Method: The Integrated Use of Mindfulness, Nonviolence, and the Body* (Mendocino, CA: LifeRhythm, 2015).

If, as a child, I learned that I was not good enough, I might have become "the doer" in an effort to be perfect. I might have stayed busy and worked very hard. As a result, I didn't learn to play and take care of myself. If my caregivers were undependable, I might have learned that I'm alone and might have adapted by being "the independent one" and taking control of every aspect of my life. As a result, I didn't learn to trust others or to ask for help.

We might become the "invisible one" because disappearing allows us to survive. We might become "the rock" who endures all suffering. We might become "the chameleon" who manipulates others or "the needy one" who gets attention and has his needs met by others. We can see all these characters as extreme roles adopted by parts of the self-system.

All these adaptations and extreme roles were once solutions. The problem is that we hold on to these solutions even when they no longer serve our current goals. Having a hero part might have worked as a teenager to deal with pain, but now it might be preventing me from connecting with others with authentic emotions. Having an emotional part might have enabled me to connect with others' feelings, but now it is preventing me from being able to self-soothe.

It is quite possible that one's current problem in life was once a solution. Our parts can learn to adapt in new ways as we identify their burdens, help them release those burdens, and offer them now what they always needed. Our invisible part needs to hear that she is safe now. Our rock part needs to learn that what he wants matters. Our doer part needs to absorb that she doesn't have to work so hard.

When a part adopts a role, such as the hero, the chameleon, the invisible one, or the doer, the part also takes on a set of attitudes, perceptions, and beliefs. The negative beliefs are the burden that keeps the part locked in his role. The part is afraid that if he sets down the burden, the truth of that belief will overwhelm the system. It is very important that we begin by validating that fear. At one time, that fear was extremely reasonable! At one time, the part felt that he was in danger, or that he was alone, or that he was not safe, or that he didn't matter, or that he was helpless.

The key is to help bring this part into the present and reevaluate whether that is still true. These parts will have to enter a new relationship with the inmost self, with his current wisdom and resources, to offer the part what he always needed: safety, boundaries, trust, action, honesty, authenticity, rest, connection, and compassion.

Self-Energy

We may have parts in conflict with each other. For example, we may have an independent or hero part in tension with a needy or invisible part. We may have a stressed doer part working very hard to meet a deadline while a critical part berates him for not planning his time better. These conflicts create anxiety for the whole self-system, and this is often externalized in the body. Examples of bodily reactions to anxiety include hypertension, muscle tightness, shallow breathing, and panic attacks. We therefore begin any internal work by taking a deep breath and noticing what may be active in the body.

We can often connect with a part by noticing where in the body the part is active. My doer part, for example, will sometimes express himself in shoulder tension. When my parts are fearful, they often express themselves as tension in my chest.

If a burdened part is the "executive" or is in the "driver's seat" or is "running the show," we can say that the self is "blended" with that part. In this situation, when the part is burdened, the person behaves in ways that may be unhealthy or hurtful to himself and others. This will typically generate a negative reaction from other parts of the self-system, and an inner battle will begin. As we "unblend" from these competing parts, the inmost self gets some measure of differentiation or distance from them.

When the inmost self dialogues with burdened parts, the inmost self will often unblend, and the anxiety will begin to subside. The inmost self can even ask parts to reduce their intensity so that he might better connect with them. When the parts experience the compassionate presence of the inmost self, they begin to feel secure again. The entire self-system begins to relax. This may or may not be the time to do the inner work of healing, unburdening, and integrating, but it will at least bring a measure of comfort and a reduction of anxiety.

When the inmost self is present, engaged, and connected, we can say that the self-system has "self-energy." This means that the inmost self extends feelings of compassion and offers new perspectives to the parts of the self-system.

He or she can promote courage in the face of adversity, foster creativity, bring clarity to a difficult and complex problem, and even be fun and playful. The inmost self has no agenda other than to connect, to heal, and to love. He or she is patient and kind.

The Redeemed Inmost Self

By virtue of being created in the image of God, even the unredeemed inmost self is capable of greatness. The creativity of the inmost self explains the beauty of Michelangelo's *Pietà* and the lofty music of Schubert's *Ave Maria*. It explains the development of railways and air travel, the desire to climb Mount Everest, and man's exploration of outer space. The courage and persistence of the inmost self inspired the nonviolent activism of Gandhi and Martin Luther King Jr. Human rights achievements such as the United States Bill of Rights, the fall of the Berlin Wall, and the end of apartheid all speak to the spirit of the human heart.

On a more personal level, the inmost self fosters deep, abiding friendships, the love of a mother for her child, and heroic acts of self-sacrifice for others. Indeed, as human beings made in God's image, we are capable of great love and great accomplishments.

What happens when the inmost self is redeemed and we realize our fullest potential as image bearers? If the inmost self is the faculty of the soul where we connect with God, shouldn't this spiritual reality make a difference in the real world? Shouldn't Christians, as a result, be kinder, more compassionate, and more courageous than non-Christians?

St. Paul thought so but was also frustrated at times with Christians. He accused the Corinthians of having some members who acted worse than the pagans (1 Cor. 5:1). The reason that we, as baptized Christians who have professed our love for and commitment to Jesus, sometimes fail in disappointing ways is that, despite our positive intentions and our church attendance, we have burdened and blended parts we haven't dealt with.

When we are baptized, we receive a share in the threefold office of Christ as "priest, prophet, and king" (see *CCC* 783–786). Recall the various characteristics of the inmost self from chapter 3. The priestly role reflects how Christ is the bridge builder, who creates and restores connections with God and others. The prophet role aligns with the pathfinder, who guides us and directs us into a right relationship with God. The king role reflects our inner dignity as adopted children of God, but it also represents the protector role, as it is the king's job to ensure the safety of everyone in the kingdom, especially the most vulnerable. To realize our full potential as future saints and to actualize these baptismal roles, we need to bring harmony to our inner system. This means we need to address our very real attachment needs and unresolved trauma at a human level before we can achieve greater levels of sanctification.

This is not to say that we are alone in doing this. God works with us through the inmost self to bring about inner healing, on both human and spiritual levels. After achieving a measure of unblending — by taking a few deep breaths, noticing any body tensions, looking inside, and connecting with our parts — we can invite our self-system to notice and be present with God.

The act of connecting with our parts and inviting them and our inmost self to sit with God is called recollection. This may then lead to an experience of mental prayer or contemplation,[81] but in busy daily life, it can also lead to a general sense of peace and serenity.

The Unending Melody

In a state of recollection, all the parts of the self-system are invited into communion with God by the inmost self. We notice a calming effect. We can stay in this mindset even when we are busy doing daily tasks because there is a perpetual awareness of God's presence. God works through our inmost self to our parts, who carry out the actions. Dietrich von Hildebrand expresses it this way: "We divert our vision from God to some concrete creaturely thing, and actualize a partial aspect of our being. Yet we do not separate ourselves from God; we do not sever connection with the profound and ultimate center of our being. We remain wakeful and alive."[82] Although von Hildebrand did not refer to parts, his

[81] Contemplation is a mystical or prayerful state where one experiences union with God.

[82] Von Hildebrand, *Transformation in Christ,* 108.

use of terms such as "intimate selves"[83] and "partial aspect of our being" speaks to an understanding of multiplicity within the self-system.

Von Hildebrand describes the awareness of God acting in our soul "like an unending melody."[84] St. Paul exhorts us to "pray without ceasing" (1 Thess. 5:17). Our union with God becomes so much a part of us that it is like the air we breathe. This topic is explored further by the author of the nineteenth-century Russian story known as *The Way of a Pilgrim*. The pilgrim unites himself to God through the Jesus Prayer, a simple rhythmic prayer that says, "Jesus, Son of the living God, have mercy on me, a sinner." This simple prayer becomes part of the soul. It allows Jesus to be breathed in and all the stresses of the world to be breathed out. Even without the words of the prayer, when this prayer and this way of being with God enters into our very being, it becomes a part of us. It is breathed into the heart, the inmost self, and then it flows out to all the parts of the self-system, just as the heart pumps blood to the whole body.

SCRIPTURE STUDY: HEALING OUR PARTS THROUGH ST. PAUL'S FIRST LETTER TO THE CORINTHIANS

St. Paul begins his First Letter to the Corinthians with some distress about the divisions in the community and urges the people to be "united in the same mind and the same purpose" (1:10). That purpose is to be spiritual, to have "the mind of Christ" and to "receive the gifts of God's Spirit" (2:14, 16). The "spiritual" person can be understood for our purposes as one in whom the inmost self is regenerated and intimately connected with God. The inmost self, like Christ, embraces the cross to express love. The inmost self notices and cares for the parts of the self-system that are burdened, outcast, hurting, shamed, fearful, or in pain.

St. Paul writes, "Fornicators, idolaters, adulterers, male prostitutes, sodomites, thieves, the greedy, drunkards, revilers, robbers — none of these will inherit the kingdom of God" (6:9–10). While there is a literal truth to this statement, which speaks to the results of living in a state of unrepented mortal sin, we can also view this in IFS terms: these problematic people can be understood as

83 Ibid.

84 Von Hildebrand, *Transformation in Christ,* 112.

firefighter parts. Remember that firefighters are protectors that take on extreme roles to avoid or numb painful and overwhelming feelings held by exiled or wounded parts. They don't care about anything but snuffing out the fire. They don't consider the consequences. We may have firefighter parts who act out in unhealthy ways, perhaps sexually, perhaps with alcohol, or perhaps by taking it out on others. These parts temporarily blend with the self and take charge. As a result, we become disconnected from our inmost self, disconnected from Christ, and disconnected from friends, family, and community. In a sense, we don't "inherit" the kingdom because we have put ourselves outside of it.

When firefighter parts take over, we become numb or dissociate from who we are, and we therefore break communion with ourselves. But St. Paul calls us back to our true identity: "You were washed, you were sanctified, you were justified in the name of the Lord Jesus Christ in the Spirit of our God" (6:11).

Richard Schwartz, the founder of IFS, does not address morality and parts in depth. He insists that parts always have good intentions. A Christian synthesis would admit that when a person sins, he is most likely influenced by a blended part of him acting outside of connection with the inmost self. It is still the conscious person who chooses to commit the offense. The "good" intention of the part might be some form of perceived self-preservation, but if the object of the moral action is to harm an innocent person, for example, then it is objectively morally bad, and the person is accountable for that action. St. Paul reminds us not to sidestep this reality and says that the body "is meant not for fornication" because you are "members of Christ" and your "body is a temple of the Holy Spirit within you" (6, 13, 15, 19). Indeed, St. Paul calls the sinner to "examine himself" and "discern"; in other words, he is to recollect, look inside at his interior world, and see if there is dysregulation or unhealthy, harmful, or sinful behaviors. The sinner then unblends parts from the inmost self and helps them release their burdens. The path to healing is to restore the inmost self and all the parts to harmony in accord with God's law of love. We do not ever condemn ourselves or our parts; rather, we seek to understand and empathize. Our goal is healing and rehabilitation rather than punishment.

We know that Christ Himself dined and socialized with sinful people; in other words, He met them where they were and *then* called them to repentance and change. We may have a temptation to judge others and ourselves too quickly or too harshly, but the Gospel message is that no matter how grievously sinful we have been, we are all called to repentance and new life in Christ.

There is a double healing that needs to happen here. First, we need to be recollected and bring harmony and restoration to our inner world. Then we need to have harmony with our outer world and, in particular, with our family, our friends, and the Church. The Eucharist is perhaps the best example of communal recollection in which all the people come together in a moment of deep connection with God. The celebration of the Eucharist involves both a shared experience of God within the community and an internal experience in which the inmost self and the self-system encounter God. It is in receiving the Eucharist that we return to our true identity as children of God and reenter the story of God's intimate love and salvation of His people. St. Paul directly connects the Eucharist with the Body of Christ, the Church:

> The cup of blessing which we bless, is it not a participation in the blood of Christ? The bread which we break, is it not a participation in the body of Christ? Because there is one bread, we who are many are one body, for we all partake of the one bread. (1 Cor. 10:16–17)

At the Last Supper and culminating in His death on the Cross, Christ frees us from sin and invites us to release our burdens. Every time we celebrate the Eucharist, we are invited to receive that truth anew. We can imagine our whole person, the inmost self and all the parts, united and receiving Communion, relieved of burdens and finding inner harmony as well as belonging to the Body of Christ, the Church. It is Christ who invites us into this communion of love because of His great desire for intimacy and connection.

St. Paul describes Jesus at the Last Supper:

> The Lord Jesus on the night when he was betrayed took a loaf of bread, and when he had given thanks, he broke it and said, "This is my body that is for you. Do this in remembrance of me." In the same way he took the cup also, after supper, saying, "This cup is the new covenant in my blood. Do this, as often as you drink it, in remembrance of me." For as often as you eat this bread and drink this cup, you proclaim the Lord's death until he comes. Whoever, therefore, eats the bread or drinks the

> cup of the Lord in an unworthy manner will be answerable for the body and blood of the Lord. Examine yourselves, and only then eat of the bread and drink of the cup. For all who eat and drink without discerning the body eats and drinks judgement against themselves. . . . But when we are judged by the Lord, we are disciplined so that we may not be condemned along with the world. (1 Cor. 11:23–29, 32)

There is a powerful symbolism in Jesus' taking the bread, His own Body, and offering it to the apostles. He institutes a new covenant, a new kingdom, a new Church, a new relationship between Himself and His people. Jesus invites us into this relationship, which is based on secure attachment, belonging, and intimacy. This new bond is one that is rooted in sacrificial love.

Let us examine what St. Paul says about this love and think about how we can understand it in terms of the relationship between the inmost self and our parts:

> If I speak in the tongues of mortals and of angels, but do not have love, I am a noisy gong or a clanging cymbal. And if I have prophetic powers, and understand all mysteries and all knowledge, and if I have all faith, so as to remove mountains, but do not have love, I am nothing. If I give away all my possessions, and if I hand over my body so that I may boast, but do not have love, I gain nothing.
>
> Love is patient; love is kind; love is not envious or boastful or arrogant or rude. It does not insist on its own way; it is not irritable or resentful; it does not rejoice in wrongdoing, but rejoices in the truth. It bears all things, believes all things, hopes all things, endures all things.
>
> Love never ends. But as for prophecies, they will come to an end; as for tongues, they will cease; as for knowledge, it will come to an end. For we know only in part, and we prophesy only in part; but when the complete comes, the partial will come to an end. When I was a child, I spoke like a child, I thought like a child, I reasoned like a child; when I became an adult, I put an end to childish ways. For now we see in a mirror, dimly, but then we will see face to face. Now I know only in part; then I will know fully, even as I have been fully known. And now faith,

> hope, and love abide, these three; and the greatest of these is love. (1 Cor. 13:1–13)

Here St. Paul lays out the imperative to love. It is in the very nature of the inmost self to be patient and kind. Just as "God is love" (1 John 4:8), so the inmost self, created in His image, is nothing without love. Envy, arrogance, and rudeness are all signs of a burdened part. The inmost self can bear all things and endure hardships because of love. If we have amazing parts doing remarkable things but they are not self-led, then those things are done with some agenda and not with love. St. Paul's passage is the manifesto of the inmost self.

Through Christ's death on the Cross, through our Baptism, and in our weekly Eucharist, we celebrate the undoing of the Fall of man. We celebrate that man is no longer out of relationship with God. We receive His grace, and we freely choose to sit with God. In the words of Jesus' Mother, "Here am I, the servant of the Lord; let it be with me according to your word" (Luke 1:38), we cooperate in the undoing of the disobedience of Adam and Eve, renounce pride, and accept that we are dependent on God. This is not an instinct but a choice, and therefore it is an act of love. God calls us in love as He seeks to be reunited with us, and we respond with love.

It is this relationship of love that we celebrate in Holy Mass or in the Divine Liturgy or in the Lord's Supper. We live in hope and with faith that we will ultimately receive a new "spiritual body": "The first man Adam became a living being; the last Adam became a life-giving spirit.... As was the man of dust, so are those who are of the dust; and as is the man of heaven, so are those who are of heaven. Just as we have borne the image of the man of dust, we shall also bear the image of the man of heaven" (1 Cor. 15:45, 48). This "new man" is the redeemed inmost self and all the parts in full communion with each other, with the self, and with Christ. This is the radical transformation of the redeemed and regenerated inmost self reflecting the light of Christ. We are on a journey as we work toward that fullness of life with Christ.

LIFE APPLICATIONS FOR INNER TRANSFORMATION

Meditation — Inviting Our Parts to a Calm Place

I'm going to walk you through an exercise called "going to a calm place." It is a visual technique that may help you in your everyday life to manage challenging situations and anxieties. As you practice this technique, you can adapt it to other situations and use it quickly and easily within the context of a stressful situation.

I invite you to find a comfortable place to sit.

Invite the Holy Spirit to be present as you begin this exercise. Reflect on the following passage from Scripture:

> Be merciful to me, O God, be merciful to me,
> for in you my soul takes refuge;
> in the shadow of your wings I will take refuge,
> until the destroying storms pass by.
> I cry to God Most High,
> to God who fulfills his purpose for me.
> He will send from heaven and save me,
> he will put to shame those who trample on me.
> God will send forth his steadfast love and his faithfulness. (Ps. 57:1–3)

Direct your attention to how you are sitting. Notice the chair or sofa you are sitting on and how it holds your body and supports it. Gently relax your muscles and invite any tension to release. Now turn your attention to your breathing. Take several deep breaths. As you inhale, hold your breath for a moment, count three seconds, and then gently release. As you exhale, notice that tension flows out of your body, and rest even more deeply into your chair. If your feet touch the ground, notice the contact point between your feet and the floor. Continue to take deep breaths until your body begins to feel a greater sense of calm. (Option: You may choose to gently tap the sides of your legs; see the exercise in chapter 1.)

Next, I'd like you to imagine a peaceful place that brings about a sense of comfort — a beach, a mountaintop, a vacation spot, a beautiful church. Make it whatever you like. You can even choose an imaginary place.

Ask yourself what it is about this place that makes it feel safe.

Imagine that you are really there; look around, and feel the peacefulness.

Notice the things you can see there. Perhaps it is a detail on a tree or the colors in the sky. Take in all the sights.

Notice physical sensations — perhaps your feet against the ground, the wind, the sun, or anything you can touch.

Notice the different sounds — perhaps birds, the wind, a bell, children laughing, or maybe just silence. Notice everything you hear.

Notice the different smells. Maybe it's incense, or something baking, or the sea. Take in any particular scents.

Take a moment just to experience what it is like to be in this place. Pay attention to how your body feels, your breathing, and your sense of peace and tranquility.

If there's one word that you would use to describe that place, what would it be?

Now I'd like you to redirect your attention to something that happened either earlier today or earlier this week. Choose an experience that elicited a small amount of anxiety.

Once you have selected a recent memory, sit with that memory for a moment. Notice where in your body you are carrying that stress. Maybe it is your chest or your arms or your shoulder or your head. I invite you to notice the anxiety. Just notice that it's there.

See if your protectors would allow you to accept that the anxiety is there and turn toward it. See if it would be okay to just accept that the anxiety is present.

Ask the part of you who is anxious not to overwhelm so that you can be in relationship with him. See if it is possible for the anxious part to hold the anxiety and reduce the intensity so you can connect with that part.

If the protectors give you enough space to work with the anxious part, just be with the anxiety, allow it to be present, separate from you but nearby. And now just listen to your anxious part with a big, open heart.

Take some time be with the anxious part. You can invite the part to look at you and be with your inmost self. It might be new for this part to know that you, as the inmost self, can be present. I invite you to recall the calm, peaceful place. Recall that one word that best describes that place. If it feels right for you and the anxious part, invite that part to join you in this restful place.

Notice again the things that you see there: the physical sensations, the sounds, the smells . . .

Notice what it is like for this part to be there with you in that calm, peaceful place.

This is a place where this part can be seen and known and understood.

What does this part need?

What would he like you to know?

Notice what happens in your body as you listen to and extend compassion to this part.

Notice how your breathing changes, and notice how the part releases any tension or stress.

Spend as much time with this part as you need.

As you return to the present, let this part know that this doesn't have to be the end and that you can come back here with him whenever you need to.

Thank your part for being willing to come with you on this journey.

Recall the words of the prophet Jeremiah: "Thus says the Lord: Stand at the crossroads, and look, and ask for the ancient paths where the good way lies; and walk in it, and find rest for your souls" (6:16).

Now let's pause and work our way back to our present location. Take a moment and consider how your part feels now. More relaxed? Rested?

I find this calm-place exercise to be very useful in everyday life, and I use it often to reduce anxiety, regulate emotions, and help my parts when they are distressed.

Reflection Questions

1. How do you experience anxiety in your body? In your mind? In your emotions?

2. Pause for a moment and notice where you might be experiencing anxiety. Where do you feel it in your body? What emotions does it intensify?

3. Anxiety implies that you are responding to a real or perceived threat. What sorts of threats trigger anxiety for you most often? (Examples could be relational threats, financial threats, or physical threats.)

4. Identify the part of your self-system that is triggered by the perception of a threat. Connect with that part. If the perceived threat

is not imminent, remind yourself that you are safe in the present moment. How does your body respond? What emotions do you notice?

5. How old is the part you identified in the previous step? How old does that part think you, as the inmost self, are? What year does the part think it is right now?

6. Imagine bringing an anxious part to Jesus in prayer or at Mass. What happens to this part in the presence of Jesus?

7. As you bring kindness and patience to your anxious part, what happens in your interior world? As you recollect, how does your inmost self console your part? How does your self-system experience God's love and calm?

7

THE CLOSED HEART

Aaron's Story: The Older Brother

I was only twelve when my father died, and as the eldest brother in a Korean family, I assumed the role of parent for my three younger sisters. I passed up a scholarship at SJA Music Institute in Seoul and postponed going to college for eight years because my mother was sick. I worked at the music store, selling guitar strings and giving lessons to wealthy kids. When I finally earned my degree, I passed up an opportunity to go on tour with Cuban classical guitarist Manuel Barrueco so that I could be near my mother before she died. Instead of becoming a famous performer, I taught music to high school students.

When my sisters were settled, I moved to America and began graduate school at Berklee College of Music in Boston. That's where I met Victoria, the woman who would both steal my heart and destroy it. She played the clarinet and described music as the universal language. She introduced me to jazz, and together we played in a jazz band as I developed — to the shock and dismay of all my friends — a love for hollow-body electrical guitars. How Victoria changed my life! We dated for two years and then married when she became pregnant. I was happy to marry her because she was the girl of my dreams and had brought so much goodness to my life.

When she was seven months pregnant, I was working at a club, and the patron, a wise-cracking, tipsy fellow, asked how Victoria was doing. "Fine," I replied. In a casual way, he said, "Mighty good of you. I can think of at least three guys who were relieved when you stepped up." I was confused and shocked, "What do you mean?" I paused. "What are you saying?" He just laughed dismissively, as if everyone in the world already knew, and he went back to tending the bar. I soon learned that Victoria had been having sex with countless men while we were dating. I confronted her, and she didn't deny it. I was furious, and I lashed out at her. She promised to stay faithful to me, and I repressed my feelings and stayed by her side.

It has been twenty years, and Victoria and I are still married. We have four children, and we both became committed Christians more than ten years ago. She's very active in our local parish, and I am confident that she has completely reformed her life. She is on the parish council, she runs the Meals on Wheels program, and she hosts a women's prayer group at our house. She is respected by the parish priest and the community. She has on occasion expressed gratitude that I stayed with her, and I forgave her for the affairs that happened while we were dating. We rarely talk about those years now. Meanwhile, I've been successful working with a company to develop, patent, and sell guitar products, including a breakthrough line of humbuckers. My kids are mostly well adjusted and happy. Things are good. So why do I hate my life?

I have always done the right thing. I had plenty of opportunities, especially when I played in bands, but Victoria is the only woman I have ever slept with. I could have lived a wild party lifestyle, but foolishly I never did. I might have been successful as an extraordinarily talented classical guitarist if I hadn't postponed college to help my family or skipped the tour to take care of my mother. I have always been the "good guy," but I have nothing to show for it. I know plenty of musicians who have been with many women as they "sowed their wild oats" — but not me. Everyone, including my wife, has a redemption story, but I'm just standing on the sidelines, as always, doing the right thing.

Then things came to a head last year when Victoria discovered that I had been viewing pornography. It was my secret shame and my way of self-soothing. She yelled at me and said that pornography was the same as adultery. She threatened to kick me out of the house. I raged back that we hadn't had sex in months. She accused me of being insensitive and said that I didn't understand how much pain she was in as her endometriosis had been flaring up with all the stress she had been under. In the end, I apologized and promised I'd never look at pornography again. But inside I fumed. How dare she recriminate me for looking at porn when she ran around with many men while we were dating? I wanted to throw that in her face, but I held back. It would only make things worse.

But holding back made me hate myself even more. I always hold back my feelings, taking the higher road, ignoring my needs. Heck, I don't have needs. I'm just a sap. A cuckold. A loser. Second best. An afterthought. Every year I bristle when I hear the parable of the prodigal son. Everyone loves the guy who comes back home after wasting money and sleeping with prostitutes, but no one cares about the guy who always did the right thing. The older brother is the one who gets a raw deal.

THE PSYCHOLOGY OF THE INTERIOR WORLD

Aaron's story is told in the first person but from the perspective of a blended protector-manager part who plays the role of victim and martyr. The manager part always does the "right thing." He sacrifices his career for his family when his mother is sick. He sacrifices his feelings when he finds out that his wife cheated on him. Like the older brother in the parable of the prodigal son, he has never gone astray. This is a remarkable part who deserves to be appreciated. And yet Aaron has another part who sees this older-brother part as weak. This other part is angry because he was never allowed to explore his full potential. This resentful critical part is relentless in his contempt. When this inner conflict becomes too much and Aaron cannot turn to his wife for comfort, he turns to pornography to release the tension. This activity only gives the critical part more fuel for the fire. The critical part argues with the manager part's sense of self as the good guy who does no wrong.

Aaron learned early on in life that he needs to be responsible for others and that he must put his needs beneath the needs of his family. His manager part accepted the identity of a noble son and husband tied to being hardworking and self-sacrificial. This noble manager part ensures that the parts holding grief, pain, and shame never get triggered. This manager part, with all its good intentions, does not allow Aaron to grieve the loss of his father, the loss of his mother, the loss of his career aspirations, and the terrible betrayal of his wife. These feelings remained closed off and keep Aaron in an internalized self-hatred characterized by bitterness, resentfulness, and angry self-loathing.

Aaron's noble protective manager part is understandably concerned that if he felt all his grief and loss, his feelings would overwhelm him. He is afraid of "flooding" his system with all that intense emotion. The same part may be concerned that if Aaron allowed himself to feel his pain, he would lose his relationship with his wife and the stability provided by his family.

The key to healing for Aaron will be to connect compassionately with each of his parts: the noble manager, the critical protector, the part turning to pornography, and the grieving exile. Would these parts be able to share their thoughts, feelings, assumptions, and memories without overwhelming the system? If the protectors and managers can soften and allow some space, would the exile be willing to share his story? If so, some parts might be triggered by the intensity of the story and want to use distracting or comforting strategies, such as rage, workaholism, alcohol, drugs, or porn to quiet or numb the exile.

There may be a protector part who shows up to minimize the problem or shame the exile. We can recognize that these are all ways the system uses to provide relief. The inmost self can be aware of these strategies and, with gentleness, courage, and creativity, can calmly ask the protectors to soften and redirect the attention to the exile.

With grace from God, Aaron's inmost self can take on the role of the loving and present parent who was missing first when Aaron's father died and then again when Aaron's mother became sick. The loving parent would be attuned to Aaron's feelings — all of them, including the anger and the shame and the self-loathing. The loving parent would empathize with Aaron's experience of grief and loss, with his willingness to self-sacrifice, and with his feelings of betrayal. The loving parent would see through all the tangled resentments and hurt feelings and remind Aaron, "Son, you are always with me, and all that is mine is yours" (Luke 15:31).

And when the older-brother protector part softens, the inmost self can be with the exile and love the exile. This exile is the wounded child who lost his father. It is the young man who had to give up his dreams to be with his dying mother and take care of his siblings. This exile can begin to feel the unfathomable love and mercy of God through the inmost self because, perhaps for the first time, he is seen and known. Is there a need that the inmost self can provide for this wounded part? Can the exile receive the goodness of being in relationship with the inmost self? The inmost self can enter the painful memories with the exile and be a witness to his experience. The wounded part can feel seen, known, treasured, and loved.

In time, as Aaron's wounded part is able to let go of his burdens, he can be invited to be fully part of Aaron's self-system and interact positively with the other parts. Meanwhile, the protector can let go of the victim-informed role of older brother, and Aaron can forgive his wife in a deeper, more meaningful way.

SCRIPTURE STUDY: THE TRANSFIGURATION

The Transfiguration is described in all three Synoptic Gospels: Matthew, Mark, and Luke. Jesus takes His apostles Peter, James, and John up a mountain, where He appears to them in radiant glory. He shines with bright rays of light, and even His garments are a bright white. To the apostles' astonishment, Moses and Elijah appear at Jesus' side. Moses, of course, is the great lawgiver who gave the Israelites the Ten Commandments and brought that people out of slavery in Egypt. Elijah is the great prophet who faced off with the prophets of Baal and raised a child from the dead.

The Transfiguration occurs on a mountain, the meeting place between the natural and supernatural realms. Jesus is the connecting figure between the temporal and the eternal. In this moment, if there was any doubt, Jesus' true identity as the Son of God becomes clear.

It is fitting that God the Father and God the Holy Spirit appear again in this deeply relational and trinitarian moment — the Father in the voice and the Holy Spirit in the cloud. The Father's words echo His words at Jesus' baptism: "Then a cloud overshadowed them, and from the cloud there came a voice, 'This is my Son, the Beloved; listen to him!' " (Mark 9:7).[85] Jesus' identity is again revealed and reaffirmed, but this time, God the Father says, "Listen to him." The apostles are being called to listen and to respond to what Jesus is asking of them. Jesus is clearly now the inheritor of the law and the prophets. He is taking the next step in assuming His role of King and Savior.

[85] In Mark 1:11, at Jesus' baptism, God the Father says, "You are my Son, the Beloved; with you I am well pleased."

Like Jesus, the higher, regenerated inmost self assumes the role of inheritor of the law and the prophets. In this, the self completely embraces the law (the teacher of morality) and the prophets (the proclaimer of the will of God). He is devoted to God and to God's will because he knows it is directed to the good. The goal of the inmost self is to help the parts as they realign to this new focus.

When we read the story of the Transfiguration and look at Peter, James, and John, who can be seen to represent our various parts, we can understand how our parts act and react. And we need to remember that, just as Jesus is always there to redirect His disciples and to help them become who they are truly meant to be, He is there for us as well.

Peter has enthusiasm but sometimes lacks faith. There are many instances in which he shows excitement but fails to follow through. When Jesus invites Peter to join Him in walking on the water, Peter soon begins to sink (Matt. 14:28–31). At the Last Supper, Peter says that he will never deny Jesus, and then he denies Him three times (Matt. 26:33–35, 69–75). Peter may be enthusiastic, but he fails in the face of fear. Don't we have parts like that? We are excited, but we lack follow-through. We are ready for a full commitment, but then we bail. We can play the part, but we are undependable and unreliable.

Peter is notoriously impulsive. He acts before he thinks. His faith is challenged on numerous occasions, and he fails. He refuses to allow Jesus to wash his feet until Jesus insists that he can't inherit the kingdom otherwise; then he asks Jesus to wash his hands and his head as well (John 13:8–9)! He is a man full of energy and life. He wins big and falls big.

James and John are ambitious and strident, but they may at times lack love. They are described as the "sons of thunder," and some scholars believe they were zealots, political activists. They wanted a major overthrow of the Roman Empire and the liberation of the Jewish people. They were ready to fight. But Jesus challenges them: "Are you ready to die?" This must have been confusing for them. They are the same two apostles who asked Jesus if they could be on His right and left side on His throne in Heaven (Mark 10:37). They are the same disciples who wanted to call down fire on a town that would not receive Jesus (Luke 9:51–55). And one of them forbade a non-disciple from exorcising demons (Mark 8:38–39).

Aaron also has an agenda. He is angry at the way he has missed out on life and been mistreated by his wife. He resents missed opportunities and disregards his own noble and self-sacrificing choices. He lashes out by using pornography, but deep down, he feels shame, loneliness, and sadness. In his self-righteous anger, he becomes self-absorbed, irritable, and withdrawn.

We, too, have self-absorbed parts, enthusiastic parts, ambitious parts, holier-than-thou parts, self-righteous parts, and crusader parts. We want to change the world, take down our enemies, and rise in glory. Jesus turns this all on its head. He tells James and John they need to die to self to be glorified. Jesus says that "the Son of Man came not to be served but to serve, and to give his life as a ransom for many" (Mark 10:45).

It is the role of the inmost self to help these parts embrace humility. This humility is not shame and not self-deprecation. It is quite the opposite. It is accepting one's true identity, which is rooted in God, who is love.

In this way, we become truly alive. We can affirm with Jesus that He is "the God of Abraham, the God of Isaac, and the God of Jacob.... He is God not of the dead, but of the living" (Matt. 22:32). Moses and Elijah appear with Jesus alive! The apostles, like us, are called to new life and to become transformed.

Peter must be unburdened from his impulsivity and his fear. James and John must be unburdened from their aggression and ambitions. Jesus is gentle and patient with them. He knows it is a process that will take time. And we see that the apostles *are* transformed.

Peter repents of his denial of Jesus and runs to the empty tomb to seek Jesus. He becomes a leader and a fisher of men, and he embraces Jesus' threefold command to "feed his sheep" (see John 21:15–17). Jesus had appropriately given him the name Peter, which means "rock," as Peter becomes the leader and spokesman of the Church (Matt. 16:18). He founds the church in both Antioch and Rome. With the apostle John, and James the Just, he is called a "pillar of the church" (Gal. 2:9).

James and John are rebuked by Jesus several times, but despite their faults, these two witness the raising of the daughter of Jairus. They witness the Transfiguration, and they witness Jesus' agony in the garden.

John and Peter are sent to make the preparations for the Last Supper. They follow Jesus after His arrest when He meets with the high priest. John and Peter heal a lame man after Jesus' Ascension. They are both thrown into prison, and they later visit Samaria to see new converts.

John is called the "beloved apostle" and he leans against Jesus' chest at the Last Supper. He is the only apostle at the foot of the Cross. At Jesus' request, he takes Jesus' Mother, Mary, under his care. John is the first apostle at the tomb of Jesus. He is the disciple "whom Jesus loved" (John 13:23). The son of thunder becomes beloved and becomes a man who loves.

Can Aaron hear the words of the father in the parable: "Son, you are always with me, and all that is mine is yours"? Can he be transformed by these words of affirmation?

The transformation for Aaron will involve coming to Christ with humility, recognizing that he has been carrying a burden of self-righteous anger, and asking forgiveness for the ways he has justified his sins in the name of justified resentments. As his protector parts soften and his wounded part receives comfort and compassion, Aaron's admirable qualities, which involve compassion, noble self-sacrifice, creativity, and courage, will flourish. He will be free to forgive and love in freedom.

LIFE APPLICATIONS FOR INNER TRANSFORMATION

Praying the Litanies

An intentional flow exists in each of the litanies of the heart. An opening prayer is followed by an initial offering of our hearts, with all their troubles, to Jesus. Here we are admitting to God that we have sufferings, doubts, hurts, fears, and burdens. We are also offering our hope, joy, and love, as well as — and perhaps more importantly — our lack of hope, lack of joy, and lack of love. In this opening, we are admitting that we are broken and that we need help.

In the next section of the litany, the petition-and-response portion begins. Here, the petitioner brings to Christ the specific negative feelings and thoughts that are burdening the heart. These are different in all three litanies because each attachment style has different concerns. The response here is "Lord, have mercy." This is the most ancient and traditional of Jewish and Christian responses. We find it in multiple psalms in the Old Testament. In the New Testament, we hear the Canaanite woman cry out, "Have mercy on me, Lord, Son of David" when she asks Jesus to cure her daughter of a demon (Matt. 15:22). It can also be found in the parable of the Pharisee and the tax collector (or publican), in which the Pharisee is self-righteous and the tax collector says, "God, be merciful to me, a sinner!" (Luke 18:13). Jesus says that the tax collector's humility is what justifies him. His act of repentance is to say "Lord, have mercy," which is also an act of surrender and trust in God. As we offer Him the burdens of our hearts in the litany, and we exclaim, "Lord, have mercy," we are, in effect, saying, "I give You this burden. I trust You with this pain. I can't do it on my own."

The next section is shorter, but here we identify *who Jesus is in relation to ourselves*. Jesus is a consoler; He is tender; He is our dignity; He is our hope. And in response to this, we exclaim, "Open my heart." Here, we are opening our hearts to Him because the litany is revealing to us exactly who He is. We may know these truths about Jesus intellectually, but we are asking Him to open our hearts to receive these truths at a deeper level.

In the next section, we identify *what Jesus does for us*. He created us, sees us, knows us, comforts us, values us, and encourages us. These are all the actions of a secure attachment figure, a good and loving parent, a God who is love.

Occasionally someone will ask, "Is Jesus our Creator? I thought God the Father is the Creator." Theologically, all three Persons of the Trinity are involved in the creation of the world and everything in it. The Gospel of John identifies Jesus Christ as the "Word" and says that "all things came into being through him, and without him not one thing came into being" (John 1:1, 3). *The Catechism* states that "everything that belongs to the Father, *except being Father*, the Son has also eternally from the Father, from whom he is eternally born" (246, emphasis mine). Jesus, with God the Father and God the Holy Spirit, is indeed our loving Creator.

In this section of the litany, we turn to Christ, who is our God, and we acknowledge what He does for us out of love. He created us in love, for love, and to be loved. He meets all our intimacy needs, and we respond, "Hold me in Your arms." This is where we allow ourselves to be held by the One who loves us so deeply. We acknowledge that we are His beloved.

I love the response "Hold me in Your arms," as it evokes a warm embrace. But, in composing the litany, I contemplated simply saying "Hold me." I want to encourage you to adapt the prayer to your needs. If a line doesn't apply to you, feel free to delete or change it. If you would prefer to say "Hold me" instead of "Hold me in Your arms," that is perfectly acceptable. I hope you'll make the Litanies of the Heart your own; after all, other than God, you know your heart better than anyone!

In the final section of the litany, before the closing prayer, we offer a series of petitions. Here we *ask Jesus to act in our lives*. As Jesus is invited to hear, draw near, help, and soothe, we respond with "I trust in You." Now our surrender is complete, as we are truly open to receiving His healing mercy and comfort. For me, this evokes the Divine Mercy devotion of St. Faustina. In it, we find the message of God's great compassion.

In the closing prayer, we acknowledge Jesus' work as Healer of both soul and heart. We ask Him to help us become more like Him. As our hearts are transformed, we find renewed fervor in spreading God's love and mercy to others. We are perhaps inspired to acts of charity, works of mercy, and more meaningful relationships based on intimacy and trust.

There are times when we want to withdraw and disconnect to protect ourselves from pain, shame, and fear. The Litany of the Closed Heart is designed to help us bring our feelings of disconnection to Christ and allow Him to soften our hearts and trust in Him.

LITANY OF THE CLOSED HEART

In the name of the Father, and of the Son, and of the Holy Spirit. Amen.

Lord Jesus, You created me in love and for love. Bring me to a place of vulnerability within the safety of Your loving arms. Help me today by transforming my closed heart into a heart that can love You, myself, and my neighbor as You intend.

Jesus, I offer You my heart with all its sufferings.
Jesus, I offer You my heart with all its doubts.
Jesus, I offer You my heart with all its hurts.
Jesus, I offer You my heart with all its fears.
Jesus, I offer You my heart with all its burdens.
Jesus, I offer You my heart with all its hope and all its lack of hope.
Jesus, I offer You my heart with all its joy and all its lack of joy.
Jesus, I offer You my heart with all its love and all its lack of love.
Jesus, Son of God, *have mercy on me.*

When I'm withdrawn, *Lord, have mercy.*
When I'm consumed with worry, *Lord, have mercy.*
When I numb out, *Lord, have mercy.*
When I feel cynical, *Lord, have mercy.*
When I lose trust, *Lord, have mercy.*
When I'm distracted, *Lord, have mercy.*
When I try to escape my feelings, *Lord, have mercy.*
When my body holds my stress, *Lord, have mercy.*
When I'm under pressure, *Lord, have mercy.*
When I'm filled with anger, *Lord, have mercy.*
When I become obsessed with tasks, *Lord, have mercy.*
When I feel the urge to act out, *Lord, have mercy.*
When I feel ashamed, *Lord, have mercy.*
When I feel unforgiven, *Lord, have mercy.*
Jesus, I know You love me in all my wounds. *Lord, have mercy.*

Jesus, my helper, *open my heart.*
Jesus, light of my mind, *open my heart.*
Jesus, my guide, *open my heart.*
Jesus, my teacher, *open my heart.*
Jesus, Bread of Life, *open my heart.*
Jesus, face of mercy, *open my heart.*
Jesus, my Redeemer, *open my heart.*
Jesus, my life, *open my heart.*
Jesus, my desire, *open my heart.*
Jesus, my comforter, *open my heart.*
Jesus, my trust, *open my heart.*
Jesus, my safe haven, *open my heart.*

Jesus, You created me in love; *hold me in Your arms.*
Jesus, You created me for love; *hold me in Your arms.*
Jesus, You created me to be loved; *hold me in Your arms.*
Jesus, You created my heart; *hold me in Your arms.*
Jesus, You see my heart; *hold me in Your arms.*
Jesus, You know my true heart; *hold me in Your arms.*
Jesus, You comfort my heart; *hold me in Your arms.*
Jesus, You treasure my heart; *hold me in Your arms.*
Jesus, You encourage my heart; *hold me in Your arms.*
Jesus, You created me as Your beloved; *hold me in Your arms.*

Jesus, awaken and restore my stony heart; *I trust in You.*
Jesus, receive my new heart; *I trust in You.*
Jesus, draw close to me in my struggles; *I trust in You.*
Jesus, forgive me; *I trust in You.*
Jesus, give me new life; *I trust in You.*
Jesus, hold me; *I trust in You.*
Jesus, contain my stress; *I trust in You.*
Jesus, relieve the pressure; *I trust in You.*
Jesus, comfort my pain; *I trust in You.*
Jesus, help me see that I'm not defined by what I do; *I trust in You.*
Jesus, let all my actions flow from Your love for me; *I trust in You.*

Jesus, You give meaning to my life; *I trust in You.*
Jesus, help me love and forgive others; *I trust in You.*
Jesus, help me embrace my vulnerability; *I trust in You.*

Lord, You are the healer of my soul and my heart. I ask that through this prayer, You will transform me more and more into the likeness of Your precious and Sacred Heart. Let Your kindness and compassion transform my heart and bring me always into the security of Your loving embrace.

In the name of the Father, and of the Son, and of the Holy Spirit. Amen.

Reflection Questions

1. How have we sometimes closed our hearts in the name of religion or doing the right thing?

2. It can be hard to love someone when we see that person messing up. Why do you think it's so hard for us to love someone when we see him or her messing up? What does this say about our own burdened and wounded parts?

3. How do we love others when they have wronged us?

4. What would it take for Aaron to see how much God loves him? Do we have parts like Aaron's that resent God and others because we feel unjustly treated? How do we sometimes identify with the older brother in the prodigal son parable? How can we help that part of ourselves to experience the love of God in a deeper way?

8

SPIRITUAL CONFIDANTS

Camila's Story, Part 2: Our Lady of Guadalupe[86]

My first three children were born in the comfort of my home with the help of my doula, who provided physical and emotional support, and my midwife, who delivered the babies. I wanted a more personal, natural pregnancy and childbirth experience. Although never easy, each birth was a beautiful experience in which I felt truly supported and cared for. I believed that childbirth expressed the fullness of my womanhood.

Unfortunately, during the third trimester of my fourth pregnancy, I suffered a fall and was taken to the hospital. As soon as I arrived at the hospital, I could feel my anxiety rise. I was reminded of how, when I was eight years old, my mother was taken to the hospital, diagnosed with pneumonia, and died the following day. Everything about hospitals seemed cold, clinical, and unfriendly. The nurses were rushed and busy, and the doctors were distracted and running behind. I didn't want to lose my baby, and I was afraid that I might die and that my children would be left motherless. I asked them to contact my husband and my midwife. They said they would, but it was too late; labor had started.

I was alone and scared, and I experienced the nurses as disinterested and distant. I felt as if they dismissed my concerns and requests and treated my worries as a nuisance. They told me they would need to do a C-section and that I would be put under anesthesia. When I woke up, I was alone in my hospital room, and I panicked. After what seemed like an eternity, my husband came in with a nurse and my new baby girl. They placed her in my arms, but I had the strangest sensation. Was she really mine?

I carefully took care of and breastfed Sonia, but I couldn't bond with her. I experienced postpartum depression as I lost my sense of

86 "Our Lady of Guadalupe" refers to a Marian apparition that occurred in Mexico in 1531 to the peasant Juan Diego. It is a popular devotion with special significance to the indigenous people of Latin America.

purpose and motivation. I feared that I was less than adequate as a mother to my baby and to my other three children, but I was helpless to do anything about it.

I was desperate for things to be different, and when I reached out to my pastor, he suggested I see a counselor who specialized in the treatment of trauma. I began seeing an EMDR therapist, who asked me about my life story. The therapist helped me realize that my early childhood losses, my father's assassination, our travel to the United States, my mother's death, and my experiences of bullying and discrimination at school all had an impact on my traumatic birth experience and my issues with anxiety. My therapist asked me if I could think of someone who represented loving, nurturing, protective care. Immediately I thought of Our Lady of Guadalupe. She is depicted as a mother pregnant with the Baby Jesus. She represents unconditional love. The therapist suggested that I invite Our Lady of Guadalupe to be with me in prayer. I sat in silence for a long moment, and then, in my mind's eye, I could feel her presence, see her loving eyes, even smell the scent of fresh roses. As she placed her mantle over my shoulders, I was able to hear the words, "Am I not here, I who am your mother?"[87] I felt loved and tenderly cared for. I would take a few minutes every day and bask in the experience of a mother's love.

Later, my therapist invited me to recall the memory of Sonia's birth. I recalled with some apprehension how I was unexpectedly taken to the hospital without my doula, my midwife, or my husband. I remembered how the nurses were cold and distant. The familiar anxiety filled up my chest. As we were processing the memory, the therapist, seeing my rising distress, asked, "What did you need?" It was then, in a moment of grace, that I saw Our Lady of Guadalupe — not one but three! — with me in my hospital room. One was delivering the baby, gently guiding me to push or to wait. Another was bringing warm cloths and ice chips. And the third was by my side, holding my hand and telling me that I was doing very well and that everything was going to be all right. Before long, I could hear the baby cry and Our

[87] Our Lady of Guadalupe spoke these words to Juan Diego in one of her apparitions to him.

Lady — one of them — brought me my beautiful little Sonia. I held my baby and cried. She was mine, and we were both safe.

After that session, I could go home and feel connected to my newest daughter. I felt energy and life come back into my heart. The historical facts had not changed, but God had given me what I needed to heal, a corrective experience within my heart.

THE PSYCHOLOGY OF THE INTERIOR WORLD

In EMDR therapy, *resourcing* refers to the identifying and installing of positive coping skills. The calm-place exercise[88] is an example of a resource that helps clients experience a measure of peace and serenity. Another type of resource is a nurturing or protective figure whom someone can call upon to provide emotional support or protection, usually a positive nurturing or protective figure from one's faith.[89] Often clients choose Jesus, Mary, a saint, or an angel. Camila chose Our Lady of Guadalupe. We can ask God to work through these figures to bring grace and healing.

Recent research clearly shows the value of developing a secure attachment to God. A review of thirty studies by British researchers[90] showed that "attachment security priming," in which a therapist uses pictures, names, or guided images to reinforce the idea of an attachment figure in a client's mind, increased positive emotional well-being. Another study from California Baptist University[91] found that subjects who engaged in two weeks of *Lectio Divina*[92] meditation

88 The meditation in chapter 6 is an example of a calm-place exercise.

89 Laurel Parnell stands out as an expert in the area of attachment-focused EMDR and resource figures.

90 Angela C. Rowe, Emily R. Gold, and Katherine B. Carnelley, "The Effectiveness of Attachment Security Priming in Improving Positive Affect and Reducing Negative Affect: A Systematic Review," *International Journal of Environmental Research and Public Health* 17, no. 3 (2020).

91 J. Knabb, R. Pate, J. Lowell, T. De Leeuw, and S. Strickland, *Lectio Divina for Trauma-Related Negative Emotions: A Two-Part Study* (conference presentation), 2022, CAPS 2022 Virtual Conference, https://caps.net/2022-conference/.

92 *Lectio Divina* is a Christian practice that involves reading the Bible with meditation, prayer, and contemplation.

showed a reduction in trauma symptoms. Indeed, several studies have shown that secure attachment to God improved psychological well-being,[93] especially in those who had an anxious or avoidant attachment to God.[94]

Except in extraordinary situations, most of us do not receive visions from God, see burning bushes, or witness apparitions of the Virgin Mary. So, what is going on when we encounter a spiritual confidant during a therapeutic or meditative experience?

We draw from our experiences, sometimes direct ones, and sometimes indirect ones. Direct experiences refer to memories, sometimes forgotten, of being held, cared for, and cherished. Indirect experiences could be ones we've witnessed in real life or seen in movies or even read about in books. When we have an emotionally corrective experience in therapy, we are reconsolidating our experiences to create new, positive, healthier memories. In brain-science language, we say that we are creating new neural pathways.

When we invite God into the experience, grace can further inspire the imagination, often with delightfully unexpected results, such as that of Our Lady of Guadalupe delivering Camila's baby.

Someone may ask, "Did that really happen?" The answer is yes, but probably not in the common historical sense. These experiences are real for our parts, and the changes brought about as a result affect our everyday real life immediately. God is able to work through our spiritual and therapeutic experiences to meet our every need and heal every part of the self-system.

Making Meaning and Post-Traumatic Growth

Jewish psychologist Victor Frankl lost his wife and his parents to the Holocaust. Somehow, he survived the horrors of Auschwitz and wrote a book called *Man's*

[93] J. Leman, W. Hunter, T. Fergus, and W. Rowatt, "Secure Attachment to God Uniquely Linked to Psychological Health in a National, Random Sample of American Adults," *International Journal for the Psychology of Religion* 28, no. 3 (2018): 162–173.

[94] David M. Njus and Alexandra Scharmer, "Evidence That God Attachment Makes a Unique Contribution to Psychological Well-Being," *International Journal for the Psychology of Religion* 30, no. 3 (2018): 178–201.

Search for Meaning. In it, he noted that some people died when they could have physically lived, and some people lived when they should have physically died. What made the difference? The ones who lived found meaning in life even when all the outward aspects of our humanity were stripped away. Suffering for its own sake holds no meaning, but our response to the suffering reveals a great deal about our inner world.

> In spite of all the enforced physical and mental primitiveness of the life in a concentration camp, it was possible for spiritual life to deepen. Sensitive people who were used to a rich intellectual life may have suffered much pain (they were often of a delicate constitution), but the damage to their inner selves was less. They were able to retreat from their terrible surroundings to a life of inner riches and spiritual freedom. Only in this way can one explain the apparent paradox that some prisoners of a less hardy make-up often seemed to survive camp life better than did those of a robust nature.[95]

The truth of the beauty and integrity of the inmost self is not historical or even biological, as the experience of Victor Frankl reveals. It is a psycho-spiritual truth.

We see an example of the spiritual freedom man can find even in the midst of suffering in the movie *Life Is Beautiful,* written, directed, and starring Roberto Benigni. In the film, the main character, Guido, a Jewish man in Northern Italy, and his son Giosuè are sent to a concentration camp by the Nazis. Guido hides the true situation from his son and creates a game to keep him engaged and safe. As an act of love for his son, Guido keeps the game going right up to his death by execution. As an adult, Giosuè understands that the game saved him and was a story of self-sacrificial love.

Indeed, even in the most desperate times, such as what Victor Frankl experienced in Auschwitz, we can discover love at the very core of our inmost self:

> Love is the only way to grasp another human being in the innermost core of his personality. No one can become fully aware of the very essence of

[95] Victor E. Frankl, *Man's Search for Meaning* (Boston: Beacon Press, 1992), 36.

> another human being unless he loves him. By his love he is enabled to see the essential traits and features in the beloved person; and even more, he sees that which is potential in him, which is not yet actualized but yet ought to be actualized. Furthermore, by his love, the loving person enables the beloved person to actualize these potentialities. By making him aware of what he can be and of what he should become, he makes these potentialities come true.[96]

Trauma and suffering are redeemed through the experiences of love. We learn the value of self-sacrifice, and we learn how to see the suffering of others through the eyes of love. We experience the cross as a powerful way to experience the depth of love. This is what it means to "proclaim Christ crucified" (1 Cor. 1:23).

Two psychologists at the University of North Carolina at Charlotte, Richard Tedeschi and Lawrence Calhoun, first developed the theory of post-traumatic growth in the mid-1990s. The idea here is that some people experience growth and thriving despite trauma. As a result of, or perhaps despite, their trauma, these people experience a greater appreciation of life, improved relationships with others, greater personal strength, and spiritual growth. This is different from resilience, in which a person "bounces back" from trauma and returns to normal levels of functioning. Instead, people who experience post-traumatic growth not only stabilize but improve.

Jesus and the saints are all examples of post-traumatic growth. Jesus, of course, is the perfect case study: He experienced terrible torture, humiliation, and an inglorious death. And yet, despite all of that, He conquered death and returned in a glorified state. In His Resurrection, as in His Transfiguration, Jesus shows His true identity; He becomes hope actualized.

The saints in various ways are all examples of post-traumatic growth. St. Bernadette Soubirous and St. Thérèse of Lisieux suffered with tuberculosis and yet persevered in greater love. St. Maria Goretti suffered a deadly physical assault and yet forgave her attacker. St. Damien of Molokai ministered to lepers, and before he himself died of leprosy, he worked with energy and zeal. There

[96] Ibid., 111–112.

are thousands of examples of saints who overcame the worst kinds of torture, pain, and suffering and continued to be inspired and find a deeper purpose in their ministry. One of my favorites, St. Lawrence, while being burned alive on a gridiron, asked to be turned over ("I'm done on this side," he added), showing how little he valued his suffering compared with the glory of the martyr's crown that awaited him in Heaven.

St. Paul famously says:

> When this perishable body puts on imperishability, and this mortal body puts on immortality, then the saying that is written will be fulfilled:
> "Death has been swallowed up in victory."
> "Where, O death, is your victory?
> "Where, O death, is your sting?" (1 Cor. 15:54–55).

All kinds of trauma, even death, lose their power when our parts, united with the inmost self, are in communion with the God who sees us, knows us, encourages us, and abides with us.

Jesus Christ and all His saints understood trauma. They understand pain and suffering. Jesus responded to the death of Lazarus with tears (John 11:35). He cried out to Heaven in His pain and agony on the Cross (Matt. 27:46). And yet Jesus and the saints all believed fervently that there in a greater purpose in this life and the next. There is a kingdom that is greater than this world. This belief gave them confidence, courage, calm, and persistence to face even the most tragic and difficult life circumstances.

The examples of Jesus and His saints can help us stay focused on that greater purpose as they walk with us through our most difficult and challenging moments. We embrace those moments because they are the heroic moments of our lives in which we are called to face life and death on their own terms with courage and faith. We are challenged to face evil and work through pain and suffering with love and faith, just as Christ did. When we embrace this difficult challenge with faith, finding a deeper meaning even in our most painful life experiences, then we experience a powerful inner transformation. This post-traumatic growth often leads to greater levels of empathy for others, a stronger drive to help those who are struggling, and an enduring gratitude for the people in our lives.

SCRIPTURE STUDY: THE SELF-SYSTEM AND ST. PAUL'S LETTER TO THE EPHESIANS

In a passage that is sometimes considered controversial for some modern readers, St. Paul instructs wives to be subject to their husbands (Eph. 5:22). From an IFS or parts-work perspective, the passage is quite significant because it reveals the deeper mystery of the Church as a "system." The Church as the Body of Christ is a system made up of many important and necessary parts, including bishops, priests, deacons, religious, and all the people of God. The Christian, as a part of the Body of Christ, is also made of many parts, as we have seen throughout this book. St. Paul says, "Now you are the body of Christ and individually members of it," and "we, though many, are one body in Christ, and individually members one of another" (1 Cor. 12:27; Rom. 12:5).

St. Paul makes analogies between Christ and the Church, based on the cultural realities of his time. He compares Christ to a husband and to a master, and the Church to a wife and a servant. These analogies might be jarring for modern readers, but the underlying point is still relevant. The husband, like Christ, must love his wife even unto death. The master must love his servants and not be a tyrant. The inmost self, likewise, must love the parts of the self-system, just as Christ loves His Church.

The inmost self is even meant to metaphorically die for the parts, just as Christ died for the Church. In the same way, St. Paul compares the relationship of father and mother with their children to God the Father and the Church: "Children, obey your parents in the Lord, for this is right.... And, fathers, do not provoke your children to anger, but bring them up in the discipline and instruction of the Lord" (Eph. 6:1, 4). Children are meant to honor their parents, and the father is not to provoke his children but to instruct them. In terms of the inmost self and the parts, we can understand from this that the inmost self is like the parent, and the parts are like children. The inmost self must love the parts like an attuned and loving parent who really sees, knows, comforts, and delights in his children, and the parts respond to this love with honor and obedience.

It has been my clinical experience that when the parts are loved, they naturally want to please the inmost self and will take instruction. Before this is likely to happen, however, the parts need to trust the inmost self. The inmost self must be present (not chronically eclipsed by burdened parts) and in relationship with the parts. Children may act as if they want to be "free" and live without rules or parental guidance, but the reality is that they thrive on consistent, calm, clear, safe parental leadership. In the same way, the parts need and desire the security that the inmost self can provide.

In a similar manner, St. Paul describes the relationship between masters and their slaves as comparable to Christ and His Church, where the slaves are to be obedient to their masters and serve Christ:

> Slaves, obey your earthly masters with fear and trembling, in singleness of heart, as you obey Christ; not only while being watched, and in order to please them, but as slaves of Christ, doing the will of God from the heart. Render service with enthusiasm, as to the Lord and not to men and women, knowing that whatever good we do, we will receive the same again from the Lord, whether we are slaves or free. And, masters, do the same to them. Stop threatening them, for you know that both of you have the same Master in heaven, and with him there is no partiality. (Eph. 6:5–9)

The masters are to serve Christ as well and be kind and protective toward the slaves. St. Paul is not advocating for the institution of slavery here. He is using this example to show how all human institutions, no matter how flawed, can be transformed to reflect the incredible love of God for His people. The inmost self's relationship with the parts reflects this radical relationship of love.

Throughout these analogies, we see that love and respect (Eph. 5:33), rather than power or anger or greed, are to guide each of these relationships. Christ died a terrible death out of love for us, and His love can inspire each and every one of our relationships, including the relationship between our inmost selves and our parts. The inmost self then becomes a kind, loving leader who "nourishes and tenderly cares for" the parts, who are then meant to "do the will of God from their heart" (Eph. 5:29; 6:6). This is not a relationship of coercion but one of freedom and mutual love.

St. Paul uses military metaphors to describe "positive protectors." In IFS, we often see protectors as overwhelmed parts attempting to guard wounded exiles, often in maladaptive ways. I suggest that St. Paul here may be describing the redeemed inmost self relating to its protector parts, who are charged with saving the entire self-system, the whole person, the soul and body, from external threats.

St. Paul calls for us to be strong and to put on the "armor of God." As well as the belt of truth, this armor includes a breastplate of righteousness, a helmet of salvation, and a sword of the Spirit (the word of God) (Eph. 6:11, 14, 17). Once unburdened and then evangelized and sanctified, our parts become fierce in a good way. They work together as a harmonious whole with the inmost self to do good in the world. They are no longer burdened; they are now equipped. It is in this section that St. Paul tells us to "pray in the Spirit at all times" (Eph. 6:18), which inspired the Eastern church to pray the Jesus Prayer. Here we can be present and "in self" as we "keep alert." This is being a saint: a man or woman whose inmost self is a loving parent and whose parts are unburdened and working together for a meaningful purpose in God's kingdom.

LIFE APPLICATIONS FOR INNER TRANSFORMATION

Meditation — Spiritual Confidants

Dr. Peter Malinoski developed this exercise to help us connect with our "spiritual confidants." "Spiritual confidant" can refer to a member of the Holy Trinity: God the Father, God the Son (Jesus), or God the Holy Spirit. It can also refer to Mary, a saint, or an angel.

There are many options for a spiritual confidant. Choose someone with whom your parts feel safe. Your parts can pick how much contact there will be with your confidant. We do not even insist that the spiritual confidant be physically close.

If you have a spiritual confidant whom you can work with and whom your parts are comfortable with, I invite you to reach out to him or her: "In the name of the Father, and of the Son, and of the Holy Spirit. I invite you to be present and to guide my meditation."

Now I invite you to notice what's going on in your body. Notice what's happening inside and where you are in this moment with your parts and what parts might be blended.

Look for those trailheads: body sensations, memories, images, and so forth. Notice where you are with those eight Cs — where are you with confidence, calm, compassion, courage, creativity, clarity, curiosity, and connectedness.

See if any parts have an agenda and if any parts are blended with you.

See if these blended parts can give you some space. See if they'd be willing to relax so that you, as your inmost self, can be more present.

See if your parts can see you and look at you and sense that you can lead and guide your system.

Are there any parts who are concerned about inviting a spiritual confidant into your human formation work? If so, you'll want to hear from those parts and respect them. You can pause and work with those parts.

The inmost self is also monitoring how everything is going with the parts. Can you allow this spiritual confidant to be with all of you? The spiritual confidant has so much respect for your parts, for your integrity, and has no desire to intrude or invade. He or she will work collaboratively and cooperatively with all your parts.

There's no agenda here. No specific action plan or checklist. The spiritual confidant can be close or remote as you begin. There's lots of freedom. Take a minute or two to be with that spiritual confidant. Take it slowly. Check in with your parts to see how it's going with them. Are there any parts concerned? Your system can move away from the spiritual confidant if needed.

Express a great deal of gratitude for your parts. Check in with them. What was the exercise like for them? Appreciate the trust they are showing toward your inmost self to whatever degree they do or can. Also express gratitude to your spiritual confidant for coming and being present.

Close with a prayer: "Lord, I thank You that You know me and love me. Thank You for giving me [my spiritual confidant] to show me Your love and to aid me in my healing. I know that You want me to find rest in You, and I praise You for Your guidance. Help me to repent of my sins and live out my true identity as Your child. Amen."

Reflection Questions

1. Which saints or angels, or which Person of the Holy Trinity, feel the most nurturing to you?
2. Which saints or angels, or which Person of the Holy Trinity, feel the most protective to you?
3. What spiritual stories have the most meaning for you?
4. Do you think you have experienced growth despite traumatic experiences? How so?
5. Try to imagine what it would be like for your parts to experience your inmost self as a loving parent, a self-sacrificing spouse, or a kind, compassionate authority. How do you feel about this?

9

THE INNER KINGDOM

Alexandre's Story, Part 4: The Cloud of Witnesses

A girlfriend in high school invited me to join her on a Christian weekend retreat during which I was encouraged and inspired by other teens who shared their faith stories. We prayed and enthusiastically sang hymns together, and we continued to meet as a larger group every Wednesday night to pray and share in small groups. More importantly, we hugged each other when we met, and we hung out at parties and became friends. It was my first real experience of Christian community. I felt a deep sense of belonging; no longer was I an outsider who escaped into books to avoid others. I even developed leadership skills and organized social events. I had discovered a lost part of me that was joyful and delighted in meeting new people and bringing them together. I also discovered an evangelical part of me that wanted to share my faith with others.

I went off to college filled with spiritual enthusiasm and an evangelical spirit. I became a leader in a nondenominational campus ministry and then established a young-adult's group at a nearby cathedral. There was a spiritual and religious part of me that flourished in that environment, and I read every spiritual classic I could find, including St. Augustine's *Confessions*, St. Teresa's *Interior Castle,* and St. Thérèse's *Story of a Soul*. I also read the classic *The Way of a Pilgrim* and Timothy Ware's *The Orthodox Way*. I was "on fire for Christ" and ready to change the world!

The rector of the cathedral, Fr. Steven, noticed that I was attending daily Mass and invited me to be an altar server, an extraordinary minister of the Eucharist, and eventually an assistant sacristan. Fr. Steven became a surrogate father while I was at college, and I came to him with every theological question I could think of. He helped me make sense of difficult doctrines with his sensible and natural explanations of complex theological problems. He became my mentor and spiritual director.

At some point, I told Fr. Steven about the abuse I experienced as a child. He was kind and loving and asked me if he could pray with me. He anointed me with oil and guided me into an experience of prayer. It isn't easy to remember exactly how it unfolded, but with my eyes closed, I was able to connect with the young, wounded-child part of myself, and I could see him in my mind's eye. He was on his bed in his old bedroom and scared while his father was yelling and pounding on the door. The splintering door eventually gave, and with the force of a rhinoceros, his father forced his way in. My child part was terrified, and I could feel my current body tighten and my breathing became shallow.

Fr. Steven gently asked if we could invite Jesus to be present, and I answered with a nod. Still shaking, I saw Jesus appear with a calm and confident presence. My father began to shrink as his bluster faded and his shoulders slumped. Side by side, Christ remained tall, kind, gentle, and strong while my father became small, his brokenness revealing that he was a shell of a man, a pathetic figure. My physical body relaxed as I exhaled a sigh of relief.

Then another remarkable thing happened. Jesus' Mother, Mary, also appeared and, with her, a retinue of angels and saints. They formed a ring of protection around me as they encircled my bed. My father disappeared, and Jesus, His eyes filled with compassion, came into the circle, His arms outstretched, and I ran into His embrace. He wanted to take me to meet my real Father in Heaven. Up until that moment, I avoided thinking about God the Father. I was more comfortable with Jesus and the Holy Spirit. Fathers were a frightful business.

But in that moment, I was overcome with delight as angels swirled around me and Christ and His Mother were by my side. Jesus picked me up and held me in His arms. I was transported to a place with a giant throne, and Jesus placed me on the lap of the Father. I couldn't see His face, but I could feel His powerful but gentle presence, and He held me while I basked in His love. He gave me everything I ever wanted from my earthly father and more. In that place, I knew I was loved without any conditions. I was good enough just by being there. His words from Christ's baptism were inscribed on my heart: "You are my beloved son, in whom I am well pleased." I finally received the affirmation my young self always needed. It was a turning point in my healing journey.

THE PSYCHOLOGY OF THE INTERIOR WORLD

In the chapter 5 meditation, we envisioned an inner "living room" where we could encounter our parts. I encourage people to create the living room in their mind's eye, rather than recalling one from a past house. Past houses sometimes have negative associations even if they were mostly positive places. The inner living room, however, and the corresponding inner "house" is open to instant redecoration, and it can change and morph into whatever people desire or need.

I learned from Sandra Paulsen, an expert in Ego State Therapy and EMDR, the idea of inviting people to picture an inner "conference room."[97] It worked very well, and I still sometimes use that image. But in time, I became more comfortable with inviting people to discover their "inner living room." It is homier and you can imagine a variety of bedrooms and playrooms and dens connected to the central living room. We invite our parts to meet in the living room. It is often helpful to take a deep breath and take a moment to notice what might be activated inside of us. Visually oriented clients will "see" their parts. Sometimes it is more of a felt sense.

As we picture or sense these parts, they can choose the couch or a chair, or they can sit on the floor, if they prefer. We spend time noticing them, hearing from them, and interacting with them. This can be a powerful time of connection. After the work is done, we can thank each one for being present, and then the parts can retreat into their respective rooms.

Earlier, we looked at how we unblend the parts from the inmost self. We explored how we can identify and differentiate our various parts. We develop trusting relationships with the protectors by listening and empathizing with them. We help them adopt new roles that are more helpful. The goal here is that we befriend the protectors so that we can be introduced to the exiles. The exiles are the wounded parts, often children, who are carrying heavy burdens,

[97] This was itself adapted from George Fraser's dissociative table technique.

usually of shame, fear, and pain. We will now explore the beginning of the unburdening process for exiles.

Approaching Exiles

There is a process in IFS for working with exiles, and I'll briefly outline the steps here:

1. *Contacting the exile*: The inmost self is present with and establishes a connection with the exile.

2. *Witnessing the exile*: The exile shares whatever he needs to share so that he experiences being seen, known, and understood. The exile may need to be reminded that what happened occurred in the past.

3. *Retrieving the exile*: The exile is freed from the past situation and brought into a newer, healthier situation in the present.

4. *Reparenting the exile*: The exile has a new emotional experience in the present or as he works with the memory.[98]

5. *Unburdening the exile*: The exile ritually releases the burdens he has been holding.

A good place to start in this process is to check in with the protector parts in the "inner living room" and ask them if they are ready to introduce you to the exile.[99] At this point, the exile may have already appeared or may need to be invited in, or you may need to ask the protector where to find him. Some exiles may reside in unsafe or uninhabitable regions, and like the Good Shepherd, you need to go find them. When you do encounter an exile, approach carefully and

[98] Richard Schwartz does not use the term *reparenting*, but psychologist and IFS specialist Jay Earley does. It is the inmost self in the role of ideal parent who does the reparenting and facilitates a new emotionally corrective experience for the exile.

[99] IFS would not start the unburdening of exiles from a safe or calm place, so this represents my own integrative approach, based on my own clinical work. These techniques are more commonly associated with Ego State Therapy.

sensitively. Appreciate how much trust it took for the protector to let you go near and for the exile to be willing to meet you.

In the same way you approached the protector, take the time to really notice the exile, to see him if you can, to feel his presence, and to notice if there is any different or unusual sensation in your body. Take a deep breath and invite the Holy Spirit to be with you and inspire you. Recall how precious children were to Jesus. Gradually move closer to the part and notice how the exile responds. Stop or slow down if necessary. Is the exiled part aware of you? How does he react to you? What does this part need to feel safe with you?

Notice the exiled part's pain. Ask yourself, "How do I feel toward this part?" If you are "in self" — that is, fully present and unblended from your parts — you will likely feel compassion. See if the part can feel your compassion. Allow yourself to feel some of the exile's pain. Ask the exile if he can show you the first time he felt this way. Remind the exile that you will stay with him. If there is a story he wants to share, remind him that he is not actually traveling back in time to the painful incident itself but is exploring the memory with you in the present. Notice the exile's feelings and any sensations, and let him know that all his thoughts and feelings are important. Listen with care to anything the exile chooses to share. As you attune yourself to the exile's pain, let him know that you relate to him and you understand how painful his experience was for him.

We will also want to check in with the managers and any other parts of the self-system who are present. The goal is for the inmost self, the protectors, and the exiles to work collaboratively and create a safe internal environment for the whole internal system. We can work with the exiles to avoid flooding, which is an overwhelming emotional response to a real or perceived threat. Flooding activates the sympathetic nervous system, which involves the fight, flight, or freeze response. Exiles can agree that if the intensity of their emotions becomes overwhelming for the system, they will soften and seek out their calm place or another helpful resource. All the parts can learn to work together in a spirit of cooperation, care, and mutual empathy. The inmost self is there to ensure a safe, loving, healing environment for all, especially when we are doing difficult and sensitive work with wounded exiles. And as always, we can invite the Holy Spirit to be present and provide the gifts of counsel, understanding, wisdom, and healing.

It is important to remember that if the exile chooses to show you a memory, it is a memory in the past, and unless you own a Tardis,[100] you can't change history. But for the exile, it is still happening in the present within your internal system. Whatever you do now with the exile, it is happening in the present, and it opens the possibility of the exile's healing, growing, and discovering new ways to adapt to life. There are new ways for the parts in your self-system to relate with each other, with your inmost self, with God, and with your loved ones.

If the exile shows you a memory in which he was bullied, abused, criticized, humiliated, or scared, it is important to reflect on what that child needs now. If this were happening to a child in front of you, now that you are a grown adult with resources, what would you do? Imagine how you would intervene and prevent bullying, remove a child from an abusive environment, reassure a child of his worth, restore a child's dignity, or comfort and console a child after a fearful event. Whatever the child needs, the inmost self, with the grace of God, can provide.

Whatever initial healing work happens as you interact with an exile, notice how the exile reacts when it is done. Often the exile appears lighter, happier, and freer. If this is the case, invite the exile to notice how good this feels. Check in with any protectors present about how they experienced the healing moment. And notice how the inmost self feels about the child part.

If it feels right, invite your exiled part into the inner living room and perhaps invite him to choose a new room for himself in the larger house. You can fill this room with whatever that child enjoys the most. Be sure to thank the exile for his hard work and check in on him daily. There may be more healing work to do, but let that part know how good he is, how brave he was, and how delighted you are that he is here with you now.

St. Teresa's Interior Castle and the Inmost Self

St. Teresa of Ávila was a sixteenth-century Carmelite nun and mystic who reformed her religious order. In her classic work *The Interior Castle,* she invites the reader on a journey of self-knowledge and marvels at the fact that the more we

[100] This is my geeky reference to Doctor Who and his time-travel device.

realize our incredible God-given dignity, the humbler we become. St. Teresa's vision of the human soul supports the idea that the inmost self resides in the deepest center of our souls, where we can experience a most profound intimate relationship with God. It is a deep and powerful entry into the depths of the inner psyche, the depths of the soul.

As I reflect on St. Teresa's interior castle, I'm amazed at the similarity between her "mansions" and my inner living room and inner house. St. Teresa imagines the soul as a castle or as a collection of mansions or rooms. The outer rooms are colder, darker, and filled with little creatures that represent distractions or preoccupations. As we go deeper, we feel the warmth of a light.

Deep within is a fountain symbolizing the baptismal waters of redemption. These waters are a source of life and renewal. Christ is in the very center room, which St. Teresa depicts as a bridal chamber. In other words, at the very core of our soul is union with God. This is where we find the deepest level of intimacy with Him. This is the "living water" promised to the Samaritan woman[101] that involves a radical change in our everyday lives as well as a promise of life everlasting (see John 4).

Before we can fully encounter Christ at the center of our souls, we must at least begin the process of discovering, unblending, and unburdening our parts. We may need to be reminded of how we access our parts and what it means to take the first steps into our interior castle. It is often helpful to begin by preparing ourselves with deep, diaphragmatic breathing and initial relaxation. Most people close their eyes, but this is not necessary. We take a moment to notice what tensions we might be holding in our body. These bodily tensions often represent a part that is communicating its distress to us. As we make space inside, we connect our bodily sensations with some part of the self-system that is activated in some way. There may be a conflict, a concern, a symptom, or a threat. We simply see if we can notice this part. We may be able to picture this part in our mind's eye.

St. Teresa makes the case that as we grow in self-knowledge, we grow in humility. We must come to know both the unique nature of our inmost self and all the interesting and resourceful parts of the self-system who inhabit our

[101] Discussed in both chapters 2 and 3.

interior castle. In time, we learn that we are not fully what we can be or what we are meant to be. This recognition impels us to embrace the "new man" or "new woman" that we are in Christ. This is a powerful moment when we realize the incredible opportunity that lies before us. We can choose to stay in our old patterns or to strive toward the life God is calling us to embrace — the life in which we operate from the conscious center of the soul,[102] the inmost self, inspired and led by the Holy Spirit.

SCRIPTURE STUDY: THE KINGDOM OF GOD AND ST. PAUL'S LETTER TO THE EPHESIANS

"The Kingdom of God Is within You"

Jesus Christ proclaims the present and coming kingdom of God: "The time is fulfilled, and the kingdom of God has come near; repent, and believe in the good news" (Mark 1:15). While a modern reader may find it difficult to understand the concept of a kingdom, it is basically a system in which a ruler, the king, is responsible for providing leadership and a vision to his many subjects. He maintains tradition and provides security. He has an army to defend the country. He governs the country and makes sure that people are treated fairly. In many ways, a kingdom is made up of parts: managers, firefighters, exiles, and those parts who are integrated and in right relationship with the inmost self.

The king's job is to make sure that the managers get along and are productive and prosperous. The protectors make sure that everyone is safe from internal and external threats. There might even be special operatives, such as firefighters,

[102] I carefully chose the term "conscious center of the soul," but it can be difficult to precisely define "inmost self." It is not precise to equate terms used in different languages, in different time periods, and with particular philosophical and theological nuances, but I tend to see the inmost self as comparable to the Greek word for "heart or mind," which is *nous*. It is also comparable to the concept of the "true self" or the "cave of the heart," used often in monastic spirituality. In Eastern Christianity, *nous* connotes the "eye of the soul" or the "mind of the heart."

who take on special missions during emergencies. In any kingdom, there are also likely to be outcasts and people who are marginalized or wounded.

A good king, like the inmost self, seeks to bring prosperity and good order. He is also concerned about those in his kingdom who are troubled. He looks for ways to bring them education, good health, stability, and proper functioning. In other words, a kingdom is a system of many parts. A good kingdom, like a functioning self-system, is healthy and prosperous. The fact that Jesus preaches the coming of the kingdom of God means that there is going to be a new order, a new system, and this kingdom will be different because it will be based on love, not corruption.

But there is a battle that must be waged for this new kingdom. It is not a battle of warfare and physical violence but a battle for a new order ruled by love and inspired by the Cross. We must fight against our own pride to win over and work with our protectors and managers and heal our exiles and to liberate the parts that are being held captive in the prisons of our souls.

The battle is against complacency and vice. We must come to Christ with our blindness, with our demons, with our leprosy, with our bleeding, and with our painful and grieving hearts. We are seeking to go from death to life, from sickness to health, from obsessions to freedom,[103] from sorrow to joy. We are fighting for a kingdom based on love, not on greed, materialism, ambition, or competition. In this kingdom, every single heart is healed and transformed. This is where we hear, "Receive your sight; your faith has saved you" (Luke 18:42).

Jesus says, "The kingdom of God is not coming with things that can be observed; nor will they say, 'Look, here it is!' or 'There it is!' For, in fact, the kingdom of God is within you" (Luke 17:20–21). Here it is explicit that there is a

[103] Paul Blowers describes St. Maximus the Confessor's position this way: "The training of 'right reason' (ὀρθὸς λόγος) on creatures' part is critical, no doubt, to this process of learning true freedom, but the most dramatic struggle is the conditioning of will and desire, at the level both of the microcosm of the individual hypostasis and the macrocosm of universal creation." Paul M. Blowers, *Maximus the Confessor: Jesus Christ and the Transfiguration of the World*, Christian Theology in Context (Oxford, UK: Oxford University Press, 2018), 122. Here we see that "true freedom" can occur only with right reason and that this is a struggle on both an internal level (the self-system) and a universal level.

"kingdom" or "internal system" led by God inside of each of us. St. Paul describes it as "righteousness and peace and joy in the Holy Spirit" (Rom. 14:17). Jesus Himself describes the kingdom and its parts in the Beatitudes (Matt. 5:1–12). He says that the following will be blessed: the poor in spirit, those who mourn, the meek, those who hunger and thirst for righteousness, the merciful, the pure in heart, the peacemakers, and those who are persecuted for righteousness' sake. He also describes what each part will receive: the kingdom of Heaven, comfort, an inheritance, mercy, the bliss of seeing God, being called children of God, and other rewards. In this kingdom, the King will reward the parts and give to each what he needs. These blessings include a sense of security, comfort and care, an identity as a child of God and connection with God.

It is the same with the inmost self and the parts. There is a cooperation between the parts as they work together, despite their struggles and despite their pain. Each part in the kingdom is devoted to God, to His justice, and to a life of humility, despite what the world throws at them.

The Kingdom of God in St. Paul's Letter to the Ephesians

Let's return to the story of Genesis, where we find that God has created the world as a kind of temple, with man, the image of God, at the center, naming the animals and caring for the land. Man is, in a certain sense, a steward and even a gardener of creation, but he is also the bridge between God and all of creation. The Fall disrupted all this and created a barrier between man and God and between man and nature.

Christ came to restore the relationship between God, man, and creation. I believe this helps explain the somewhat enigmatic moment after the Resurrection when Mary mistakes Jesus for a gardener (John 20:14–16). Jesus is the caretaker of a new creation, a new garden, where love will be cultivated. When understood in this context, a great deal of what St. Paul says in his letters has a deeper meaning.

St. Paul writes that God has given Christ dominion and power; He "has put all things under his feet and has made him the head over all things for the church, which is his body, the fullness of him who fills all in all" (Eph. 1:20–23). St. Paul describes Jesus as the head of a body that makes up the Church. Jesus is the new temple, and He is also the head of the Church, which includes all who are baptized into Christ. If we can hold these images together, we end up with a picture of the kingdom that includes the temple and many parts. In addition to this, baptized Christians are also temples of the Holy Spirit.

Jesus refers to His body as the temple (John 2:21), and as we've seen, the Church is a larger, "macro" version of the temple within the kingdom. The Church is the place of union for all Christians who worship God. There is also a "micro" version of the temple within the kingdom that exists in every baptized Christian, who is a temple of the Holy Spirit.[104]

Our whole self, our body and soul, is a part of this larger temple in the kingdom, which also represents our inner temple and inner kingdom with the inmost self and many parts of the self-system. The interior kingdom is a microcosm of the exterior kingdom, and Christ is the connector or bridge between the two.

The sign and symbol of this bridge between the exterior kingdom of God and the interior kingdom within us is the Eucharist, which is sometimes called Communion or the Lord's Supper. Communion unifies the people of the Church with God and with each other. This new covenant includes an inner journey from death in sin to new life: "By grace you have been saved — and raised . . . up with him and seated . . . with him in the heavenly places in Christ Jesus" (Eph. 2:5–6). By God's love, we are given a place, a seat, in His new kingdom. We are a "part" of this new body, which was "created . . . for good works" (Eph. 2:10). What we do, once again, is an outflowing of our owning our true identity. We take our "seat" in the "heavenly places," and we express this identity because it gives our lives meaning and purpose.

[104] In *The City of God,* St. Augustine evokes the idea that the inner man is also like a city. In the *Ambigua,* St. Maximus the Confessor also describes the human person as a microcosm of the whole universe. The exterior kingdom of God is coming about, and the inner kingdom of God is within us. There is an exterior temple and an interior temple of the Holy Spirit. The Church is the Body of Christ, but when we receive Communion, and when we receive Christ into our hearts, there is an interior transformation. Our inner world reflects the complexity of these exterior systems: a city, a kingdom, a temple, or a body. All this imagery can inform our understanding of the rich inner landscape within each person.

St. Paul speaks of how, through the Cross of Christ, we who were exiled are now redeemed:

> He has abolished the law with its commandments and ordinances, so that he might create in himself one new humanity in place of the two, thus making peace, and might reconcile both groups to God in one body through the cross, thus putting to death that hostility through it. So he came and proclaimed peace to you who were far off and peace to those who were near; for through him both of us have access in one Spirit to the Father. So then you are no longer strangers and aliens, but you are citizens with the saints and also members of the household of God, built upon the foundation of the apostles and prophets, with Christ Jesus himself as the cornerstone. In him the whole structure is joined together and grows into a holy temple in the Lord; in whom you also are built together spiritually into a dwelling-place for God. (Eph. 2:15–22)

St. Paul makes it clear that this is a new covenant with new rules and that Christ brings reconciliation to those who were formerly in conflict. St. Paul was likely speaking about the division between Jews and Gentiles, but in our context, this passage could relate to any relationship problem or internal conflict. This division is not repaired through a loss of individual identity but through the unifying Spirit of God. We are citizens with the saints in the household of God! In other words, we are individual parts of a greater whole, with Jesus as the head, the cornerstone, of a new holy temple, and this new temple collectively connects us with God the Father and with the whole Church, including those Christians in Purgatory and in Heaven. And as each of us has become a "dwelling-place for God," we can understand that our inner kingdom, our inmost self and all our parts, is at least metaphorically a microcosm of the larger kingdom, the holy Church established by Christ Himself.

St. Paul also writes that the kingdom of God, both external and internal, lives in unity yet thrives in its members' multiplicity:

> I therefore, the prisoner in the Lord, beg you to lead a life worthy of the calling to which you have been called, with all humility and gentleness,

> with patience, bearing with one another in love, making every effort to maintain the unity of the Spirit in the bond of peace. There is one body and one Spirit, just as you were called to the one hope of your calling, one Lord, one faith, one baptism, one God and Father of all, who is above all and through all and in all.
>
> But each of us was given grace according to the measure of Christ's gift. Therefore it is said, / "When he ascended on high he made captivity itself a captive; / he gave gifts to his people."
>
> The gifts he gave were that some would be apostles, some prophets, some evangelists, some pastors and teachers, to equip the saints for the work of ministry, for building up the body of Christ, until all of us come to the unity of the faith and of the knowledge of the Son of God, to maturity, to the measure of the full stature of Christ. We must no longer be children, tossed to and fro and blown about by every wind of doctrine, by people's trickery, by their craftiness in deceitful scheming. But speaking the truth in love, we must grow up in every way into him who is the head, into Christ, from whom the whole body, joined and knitted together by every ligament with which it is equipped, as each part is working properly, promotes the body's growth in building itself up in love. (Eph. 4:1–8, 11–16)

It is remarkable that St. Paul ties so many powerful theological threads together to paint this picture in his Letter to the Ephesians. On one hand, he emphasizes that the unity of the members of the Body of Christ is founded on a common faith and Baptism. Each Christian is to practice virtue and treat others with love, humility, patience, and gentleness. But within this unity, by the grace of God, we receive gifts and take on different roles, such as prophets, evangelists, teachers, and pastors, in order to build up the Body of Christ. The diverse parts of the Body of Christ work together with purpose, and as a result, the Church grows in wisdom and maturity and becomes more like Christ.

This description of the external kingdom, the Church, the macrocosm, tells us how each of us is to lead our internal system. The inmost self is like Christ, and it is the head. Our parts are to work together for peace and resolve conflicts with love. We are to practice humility, patience, and gentleness with our parts. We are to encourage our parts to fulfill the healthy roles given to them by God's grace.

When our self-system, the internal kingdom, mirrors the Church, we prosper and grow in maturity and wisdom, and we become more and more Christlike. We are transformed.

LIFE APPLICATIONS FOR INNER TRANSFORMATION

Meditation

I ask you to walk with me through an exercise to invite your inmost self and the parts of your self-system to experience God's presence.

First, I ask you to become comfortable and take several deep breaths.

Notice any muscle tension and invite those muscles to relax as you exhale.

Now, let's begin with a prayer:

Dear Heavenly Father, I invite Your loving presence to protect and guide me.

Dear Jesus, I invite Your healing presence to comfort and restore me.

Holy Spirit, I invite Your wise and life-giving presence to enlighten my mind and my heart.

Dear Holy Trinity, I invite You to be present in the way I need You most today.

As you continue to take comfortable breaths, notice how your body begins to rest more comfortably in your chair. Notice how safe and comfortable you feel now. Check in with how you're doing with the eight Cs: confidence, calm, compassion, courage, creativity, clarity, curiosity, and connectedness.

Notice if you have an agenda — that is, if you are trying to make something happen. See if you can have a big, open heart. If you notice an agenda or distress, fear, anxiety, or any intense emotions, ask that part to soften and make some space. If that part cannot, take a moment and work with him.

See if you can experience a sense of calm as you slow things down and turn your attention inward.

I invite you to look inside for a moment and imagine that inner living space. It can be an inner living room, or it could be a cabin, a porch, a kitchen, or even an outside space, such as a meadow.

Now I'd like you to notice any parts that are present in that space today. Perhaps you have a "researcher" part who is busy gathering information to apply later. Perhaps you have a part who is worried about whether you fit in, concerned about how you look or what you say and whether you are accepted. Notice also if you have a part who is uncomfortable with this activity and may be critical. If any of these parts, or others, show up, just notice them with gratitude. It is a gift from God that we have so many interesting and resourceful parts of the self-system. Notice how these parts are in some way "active" or present in your body.

Now see if there are any parts who are negative about God or critical of faith or religion. And notice if there are any "religious" parts that are concerned about doing things correctly and pleasing God. It's normal to have parts that seem to be at odds with each other. We might have a part that is extremely happy to be engaging in prayer. But we may also have a part that is worried, fearful, or even resentful. We may have a part that is cautious and another that is optimistic.

Notice how your parts relate to each other. Let them know that you're not going to resolve any inner conflicts or do any deep healing work today. You're just going to notice your parts a bit more, and in a moment, you will allow your inmost self and any interested parts to have a brief moment of prayer.

As you notice all these parts of the inmost self, see if you can bring a deep sense of gratitude to each one of these parts; notice the parts that are positive, optimistic, and hardworking. Let them know you are there with them and that you care about them. Thank all these parts for how they are working within you.

Also notice the parts of the self that might be critical, fearful, ashamed, or angry. Let them know that you are there with them too, that you care for them, and that you plan to get to know them and understand them better at a later date.

If they are willing, ask these parts of the self-system to open a bit more space in your mind and your body. Allow the feeling of compassion and kindness to flow from you, your inmost self, to all your parts. Allow your various parts to see the kind, patient, loving adult that is you. You are free to provide a bit of comfort or consolation to any part who needs it today.

As you do this, be sure to notice your breathing, and take another deep, comfortable breath.

Invite all your parts to rest comfortably beside or behind you for a moment as you turn to connect with God in prayer. As you take a deep breath, notice what it is like to feel present with a sense of well-being. You are free to be playful, creative, and calm. Breathe in and notice this deep feeling of peace and comfort.

If any tension or anxiety or distraction appears, just note that this is one of your parts being active. Invite this part to step back and rest for a moment while you connect with God.

To the best of your ability, and with comfortable but full breaths, notice how restful it is to be still with a feeling of gentle warmth in your heart. This grace comes from deep within the heart and is a gift from God. In this moment of silence and peace, notice how comforting it is to be with a loving God who seeks to protect, heal, and comfort you.

Notice how you might be experiencing God in this moment:

Fatherly and caring

Motherly and nurturing

As a close and intimate friend

As a still and quiet presence

Allow yourself to simply be with God, however you are experiencing Him:

Notice how God sees your heart.

Notice how God knows your heart.

Notice how God delights in your heart.

Notice your breaths and how your body rests in God's love.

When you are ready, return your attention to the parts of the self-system. How did they feel about this time with God? Do you notice any changes, however small, in them?

Thank all your parts for participating and being there.

Before you gently shift your focus to the outside world, you are invited to pray: "Dear God, thank You for bringing me awareness and clarity about my inner world. I thank You for the rich complexity and beauty of all my parts. As I continue to bring compassion, curiosity, playfulness, and presence to my inner kindom, help all my parts work together in a spirit of unity and harmony.

Reflection Questions

1. Can you imagine an inner conference room, living room, interior castle, inner temple, or inner kingdom within? Which image do you connect with that best describes your inner world?

2. As you become more and more aware of your inner world, what parts can you identify? What roles do they exercise? How do they relate to each other as a community or as members of a "kingdom"?

3. Remember that the inmost self has certain qualities known as the eight Cs and the five Ps: confidence, calm, compassion, courage, creativity, clarity, curiosity, and connectedness; patience, persistence, perspective, playfulness, and presence. How do you express the eight Cs and the five Ps to your parts in your inner world?

4. How can love be the guiding principle for your inner world?

10

THE FEARFUL HEART

Bela's Story, Part 2: The Little Girl

In February, the roads in Montreal were often covered with ice and snow. I was in the back seat of my father's 1977 Mercury Comet as he weaved through traffic, screaming obscenities at other drivers. I didn't realize how drunk he was when I got in the car, but it wouldn't have made a difference. At ten years of age, I did what I was told; there would be hell to pay if I said a thing. He was angry because it was late, and he had to take me back to my mother's place. *I was an inconvenience.*

As we glided across the ice, swerving and fishtailing, I was gripped with fear. I disconnected from my body. This was more than merely "the Wall" that protected me from feelings of hurt and shame. Every part of me was in danger, as my body and my life itself were out of control. When someone on the road got in my father's way, he screamed, "*Maudit bâtard!*" and his rage increased. *It was my fault.* Then, as he swerved to get around the object of his fury, the car started spinning. We spun around at least four times and stopped dead in the center of the road. There was a rare moment of quiet, and he seemed to sober up in an instant. My soul returned to my body, and he took me back home in complete silence.

Years later, when I did my undergrad degree at McGill, I attended a homecoming after-party. I was drinking and laughing and having a good time. I remember meeting some new people and then talking one-on-one with a guy who seemed friendly. I felt pretty and flirty and funny. There was a moment when my head felt light and started spinning, my soul seemed to protectively leave my body, and I woke up naked in a strange bed. The guy from the night before was watching television in the next room. In silence, I found my clothes and stumbled out of the apartment into the street. I was disoriented and confused. I knew something bad had happened, and instinctively the only words I could utter were "It was my fault."

It took me years to come to terms with what had happened. The Wall served me well, bottling up emotions, as I entered medical school and became a pediatric oncologist. My people-pleasing part had a great bedside manner, and I went out of my way to create the best experience for sick children. I avoided strong, successful men because I couldn't trust them not to hurt me. The men I dated tended to be alcoholics who didn't judge me for needing to get high to relax or have sex. In time, an angry part showed up. Why wasn't I good enough for men to stay? Why did men hurt me? I channeled my anger into causes. I fought diseases in children, such as leukemia and brain tumors. But it wasn't enough.

It wasn't until I truly met and understood my Wall part that real healing began. With the help of my therapist, I realized that the Wall was a friend who protected me from being overwhelmed by all my emotions. What would happen if the Wall created an opening? There would be a tidal wave of anger: anger at my father for leaving my mother; anger at my father for always yelling at us and for being cruel and self-absorbed and drunk; anger at my mother for not protecting me from this unhealthy dynamic and for teaching me to put my own needs aside to take care of her; anger at the man who took advantage of me. I paused and thanked the Wall. What a beautiful thing. I also realized that I'm no longer the eight-year-old at the top of the stairs as her parents fought like titans hurling rocks at each other. I wasn't the ten-year-old trapped in the car on the ice with an out-of-control alcoholic. I understood the anger. It was reasonable, but I wouldn't let it overwhelm me. I can handle it now.

In that moment, an opening formed, and I was allowed through the Wall and into a deep, dark forest. I knew instinctively that the little girl was there somewhere, lost and afraid. I called to her and found her sitting in a clearing on the grass. She appeared tired and sad, weak and washed out. "What happened to you?" I asked. She replied, "No one loves me or wants me. I'm ugly and broken, tossed aside. I don't matter." Real tears poured down my cheeks as I felt a surge of compassion for her. "That's not true!" She looked up at me, "Then why didn't anyone take interest in me? Why was I discarded? Why didn't my daddy love me? Why did he hurt me, and why did he leave me?"

I held her pain for a long time, and we cried as I held her in my arms. "I can be with you in this. It's okay. You can feel all the hurt and anger and shame, and I'll be here with you. I can handle it. I looked into her eyes with the eyes of a loving mother. "Your needs were not considered, but they are important to me now. You are worthy of being comforted and loved. I will take care of you now."

With the giant eyes of an eight-year-old, she looked up to me. "Was it all my fault?"

Calmly and directly, I responded, "It was never your fault."

We played in that clearing for hours, picking flowers, flying a kite, and soaking in the sunshine as her cheeks filled with life and her smile beamed. She is truly a beautiful, loving child, and she only wanted to be good. In time, we walked back to the Wall, which now had a beautiful, opened portcullis for us to pass through. She can take her place within my interior world. I can handle the tougher emotions now, and I can also experience joy and laughter again.

THE PSYCHOLOGY OF THE INTERIOR WORLD

Exiled parts often hold all the distress and intense emotions from past experiences. They may be "frozen" in time and developmentally stuck at a young age. When an exile shares her experience, often a protector part jumps in between the exile and the inmost self to interrupt the connection. In Bela's case, the firefighter showed up as a Wall. The exile may not even be aware of the person's actual age. The eight-year-old may not be aware that Bela is now in her forties. Sometimes the exile needs help to see that the inmost self is a safe adult. In this case, the inmost self was able to be with and comfort Bela's eight-year-old part.

When the inmost self can relate to a part with compassion, confidence, connection, and curiosity, we can say that it imparts self-energy to the self-system. Without sufficient self-leadership, healing cannot occur. But when the exile experiences the inmost self as a secure attachment figure, a loving parent, and when she sees that she was always needed, then the exile can finally have her needs met and may be able to release her burdens and reclaim her true identity, filled with playfulness, calm, connection, and confidence.

Bela's exile carries a burden of shame and unworthiness. As children often do, she carries all the blame for the actions of the adults in her life. The shame tells her that she is not valued because her father left her family. Her survival instinct kicked in, and as we saw in a previous chapter, she became a people pleaser and a peacemaker. Often another part shows up, a firefighter part, who acts recklessly to protect her against abandonment or against some other intense disturbance. This firefighter may take the form of flirting, promiscuity, risky behaviors, and poor boundaries to find or maintain a connection.

When the managers and firefighters are asked to step back, when the inmost self is allowed to access the exile with a loving and open heart, it becomes clear what the exile needs and has always needed. Bela, for example, always needed to know that she was valued and that she was precious and that her feelings were important. Her father's dangerous behavior, his rage, his infidelity, and his departure were never her fault.

SCRIPTURE STUDY: GOD IS LOVE

When Bela experienced fear in the car with her father, she felt far away from the safety of a loving and attuned God. Our experiences of trauma can take us outside of our bodies[105] and disconnect us from our inmost self and our connection to God. When we do IFS therapy, we reengage with these lost parts and bring them into the present, where they can be consoled, affirmed, comforted, and loved. We recognize that even in these most disturbing and fearful moments, we were and always will be loved by God. Indeed, Scripture promises:

> You shall be called by a new name that the mouth of the Lord will give. You shall be a crown of beauty in the hand of the Lord, and a royal diadem in the hand of your God. You shall no more be termed Forsaken,

[105] Dissociation can include experiences of depersonalization and derealization. Depersonalization is the experience of feeling that one's own person is not real, usually coupled with a strong sense of estrangement from one's own being, a disconnection from a sense of one's personhood. Derealization is characterized by a diminished sense of contact with reality; perceptual processes become altered so that the experience of external reality feels strange or unreal.

> and your land shall no more be termed Desolate; but you shall be called "My Delight Is in Her, and your land Married; for the LORD delights in you, and your land shall be married." (Isa. 62:3–4)

St. John writes that this love of God is so strong that God lives within us:

> By this we know that we abide in him and he in us, because he has given us of his Spirit. And we have seen and do testify that the Father has sent his Son as the Saviour of the world. God abides in those who confess that Jesus is the Son of God, and they abide in God. So, we have known and believe the love that God has for us. (1 John 4:13–16)

This is such a powerful message. The Holy Spirit is the glue that connects us with God. We can rest in God and be with Him, and in being present with Him, we know and experience His love. St. John mentions the inmost self as the place of love where we rest in Christ: "God is love, and those who abide in love abide in God, and God abides in them" (1 John 4:16). God is with us, and we choose to rest in Him, in the dwelling place of our inmost self, our deepest heart. As we abide in Him, love is perfected in us: "We may have boldness on the day of judgement, because as he is, so are we in this world" (1 John 4:17). We literally become transformed by the love of God and become like Christ.

There is no condemnation in this sacred place within. All of our fear dissipates, as St. John assures us: "There is no fear in love, but perfect love casts out fear; for fear has to do with punishment, and whoever fears has not reached perfection in love" (1 John 4:18). This "casting out" is the way parts are unburdened. We help each part let go of fear and any other negative thoughts, beliefs, or emotions. True love involves complete trust in and surrender to God.

Once we experience God's love in this transformative way, we naturally want to share that love with others. "We love because he first loved us. Those who say, 'I love God,' and hate their brothers or sisters, are liars; for those who do not love a brother or sister whom they have seen, cannot love God whom they have not seen. The commandment we have from him is this: those who love God must love their brothers and sisters also." (1 John 4:19–21).

It is important to note that God loved us first, and thus, parents must love their children first. So often, parents fail their children by not reaching out to them. As we saw in chapter 3, Christ is a seeker, and so is the inmost self, acting in His image. Christ seeks out the lost, the oppressed, the most vulnerable in society, the ones in pain and suffering, and all the exiles.

Obeying God's commandments is framed here in the context of love. When we want the good for another, we love him or her. When we want to have a deep and healthy connection with someone, we love him or her. These commandments are not burdens. Often, we must release unhealthy burdens in order to truly love God and our neighbor. St. John captures this beautifully:

> Everyone who believes that Jesus is the Christ has been born of God, and everyone who loves the parent loves the child. By this we know that we love the children of God, when we love God and obey his commandments. For the love of God is this, that we obey his commandments. And his commandments are not burdensome, for whatever is born of God conquers the world. And this is the victory that conquers the world, our faith. Who is it that conquers the world but the one who believes that Jesus is the Son of God? (1 John 5:1–5)

The "conquering" and "victory" are not about defeating, oppressing, or coercing others: they are about loving them the way God loves them.

John beautifully expresses the love between God and His children in terms of attachment theory. Obedience may seem like a harsh or restrictive or domineering requirement, but in the context of the biblical narrative, it is about safety, guidance, protection, and love. God does not want to see us suffer; instead, He wants us to live free from the burdens of false beliefs and dysregulated emotions that keep us trapped in old dysfunctional patterns.

LIFE APPLICATIONS FOR INNER TRANSFORMATION

Going Deeper with the Litanies

Once you have prayed the litanies enough times to be comfortable with the experience, you may want to open your heart more consciously, more intentionally, during this prayer and this time of intimacy with Jesus. Here are some suggestions for how to become more aware of and further cooperate with the movements of your heart and the healing presence of Jesus while praying the litanies and to adjust them where needed.

Take time to notice and consciously reflect on your experience.

- Consider using a journal — or just a paper and pen — to take a few notes when you are praying a litany.
- You may notice that a particular line catches your attention. This can be a good line to hold on to. You can gently repeat it later at various times during the day in order to renew that grace in your heart.
- You may have been struck by a strong idea or impression to reflect on, or it may require some reflection to generate awareness of your experience in prayer. It might be helpful to consider the following questions and write down any observations, for further reflection:

  What did you notice happening in your body as you prayed the litanies?
  Did you notice a movement in your heart? What feelings or emotions did you notice?
  What thoughts or beliefs came to the surface as you prayed the litanies?
  Which lines moved you the most? Why?
  Which litany spoke to you the most? Why?

- Use the notes to reflect on and pray about what you experience in prayer. Take time to review them and consider what you have learned.

Acknowledge and respect negative reactions.

- You may have negative feelings while praying a litany. Perhaps you have difficulty relating to some of the lines in the prayer. It is normal and perfectly acceptable to have a variety of responses. Some lines may affect us, and some may not. When you are praying the litanies alone, you can skip over any lines that don't speak to you.
- If a line produces a negative reaction, this likely represents a part of you that needs attention. It is good to pause for a moment and listen

to your "reacting" or "resisting" parts. Give yourself time to attend to and care for any parts that have negative thoughts or feelings. It's normal to have inner conflicts of some kind. Perhaps part of you loves a line and another part of you is angry, upset, sad, or concerned over that line. See these conflicts as opportunities to explore and attend to your inner self at a deeper level. Christ wants you to know, hear, and care for *all* the parts of you.

- It is also possible that as you pray the litanies, negative feelings about Jesus may show up. Although we *know* about Jesus — He is good, loving, merciful, and so forth — we may have negative beliefs about Him because of our past hurts. If this is the case, the litanies are an opportunity to develop a new relationship with Jesus at a heart level. We want to acknowledge our wounded parts that were hurt and allow them to experience Jesus as He is. This will likely take time, but the litanies are an opportunity to work with our wounded parts rather than hide them, exile them, or invalidate them.

Bring your insights back to your next prayer time. If you took notes from the prior litanies, reflect on them briefly before you pray them again.

- Take additional time to prepare for and enter into your time of prayer. Invite your body into a safe and more comfortable place with Jesus. Bring to Him any distracted thoughts, worries, and anxieties as you feel more peace and a sense of relief. Invite all of you to be present, even your inner conflicts, and if any part of you is carrying a burden, allow yourself the opportunity to give that burden to Jesus. Notice your emotions as you pray; these emotions sometimes tell us about our needs and unhealed wounds. Take your pain to Jesus as needed.

LITANY OF THE FEARFUL HEART

In the name of the Father, and of the Son, and of the Holy Spirit. Amen.

Lord Jesus, You created me in love and for love. Bring me to a place of vulnerability within the safety of Your loving arms. Help me today by transforming my fearful heart into a heart that can love You, myself, and my neighbor as You intend.

Jesus, I offer You my heart with all its sufferings.
Jesus, I offer You my heart with all its doubts.
Jesus, I offer You my heart with all its hurts.
Jesus, I offer You my heart with all its fears.
Jesus, I offer You my heart with all its burdens.
Jesus, I offer You my heart with all its hope and all its lack of hope.
Jesus, I offer You my heart with all its joy and all its lack of joy.
Jesus, I offer You my heart with all its love and all its lack of love.
Jesus, Son of God, *have mercy on me.*

When I feel afraid, *Lord, have mercy.*
When I don't know how to feel safe, *Lord, have mercy.*
When life feels chaotic, *Lord, have mercy.*
When I'm confused, *Lord, have mercy.*
When I don't know how to trust, *Lord, have mercy.*
When I feel hurt, *Lord, have mercy.*
When I feel unloved, *Lord, have mercy.*
When I feel disappointed, *Lord, have mercy.*
When others fail me, *Lord, have mercy.*
When I feel let down, *Lord, have mercy.*
When I feel all alone, *Lord, have mercy.*
When I feel rejected, *Lord, have mercy.*
When I feel I don't belong, *Lord, have mercy.*
When I feel hopeless, *Lord, have mercy.*
When I'm afraid of being hurt, *Lord, have mercy.*

Jesus, help me love others when it is difficult; *Lord, have mercy.*
Jesus, help me pray for those who have hurt me; *Lord, have mercy.*
Jesus, I know You love me in all my wounds; *Lord, have mercy.*

Jesus, most compassionate, *open my heart.*
Jesus, healer of my wounds, *open my heart.*
Jesus, my shepherd, *open my heart.*
Jesus, my protector, *open my heart.*
Jesus, unspeakable love, *open my heart.*

Jesus, You created me in love; *hold me in Your arms.*
Jesus, You created me for love; *hold me in Your arms.*
Jesus, You created me to be loved; *hold me in Your arms.*
Jesus, You created my heart; *hold me in Your arms.*
Jesus, You see my heart; *hold me in Your arms.*
Jesus, You know my true heart; *hold me in Your arms.*
Jesus, You comfort my heart; *hold me in Your arms.*
Jesus, You treasure my heart; *hold me in Your arms.*
Jesus, You encourage my heart; *hold me in Your arms.*
Jesus, You created me as Your beloved; *hold me in Your arms.*

Jesus, You are present with me; *I trust in You.*
Jesus, You bring me close to You; *I trust in You.*
Jesus, You walk with me; *I trust in You.*
Jesus, You accept me; *I trust in You.*
Jesus, You calm all my fears; *I trust in You.*
Jesus, You protect me from threats; *I trust in You.*
Jesus, You delight in me; *I trust in You.*
Jesus, help me trust You; *I trust in You.*

Lord, You are the healer of my soul and my heart. I ask that through this prayer, You would transform me more and more into the likeness of Your precious and Sacred Heart. Let Your kindness and compassion transform my heart and bring me always into the safety and security of Your loving embrace.

In the name of the Father, and of the Son, and of the Holy Spirit. Amen.

Reflection Questions

1. When have you experienced fear and disconnection from yourself, your body, others, or God?

2. What negative beliefs have you adopted to make sense of those fearful experiences?

3. As you allow your inmost self, with God's grace, to connect with your exiled parts, what do you notice about those parts? What needs do they have? Describe how you can comfort their fears and provide for them what they have always needed.

4. How can you allow your exiled parts to know they are precious?

5. God is always with us, even in the most terrible moments and even when we don't know it. What do you feel as you contemplate this truth? What parts hold those feelings?

11

UNBURDENING

Alexandre's Story, Part 5: The World's Finest

My French teachers had us practice our handwriting in a floppy workbook that they called a *cahier d'exercises*. As I absorbed the twenty red pen markings on just the first page of my book, I wondered if perfect cursive penmanship was so rigorously enforced in English schools. Each oppressive red line began where my letter began but moved upward and in a rounded way to indicate how my letter should have blossomed. Instead, my capital cursive *S* slumped and dropped when it should have risen past the midline and reached the top line without surpassing it.

I paused to wonder how my five-year-old self felt about those pages of failed letter formations that filled the first eight pages of the workbook. Then I noticed that the ninth page had a drawing of a person. My stick people always had arms and legs projecting from oval torsos, and atop the torsos sat round, neckless heads with two eyes, a mouth, and some scribbled hair. Long hair meant a girl, and short hair meant a boy. Sometimes I drew feet, sometimes not. This particular figure stood in the center of the page, and there were small droplets emanating downward from his face. He was crying.

I turned the page, and there were three figures, and they were all crying. Some pages had two or three or four or five figures, and they were all crying. Page after page, nothing but tears. My *cahier d'exercises*, after its first eight pages, was chock-full of people crying. A part of me exclaimed, "What happened to this kid?"

It was then that I recalled the sharp and vicious words "Stop crying, or I'll give you something to cry about!"

"Run away, scared rabbit!"

And finally, "You're a baby! If you keep crying, I'll put you in Pampers, like the baby you are!"

And then he did it. My father came home with a large box of Pampers and dumped them on the counter with satisfaction. "If you start crying, I'll put you in a diaper."

I recalled when fear swallowed that mess of sadness, shame, and hurt, consuming all my emotions. I had forgotten about this memory, but now it was back with a vengeance.

I paused for a moment, took a deep breath, and noticed that my shoulders were tight, and my heart was racing. I invited those muscles to relax, just as my therapist told me to. "I'm safe right now; this is just a memory."

I noticed that a part of me wanted to reach for a fictional book to read, another part wanted to go walk in the rain, another part wanted to have sex immediately, and another part wanted to go fix a drink. I asked all these protector parts to soften, as my therapist asks me to do. "Just give me a moment. I've met this five-year-old before in my therapy sessions. I have a relationship with him." My managers and firefighters all softened and relaxed back, giving my inmost self space, sitting just behind me to the right and to the left.

The first thing I noticed was this boy and how scared he was. He was wearing a Batman T-shirt, and his hand clutched a Superman action figure, as the angry figure of his father, my father, loomed large. I remembered that I have a spiritual confidant, Christ Himself, and I took a moment to issue a short prayer: "Lord, be with me in this moment." It wasn't hard because Jesus helped me before when He brought with Him the cloud of witnesses. But today all I needed was Jesus. Again, the power seeped out of my father next to the presence of Christ. My father was a sad, pathetic man raging against a scared five-year-old. He had never worked on his own trauma, and he was taking out his insecurities and inner rage on his son. But that was not my problem anymore. I whispered, "You're not my father anymore, and you don't belong here." He was gone.

The little boy was still shaken, scared, and ashamed. I turned to him and felt nothing but compassion for him. He was receptive, so I held him, and I let him cry in my arms for as long as he needed it. All those tears. I may have a protector who thought the tears would never end, but that wasn't true. I could contain the child's tears and love him, abide with him, for as long as he needed. I understood his pain, his anguish.

I paused to see him, really see him. He had thick hair with a bowl cut and big blue eyes and an angelic face. He was beautiful and innocent, and I told him so. "I am always here if you feel sad." He looked around nervously. "And I am here to protect you now, and we have parts that can help with that." My managers, standing back but not too far away, waved. They were watching, and their hearts were moved now that we could really see the little boy. "We haven't done a very good job of taking care of you, but that will change now." The boy's shoulders dropped a bit, and he took a breath, maybe the first long breath he could remember. He saw me now, perhaps for the first time, as the grown-up that I am today — kind, loving, compassionate, and calm.

But something was still wrong and unsettled. The boy felt mostly safe now, and he stopped crying. He was more relaxed, but he turned a light shade of red. He pointed to the counter: the diapers.

I felt along with him a sinking feeling in the pit of my stomach, rising up into my lower chest. That box held the thoughts that I was not wanted, not quiet enough, not fast enough, not boy enough, not tough enough, and not good enough.

The box held the memories of being yelled at, being shoved, being dismissed, being hated, being an inconvenience, and being ignored.

The box held the images of an angry, disapproving face.

The box held beliefs that I could never be safe, that I could never trust anyone, and that I could never be truly comforted.

The box held all the pain, anguish, heartache, hurt feelings, sadness, and, most importantly, all the shame.

It was my box of shame.

"It's a heavy box," I said to the child. "You're not meant to carry all that shame and all that pain and sadness." He nodded. "Can we do something with the box?"

"I'd like it to go away."

I looked at the action figure in his hands. "What would Superman do?"

"He'd throw it into the yellow sun, and it would blow up."

I found a long towel and tied it around his neck, like a cape. "You can be Superman today, and I'll be your helper, Batman. Let's pick up that box of Pampers, okay?" He nodded. "Notice that it has all the bad stuff, the lies, and the bad memories and the bad feelings." He nodded. "Notice how really heavy it is." He nodded. "Now I'd like you to use all your Kryptonian strength and throw that box into the sun. I'll help steady you if you need me to." He nodded.

The box went hurtling through the air, and out of the earth's atmosphere, and into the burning rays of the sun. We watched as it burned up on contact. We just stared for a very long time, my arm around his shoulders, two superheroes side by side.

"How do you feel?" I asked.

"Lighter. Can we play? I'll be Superman, and you be Batman. We're the World's Finest!" I nodded, smiling.

For the rest of the afternoon, we laughed and played. We ran around the house with our towel-capes flowing behind us as we defeated every conceivable villain. The letter *S* on his shirt beamed with strength and vitality. We were invincible, leaping from couch to chair and in and out of bedrooms and balconies. At the end of the day, we settled in at the Hall of Justice for hot chocolate and a friendly game of Battleship.

THE PSYCHOLOGY OF THE INTERIOR WORLD

In previous chapters, we saw and experienced the process of identifying and unblending from our parts. We learned how we can access our inmost self and how we can befriend our protectors and bring a measure of healing to our exiles. We also saw how we can connect with God and our spiritual confidants.

Now that we have a relationship with our parts, and they are more comfortable as belonging to our inner family of parts, we can invite them to let go of their burdens. Begin, as usual, by finding a calm, quiet place to sit, taking a few deep breaths, inviting your body to relax, and then looking inside. Notice where you feel any disturbance in your body.

You can imagine that inner living room (or other inner space) and just notice if any parts naturally appear. You can ask if there are any parts struggling, feeling down, feeling anxious, or experiencing any disturbance. As you connect with a part, take a moment, as before, to really notice the part, see the part, and look into his eyes. See if he is doing anything or if he has something to share. Spend some time with any parts that show up.

Ask yourself, "How do I feel toward this part?" If another part shows up with a criticism or an agenda, gently invite that part to wait, and agree to check in with him later. If you feel compassion or calm or connection with this part, notice how strong that feeling is. See if the part can feel your presence and your compassion.

In IFS, there is a process called the "6 Fs" which outline the way we work with protector parts. Here is a summary of these steps:

1. *Find*: We find out which parts we will work with and where they are located in or around the body.
2. *Focus*: We look inside and bring attention to the part and notice the part's qualities.
3. *Flesh out*: We continue to learn about the part and distinguish between the part and the inmost self.
4. *Feel toward*: We see how the inmost self feels toward the part, and we build a strong connection between the self and the parts. A part may need to further unblend from the inmost self during this stage.
5. *(Be)friend*: We continue to learn about the part and establish a loving relationship between the inmost self and the part.
6. *Fears*: We ask the part about his deepest fears and how those fears influence his behavior. Often this process will lead to the discovery of a polarized part or an exile.

If the part has a story to share or something to show us, listen and attend to the part. Look for something that you believe the part is holding on to. This could be a core false belief, such as "I'm not worthy" or "I'm bad." It could be a negative cognition (lies we tell ourselves), such as "Nothing good ever happens to me" or "Everyone I love will abandon me." Identify this belief or thought as a burden. Once you feel ready, ask the part, "Where is the burden in your body?" Allow the part time to look inside and feel the weight of the burden and ask if the burden takes any shape or form. Some report their burdens as heavy backpacks, beams across their shoulders, giant boulders they are carrying, or a heavy weight on their chest.

As your inmost self connects with the part and notices with compassion the heavy burden he is carrying, ask the part if he is ready to set the burden down. There will likely be hesitation; if so, ask the part what he is afraid will happen if he unloads the burden. This will likely bring up deeper fears, and it may be important to explore these with the part. Here the inmost self may be able to console and reassure the part. If circumstances in your life have changed since your trauma, you can help the part see how things are different now and how you and all the parts of the self-system will help to make sure that things are different now.

Would the part like to put the burden down, even just for a moment? He can always pick it up again if he chooses. If he agrees to try, praise him for his courage and let him know that you are with him every step of the way.

When the part puts the burden down, it is important to watch carefully and support him in any way he needs. Some people like to release the burden to the wind, fire, or water. Others place the burden at the foot of the Cross, in front of the altar, or near the tabernacle. Once the burden is released, invite the part to stand up and stretch. Ask him to notice how it feels not to carry the burden. The part will invariably say he feels light and wonderful. If you see relief and joy, then join with him in that joy. Help him see that his worst fear did not come true when he put down the burden.

Notice how the other parts of the self-system are reacting to this turn of events. Usually the protector parts, even the old critics and former bullies and the perfectionists and the self-destructive parts, will all be paying close attention. They will likely be rooting for the liberated exile part, who is now feeling unburdened. This may be a time for dancing, playing, and celebrating. As at the end of the parable of the prodigal son, it is time to throw a party.

Ask any protector parts if there's anything they would like to unburden now that the exile is unburdened. They may have strong beliefs or feelings that no longer seem to fit. Whether those burdens are like a backpack, a boulder, or a blob of heaviness, what would your parts like to do with them? They may decide that they would like to throw them into Mount Doom, where Frodo was instructed to throw the One Ring. They may decide to put them at the foot of the Cross and let Jesus take care of them. They also may see their burdens evaporating into a puff of smoke that dissipates into the air. Be sure to let the parts know how proud you are for their courage and that you understand that this wasn't easy.

Next, you can ask the parts if they'd like to replace the burden with something new. This can be anything they choose, such as love, joy, peace, or playfulness.

Remind all the parts that although important burdens are lifted, the effects of living in a fallen world and the resulting habits that were formed mean that we still must work on sanctification. We can't assume that we are now perfect saints because of one powerful psychological unburdening experience. But the sanctification becomes so much easier without these heavy burdens. Without the heavy burdens, we feel a surge of gratitude and are more open to receiving God's grace; we experience a greater sense of freedom. As a result, we feel motivated to pray more often and fully engage in the sacramental life. The inmost self, the mediator of God's grace to the self-system, can be accessed more readily. The unburdened part is also freer to be himself and is more open to grace. But even if a part later picks up an old burden or finds a new one, we have a way to help him.

SCRIPTURE STUDY: A NEW LIFE FILLED WITH JOY

The unburdening that brings about a joyful and thankful spirit comes about only when we have a true change of heart and own our identity as beloved children of God. St. Paul underscores this when he says, "You were taught to put away your former way of life, your old self, corrupt and deluded by its lusts, and to be renewed in the spirit of your minds, and to clothe yourselves with the new self, created according to the likeness of God in true righteousness and holiness" (Eph. 4:22–24). The renewal of the mind involves bringing truth to the cognitive distortions, false beliefs, or lies that these burdened parts carry. These beliefs, such as "I am worthless" or "I am bad," keep the part weighed down, depressed, and anxious. Clothing ourselves with the "new self" means allowing our inmost selves to love, comfort, console, and bring truth to these weary and misguided parts. The old false beliefs, the overwhelming painful emotions, and the painful traumatic memories are released, and we are free to experience joy. We are free to laugh and play like Alexandre with his Batman and Superman capes.

When our parts are unburdened, we experience a deep, profound sense of joy. Our unburdened younger parts often want to play. The freedom that comes from unburdening produces a spontaneous desire to celebrate, often with music and dancing. David, who becomes King of Israel, dances freely, joyfully, and without shame before the presence of God in the Ark of the Covenant:

> David went and brought up the ark of God from the house of Obed-edom to the city of David with rejoicing; and when those who bore the ark of the LORD had gone six paces, he sacrificed an ox and a fatling. David danced before the LORD with all his might; David was girded with a linen ephod. So David and all the house of Israel brought up the ark of the LORD with shouting, and with the sound of the trumpet." (2 Sam. 6:12–15)

It is possible to see David here as representing the inmost self. He wears an ephod, which is a priestly garment, so, in one sense, he is acting as a mediator between God and the people. He leads the celebration and brings the Ark, the presence of God, to the people, who can be understood here as the parts of the self-system. David and all of Israel, dancing and shouting, represent our inmost self and all of our parts worshipping and rejoicing together before God.

The journey from a place of desolation, isolation, and disconnection to one of joy and celebration is captured beautifully in the story of the prodigal son. I referenced this parable in chapter 3 and in Aaron's story, but it is worth recalling the full Scripture passage here with my comments interspersed in brackets:

> Then Jesus said, "There was a man who had two sons. The younger of them said to his father, 'Father, give me the share of the property that will belong to me.' So he divided his property between them. A few days later the younger son gathered all he had and travelled to a distant country, and there he squandered his property in dissolute living."

[This correlates with a part, perhaps a firefighter, who made an impulsive and selfish choice, experienced isolation, and then chose to distract himself by spending money and engaging in a dissolute lifestyle.]

"When he had spent everything, a severe famine took place throughout that country, and he began to be in need. So he went and hired himself out to one of the citizens of that country, who sent him to his fields to feed the pigs."

[Here we see the exile, isolated and carrying a burden of shame.]

"He would gladly have filled himself with the pods that the pigs were eating; and no one gave him anything. But when he came to himself he said, 'How many of my father's hired hands have bread enough and to spare, but here I am dying of hunger! I will get up and go to my father, and I will say to him, "Father, I have sinned against heaven and before you; I am no longer worthy to be called your son; treat me like one of your hired hands." ' "

[Here the heart is moved, and the conscience is awakened. The son repents. Perhaps a manager part helps make the decision to return home.]

"So he set off and went to his father. But while he was still far off, his father saw him and was filled with compassion; he ran and put his arms around him and kissed him."

[*The father here represents the inmost self, who, filled with compassion and forgiveness, runs toward his son.*]

"And the son said to him, 'Father, I have sinned against heaven and before you; I am no longer worthy to be called your son.' "

[*This can perhaps be seen as the first step in the unburdening as the son approaches his father with humility.*]

"But the father said to his slaves, 'Quickly, bring out a robe — the best one — and put it on him; put a ring on his finger and sandals on his feet. And get the fatted calf and kill it, and let us eat and celebrate; for this son of mine was dead and is alive again; he was lost and is found!' "

[*The father's response to his son's humility is to release the burden of shame. The son is now free to reclaim his true identity as a beloved son, and he is free to celebrate in thanksgiving.*]

"And they began to celebrate." (Luke 15:11–24)

The Father restores the son's dignity and gives him the best robe, a ring, and new shoes. We, too, are children of God, and our Father delights in us and celebrates our return with great gifts. We know that "the fruit of the Spirit is love, joy, peace, patience, kindness, generosity, faithfulness, gentleness, and self-control" (Gal. 5:22–23). We replace our burdens of fear, shame, and self-recrimination with the Father's love and the gifts of the Holy Spirit. This brings about joy, an intense and long-lasting inner happiness that includes a zest for life.

This zeal or passion for life is powerfully captured in Jesus' invitation to drink "living water." When Jesus encounters the Samaritan woman at the well, she is surprised that He even speaks to her. Instead of rejecting her outright as a woman with five husbands and a foreigner, He offers her "living water," which represents "eternal life." Although He doesn't say the word *repent*, it is implied as He names her sins. He calls her, however, to something beyond repentance: to joy and to living a new life filled with a new kind of worship. He invites her to a change of heart, to be unburdened through faith, and to receive a new life. Jesus tells her, "But the hour is coming, and is now here, when the true worshipers will worship the Father in spirit and truth, for the Father seeks such as these to worship him" (John 4:23). This worship speaks to a new, festive, life-giving celebration like the merrymaking in the household of the prodigal son.

With this new zeal and spirit of joy, we can join the psalmist, traditionally identified as David, who celebrates:

> Make a joyful noise to God, all the earth;
> sing the glory of his name;
> give to him glorious praise.
> Say to God, "How awesome are your deeds!
> Because of your great power, your enemies cringe before you.
> All the earth worships you;
> they sing praises to you,
> sing praises to your name. (Ps. 66:1–4)

LIFE APPLICATIONS FOR INNER TRANSFORMATION

Meditation — Identifying and Witnessing a Burden[106]

Let us begin: "In the name of the Father, and of the Son, and of the Holy Spirit. Amen. Holy Spirit, I ask You to be present as I explore my inner world for difficult and perhaps painful burdens. I ask You to help my inmost self to express the gifts of love, joy, peace, patience, kindness, generosity, faithfulness, and gentleness as I approach the parts of my self-system. Amen."

You are invited to connect with your protector parts and consider the idea that no part is itself a burden. The reason parts are rejected and we have exiles is that other parts assume that the burden *is* the part. The burden is not a part, nor is the part a burden. The burdened part is precious and indispensable; we never want to leave a part behind. The burden is something we can resolve, or let go of, or put on the back of the scapegoat and allow to be released.

I invite you to check in with your system. Take a couple of breaths. Just notice what's happening inside at this moment, especially concerning this topic of burdens.

Even as you read the word *burdens*, do you feel anything about that word? What are your reactions inside?

If there's something your protectors are protecting against, avoiding, or guarding against, it is likely a burden.

As you check in with your protectors, try to find out what they are afraid of. If you can get a sense of what they are afraid of, you can better understand the burden that the exile carries. It could be an emotion, such as grief, rage, anger, or shame. It could be a belief or an assumption, a desire, or an impulse. It could be an attitude or a body sensation.

When you know what your protectors fear, you have an important clue about the burden. But you don't just want to figure it out; it's not a deductive exercise. You want to be able to get in touch with the parts. This is an opportunity to connect with your

[106] This meditation has been adapted from an exercise developed by Dr. Peter Malinoski for the Resilient Catholics community.

protectors about their fears and potentially gain access to the exiles that they protect. Can they be candid with you about their fears?

You can allow your protectors to draw or write about their fears. Let them know that you, the inmost self, care; that you won't bring exiles in without patience and solicitude; and that you understand about the possibility of feeling overwhelmed. If that happens, you can step back to a place of safety and calm.

You want to reassure all the parts that the exile is not the burden, and the burden is not the exile. The burden is what the part carries, not who the part is. Can your protectors understand and accept that? What questions might they have about that?

If the protectors are accepting and willing, you will want to connect with an exile and gain an understanding of the burden he is carrying. You will want to do this with an open heart, with calm, compassion, confidence, courage, and connection.

You should pause if there are parts that are blended or resistant. If a part is concerned that you're working with an exile, you will want to ask him to give you space.

Invite your parts to increase some trust in you, in your inmost self, to lead and guide your system.

If you're "in self," so many good things are going to happen.

I invite you, with your protector parts' permission, to work with an exile or a wounded part.

See if this exile can recognize that you, the inmost self, are present.

Notice that your heart is going out to this part with a sense of curiosity and a desire for connection. Notice how your inmost self is calm.

Maybe this part has already shared something about his childhood origins, what happened back in the day.

If not, I invite you simply to be with that part — separate but nearby. There's no agenda here, and you're not rushing anything.

Maybe the exile has already given you an image or a memory or an event from the past. I invite you to be with that part as he shows you his experience of that. He may share an image or a memory of what happened when you were young and when he took on a burden or a role.

He may show you how he came to believe what he believes.

Maybe he is willing to show you his burden and how he understands his burden. Sometimes the burden can be like a huge backpack that weighs down the part. It can be a growth or a sticky, tarry mass on the part's body. There are many ways that parts describe burdens. How does this part describe his burden?

I invite you to check in to see if you're *really* hearing from this exile. Other parts might want to speak for this part; ask them to allow you to hear directly from this exile.

With gentleness and compassion, allow the part to show you whatever he wants you to know about the memory. It might be helpful to write this all down in a journal. Simply be with this part as he shares his experience.

If the part has shared with you the event but not the emotion, see if he can share more about the emotion and about the meaning of the event. What does that event say about that part? What does it mean? What does it say about God? Who does the part think God is?

If the part is not ready to release a burden, that is perfectly all right. You want to allow each part to take the time he needs. You want the part to feel safe and develop a sense of trust. This may take time. Thank the part for making himself known today.

If the part is ready to release a burden, invite your inmost self to be present with him through that process. Allow the burden to be taken to the foot of the Cross or released into the air, into the sea, or into space — whatever makes the most sense for that part. If the unburdening happens, notice how the part feels a sense of relief. Allow the part to bask in this feeling of freedom. Allow calm or playfulness or joy to fill the void left by the burden.

I invite you to extend gratitude to all your parts, especially to your protectors, for the space they've given you. Be grateful and thankful to your exile for what he was able to share. Let him know that you can connect with him again.

And let us join with the psalmist in this prayer of thanksgiving to God:

> O come, let us sing to the Lord;
> let us make a joyful noise to the rock of our salvation!
>
> Let us come into his presence with thanksgiving;
> let us make a joyful noise to him with songs of praise! (Ps. 95:1–2)

Reflection Questions

1. When we witness to the stories of our hurt, wounded, and exiled parts, what do we learn? What do these parts want us to know? How do they respond when we listen with the ears of a loving, caring, parent-like adult?

2. What burdens do your parts carry from your childhood? What are the beliefs, thoughts, emotions, or attitudes that make up those burdens?

3. As you allow your parts to let go of burdens, what is it like to experience relief, even for a few moments? As you allow yourself to feel that relief, what new emotions do you experience now?

12

INNER HARMONY

Leo's Story — As Told by His Counselor[107]

Background

Leo initially came to counseling because his wife made him do it. In fact, I initially saw Leo with his wife for several weeks. It was in this context that I developed a rapport with him, and we discovered that Leo had a great deal of repressed and unresolved trauma. After some reflection, it was decided that Leo should do some individual work. Once he felt safe enough with me, he was willing to open up and explore his family-of-origin story and even address his current personal "demons." Sometimes Leo had to be reminded that he wasn't dishonoring his parents by talking about his childhood struggles.

Leo grew up in a rough neighborhood in New York City. His father was a cop, and his mother was a social worker. His parents were devout Catholics who attended Mass every Sunday and several times during the week. The family prayed the Rosary every Wednesday and Friday night. Leo's parents worked long hours, and they also helped at the soup kitchen once a month and participated in many of the parish service activities. A strong work ethic was instilled in Leo. Service to the less fortunate was considered a duty. Their parish priest visited Leo's family regularly and baptized him and his five siblings. Leo was an alter server, his father was a Knight of Columbus, and his mother was in the Legion of Mary.

Leo was not a top student, but he scored very high on the ACT and went to New York University to study economics and then earned an MBA at an Ivy League school. He worked for a prestigious consulting firm for ten years and then accepted an executive-track position at a technology company. He is now the CEO of a successful start-up. He

[107] Leo's story is a longer vignette. Here I want to bring together multiple elements of a parts-work approach to show how it can all come together. This vignette, while still a narrative, is also different because we are hearing it from his counselor's point of view.

is married to a devout Catholic woman, and they have four healthy children who attend a prestigious private school. He drives a Lexus, and they live in a beautiful home in Forest Hills, Queens. From the outside, Leo has achieved the American dream.

Leo has always done his duty. He never misses Mass and often serves as an usher. He arrives at work early and leaves late. He has always been a top performer. He knows how to "booze and schmooze" with clients, but he never gets drunk or loses control. His yard is immaculate. He owns a vacation cabin in the Outer Banks. He votes Republican, and he gives generously to charity.

Leo's wife is attractive, attentive, and intelligent. She studied psychology in college and then chose to be a stay-at-home mom. She is devoted to their children, and she cares deeply for Leo. She works part-time at the library now that the children are all in school. She is sexually available and makes an effort to consider Leo's stresses at work.

So why did Leo have an affair?

Leo's Parts

Let's start by acknowledging Leo's successful manager parts. Leo has a strong independent part who values competency and the ability to manage any situation successfully. He also has a "rock" part that is strong and dependable. He has a taskmaster part who has a great deal of energy and works hard.[108] These high-functioning parts were developed in Leo in childhood. They formed in response to the way he was raised. His culture and home life promoted independence, a strong work ethic, achievement, reliability, and self-sacrifice. These three powerful parts are very well developed in Leo, and they have allowed him to be successful at work and in the community. He earns a high salary with regular bonuses. The board respects him, and his employees fear him.

108 These names for the parts, "independent," "rock," and "taskmaster," were chosen by Leo's parts as Leo got to know them. There are no official names for any of these parts. They are just helpful descriptors to remember them and understand them. A client and his or her parts can also change the names of parts as the parts change or adopt new roles.

At home, Leo has another part that holds anger and resentments. He notices every mess around the house, and he becomes angry when one of his children gets a B or gets into any trouble at school. He complains that his wife shouldn't work so much outside the home and grumbles when anything doesn't work in the house. His oldest son, Matthew, is a high academic achiever, but Leo doesn't praise him. His second child, Joseph, is artistic, but Leo doesn't encourage him in the creative arts. His son Andrew is funny and charismatic, but Leo doesn't respect him. He coddles his daughter, Leah, who is the bridge builder and the people pleaser.

Leo also has a part that is distant and withdrawn. He and his wife rarely have marital intercourse and don't have date nights. They go on vacations only with the family or with other couples, but never just the two of them. His wife is focused on raising the children, but she is sad and disappointed that she and Leo have lost what little emotional connection they ever had. None of his children feel close to him, but they all recognize he is an influential and respected man at work and at church. Leo's wife and children feel they must tiptoe around Leo and his moods. In public, he is a devoted and engaged father, but in private, he lives in his own world.

The angry part and the withdrawn part are both protector parts. When the independent part, the rock part, and the taskmaster part are tired or overwhelmed, the protector parts function in Leo's system as a last resort. If you ask Leo how he feels about the angry part, his independent, rock, or taskmaster part may speak up and say that Leo is justified. "I work very hard and live by high standards, and so should everyone else. I expect perfection of myself. Why doesn't everyone else expect perfection of themselves? I deserve respect for the way I suppress my needs. Why is everyone else so selfish and ungrateful?"

If you ask Leo how he feels about the withdrawn part, he will say that he understands. "Of course, he is distant; no one appreciates him. I will just suffer in silence, and tomorrow I'll get up and do the same thing I've always done: work hard, provide for my family, and ignore my needs." The taskmaster part and the withdrawn part collude to protect him against anger, shame, and any hurt feelings that might overwhelm his system.

Leo Connects with His Parts

If the three manager parts, the independent one, the rock, and the taskmaster, can step back for a moment, we can try to look a little more closely at the angry part. I ask, "What is really going on for him? Why does he feel that bitterness is his only option? What would happen if he let go of anger?"

There is a very long pause. The part shares, "I would have to feel pain, hurt, and disappointment. It is easier for me to be irritable and unhappy than it is for me to acknowledge, let alone express, how bad I feel inside."

"So the anger protects you from feeling bad feelings?"

"Yes," the part admits.

I encourage Leo to thank the angry part for letting us know this important truth. "You've been protecting Leo's system with anger for a very long time?"

"Yes."

"You must be exhausted. And you must be frustrated that it's still not working?"

"Yes."

"Would you be willing to try for a moment, just for a moment, to try something different?"

"Yes."

I ask Leo, his inmost self, "How do you feel about this angry protector part now?"

Leo says that he feels very bad for the part and sees for the first time how hard it has worked to keep him from feeling pain. His manager parts have justified his behavior, but he also has parts that just assumed he was a first-class jerk. Now he feels compassion for the angry part, and he notices for the first time that the angry part is carrying a burden of negative criticism that he unleashes on himself and others as a kind of self-defense. Leo notices that the angry part reminds him of his mother, who was always critical and unsatisfied. She complained loudly and with expletives when his room wasn't perfectly clean, when he got any grades less than an A in school, and when the chores weren't completed perfectly and on time. She was angry about her husband, her kids, and her job. This part learned from her and has been carrying her burden all this time.

"Angry part," I ask, "do you know that your criticism is overwhelming the system? Do you know that you don't have to be angry anymore? You have choices you didn't have back then. Would you like to experience something new? You don't have to carry the burden of anger any longer."

The angry part agrees to give space and unblend from the inmost self. Leo can spend as much time as he likes experiencing the relief of not needing to hold on to resentments and bitterness. He approaches this formerly angry part with love and gratitude for a lifetime of thankless service. And he knows that now this part can be something new.

Discovering Leo's Exiled Wounded Part

Leo's formerly angry part is now willing to let Leo approach his wounded part.

A wounded part, sometimes called an exile, is usually in the form of a child. In this case, Leo notices that the child is about ten years old. He looks scared, and he is looking away. Leo feels a burst of compassion for this kid. When he approaches, the child flinches. Leo moves slowly and gets down on one knee. "I'm here to help you." Leo turns the child to him gently and notices a large bruise on the right side of the child's face. "What happened to you?"

The child does not immediately answer, but Leo starts to remember. His father used to come home after work and heavy drinking. His mother would get angry, and the two of them would yell at each other for hours. It usually ended in broken furniture and Leo's mother crying. One night, Leo decided to intervene, and his father struck his head with great force. His mother looked at Leo with scorn and yelled at him: "Go clean your room; it's a mess! And get your homework done! I don't want to see another C on your next report card!" Ten-year-old Leo scurried upstairs, alone and in pain, holding back tears as his body shook in fear and shame.

At this point, as Leo remembers this incident, he expresses strong emotion, tears flowing down his face.

"Leo," I ask, "what would you like to do for the ten-year-old now?"

"I want to hold him. I want him to know he was courageous for standing up to his dad like that, and his dad was wrong to hit him. I want him to know that his mom was wrong to yell at him. She was reacting from a place of shame and anger. She took it out on me. I also want him to know that his room doesn't matter, and the stupid grades don't matter. The only thing that matters is that this kid needs to be loved. The kid matters. His needs matter. Yes, my needs matter. I don't have to be a rock anymore and suffer alone. I want to hold the ten-year-old in my arms and let him cry with me."

"What does the ten-year-old need now?" I continue.

"Honestly, he just needs to be in a happier place with nurturing parents, and he needs to play."

"Can we find that for him in your system? Let's check first with the formerly angry part. What did you think of what just happened?"

"It moved me to tears!"

"Would you be willing to take on a new role, not as critical person, but as an encourager?"

"Yes, but I'll need some help to get there."

"No problem. What about the managers? Can we refocus our efforts? Would the independent part be willing to channel his competency into helping the ten-year-old ask for support when needed? Would the rock part be willing to channel his dependability into checking in on the ten-year-old's needs? Would the taskmaster part be willing to channel his energy into making sure the ten-year-old has time to play?"

All the parts agree, as long as Leo, the core Leo, his inmost self, is there to oversee and lead this effort. These parts may need guidance and frequent reminders, especially since this is all so new.

Working with the Parts toward Inner Harmony

Leo continued to work on his parts. The withdrawn part turned out to be a protector who shielded Leo from strong feelings of loneliness and sadness but who also longed for love and connection. As a child, Leo wanted his father's affirmation and his mother's nurturing, but his unpredictable father was often in conflict with his mother, and his mother, though sometimes nurturing, often criticized Leo. Leo felt that the people who were supposed to be sources of loving and secure attachment did not really see him as a person; they did not encourage him or find joy in him. The people Leo needed for regular everyday family functioning instead felt unsafe, dangerous, unpredictable, and often toxic.

Leo unconsciously replayed this unhealthy dynamic in his own family life. At times, he played the role of his distant father, and at other times, he played the role of his critical mother. He consoled himself that he wasn't like his parents. After all, he didn't overindulge in alcohol, and he was never physically violent. But he had parts that were carrying burdens from the trauma he experienced. And when the burdens became too great and his managers and firefighters were overwhelmed, a firefighter part appeared to make sure that Leo felt no pain, shame, fear, or hurt.

Leo turned to a female peer at work who appreciated his good looks, his masculine demeanor, and his powerful corporate presence. She made no demands on him. She acted as if he was the only one who mattered. She admired him for his business acumen and his ability to influence others. She offered help in a nonthreatening way. And she was there to offer him an escape, a time to play, a stress-free zone with no expectations or demands. She was a fantasy person, and together they created a fantasy world where the independent part didn't need to be in control, where the rock part could be soothed, and where the taskmaster could take a break.

The problem with most fantasies is that they are not real, and they don't last. They provide an escape for the parts, or they numb all the parts, but they don't solve real-life issues. Some people try to escape reality through pornography or gambling. Some turn to alcohol or drugs. Others simply watch hours of television or immerse themselves in video games. But Leo's female colleague wanted more than a fantasy life. She wanted an escape from her own marriage. She was threatening a sexual-harassment lawsuit if Leo didn't leave his wife. Leo's job was now in jeopardy. When Leo's wife found out about the affair, she was understandably angry. Leo's betrayal scarred her in a deep way, and it took them years of marriage counseling to heal the damage. Leo also had to manage his own parts' reaction to the situation. His independent part wanted to run away by leaving his marriage. His rock part wanted to suffer in silence and self-loathing. His taskmaster part started reading books, going to therapy, and working overtime to win his wife back. The critical-mother part unleashed scorn and vitriol, and the ten-year-old ran back into his room, wounded and in pain.

As you may recall, Leo was raised in an actively Catholic family with a strong emphasis on discipline and service. He also had a strong sense of right and wrong and prided himself on sticking to his values. He was a rule follower. He believed that the main reason his wife had married him was that he was dependable and loyal. Leo looked down on people who didn't follow the rules, and he couldn't understand how God could reward people who broke rules. He was the man who pulled himself up by his bootstraps and worked hard when others slipped into self-pity and succumbed to addictions. His affair was so overwhelmingly out of character for Leo that it caused him to feel tremendous shame and self-hatred. He violated everything he believed in.

In this case, Leo's withdrawn part was protecting his lonely, wounded part, but the turmoil caused by protecting the exile only caused everything the exile feared. This exiled wounded part needed love, connection, and intimacy, and Leo's affair instead damaged his marriage and hurt his family. The firefighter part caused a lot of damage to the internal system and to Leo's external life as well. Leo would have to attend to all of his parts, another round of checking in with them, unblending, unburdening, and providing them with what they truly needed.

Leo learned to bring compassion and understanding to his parts as he gained self-awareness. The withdrawn protector part learned to be a new kind of protector. This new protector could be a comforter and a helper, maybe even an advocate. This part could be there to provide emotional support and to help Leo confront others when appropriate or seek help with good friends and loved ones. It would continue to be a challenge for Leo to learn not to repress his feelings, but with the guidance and leadership of his inmost self, Leo will get there.

Leo's Inmost Self

As the parts of Leo — in this case, the independent part, the rock part, the taskmaster part, the angry (now encourager) part, the withdrawn part, and the ten-year-old part — were revealed, the core Leo emerged: the inmost self.

Leo's inmost self is naturally compassionate, kind, and loving. Once Leo's inmost self was able to lead the parts, the parts were able to let go of their burdens and work together for the good of his whole self-system.

As Leo's internal system became healthier, it had the effect of improving Leo's relationship with his wife and children. He became less rigid and less demanding. He became more appreciative of his family and more curious about their activities because he started to really see and understand them as unique human beings with diverse resources and talents. He began interacting with his family members and friends not from the perspective of a blended and burdened part but from his inmost self. This approach even improved his situation at work. He was still hardworking, dependable, able to take control, and competent, but he was also able to relate better to his employees and bring out the best in them without resorting to fear tactics. Leo found a deeper sense of fulfillment and peace in all the aspects of his life.

Leo Cultivates Humility

Leo's affair and the work he had to do in the recovery process was a true crucible for him. It was the "belly of the whale"[109] experience for Leo that moved him to the next level, not just in the natural realm but in the spiritual as well. It involved a great deal of interior work as well as the necessary repair work with his family.

The first stage in this repair process for Leo was discovering true humility.[110] First, Leo had to discover at a heart level his total dependence on God. As a creature affected by the Fall and therefore with an inclination toward sin, he was also affected by the sins of others, including those of his father, his mother, and his female co-worker.

[109] This is an allusion to Jonah, who was consumed by a "large fish" and remained in its belly for three days and three nights (Jon. 1:17; Matt. 12:40), and refers to a soul-searching and transformative experience in the face of a difficult task.

[110] Incidentally, the first three steps in any twelve-step program involve recognizing that life is unmanageable, that a Higher Power (God) can help us, and that we must surrender our will and accept that we need help.

Leo's trauma caused him to develop defense mechanisms and means of coping that were not always healthy, and in order to fully heal, Leo had to surrender to God his self-reliance, his overindependence, his rocky exterior, his overachievement, and his need to be perfect. That's a lot to give up for a man who has relied on those things to succeed in life. You might think that those things constituted his identity, but that is not true.

Leo's real identity is that of a son of God, adopted by the Father through the work of Jesus Christ. This statement must not remain a theological equation or a sort of stale dogma. It must be received at the level of the heart. Leo's real identity is not based on his burdens and overdeveloped talents. His identity is certainly not the sum of his sins and failures in life. St. John Paul II emphasized this idea in his homily at World Youth Day in 2002: "We are not the sum of our weaknesses and failures; we are the sum of the Father's love for us and our real capacity to become the image of His Son."[111] Leo's identity is based on the fact that a loving God created him in love and for love. We are all created to be in communion with a relational God.

The double realization of Leo's total dependence on God and his true identity as a son of God brought about contrition for his affair and for all the ways he had hurt others. Leo's deep repentance moved God to take this child to the next level of spiritual growth and transformation. It was there that Leo could hear the words that God the Father said to Jesus and to each of us at our Baptism: "You are my beloved son in whom I am well pleased." This love is based not on achievement or works but on faith, repentance, and surrender.

With this conversion of heart, Leo discovered the heart of Jesus' message of the kingdom of God, which is nothing less than the transformation of the world into a place dominated by God's love. Leo has been praying it every day in the Lord's Prayer: "Thy kingdom come; Thy will be done, on earth as it is in Heaven." The true heroes and the true saints do not transmit pain; they transform it. We are

[111] Pope St. John Paul II, Homily, Seventeenth World Youth Day Solemn Mass, Toronto, July 28, 2002. Good friend and Catholic psychologist Dr. Peter Martin was in attendance and reminded me of this powerful quotation.

all called to bring love to every aspect of our lives, to ourselves, to every person we interact with. This Christlike response involves all our parts. As Leo worked with his formerly angry and withdrawn parts, they became encourager and comforter parts. Now, as Leo grows in the spiritual life, those same parts continue to be strengthened and renewed. Leo discovered that the service-oriented part that was developed in his childhood out of duty became a servant leader who found true fulfillment in making a positive difference in the lives of the less fortunate. In time, he may discover and nurture healer parts, wise parts, and teacher parts. These newly renewed parts, filled with the gifts of the Holy Spirit, become truly active members of the kingdom of God.

THE PSYCHOLOGY OF THE INTERIOR WORLD

The goal of IFS therapy is self-leadership. This means that the self listens to the parts, helps them, and leads them. With the inmost self fully engaged, the interior world of the person embodies the eight Cs: confidence, calm, compassion, courage, creativity, clarity, curiosity, and connectedness.

When the exiles share their stories and the inmost self compassionately listens, deep transformation takes place. It is even possible for the self to engage with the exile and finally meet its true needs. The inmost self can hold the old painful feelings and negative beliefs and release the exile from those burdens.

The unburdened exile can take on new qualities and new beliefs. The exile no longer believes he is unworthy or unlovable, and the protectors can relax and take on new roles. These exiles, often young parts, are experienced in entirely new ways. Their inner playfulness and creativity and lovability become obvious, and the inmost self can see them and delight in them in a new way. The protective managers can exercise their true talents and gifts in tandem with, not in opposition to, the inmost self. The diversity of our parts is no longer expressed in inner conflicts and polarization but is celebrated as a rich resource. The inmost self loves each and every part for what he brings to the system, and each part feels that love and appreciation.

The Monastic Tradition and Humility

The redeemed inmost self is not a monolith or a fusion of all the parts. It is a diversity within a unity. The parts of the self are in harmony. It is a symphony working together perfectly to create beautiful music. With God's grace, this music is transformative for both the orchestra itself and for the world at large. It makes a positive difference in the world and builds God's kingdom. When all the parts experience themselves as loved by the inmost self with a unique identity and a meaningful purpose, there is an energizing zeal and a passion for life. When the inmost self accepts his or her baptismal roles as priest, prophet, and king, all the parts of the self gain a sense of purpose and feel safe. The inmost self is called to exercise the virtue of humility and the faculties or qualities of reason, conscience, true consciousness, freedom, creativity, relationality, and gratitude. As the parts of the self-system feel secure and cared for, they, in turn, can adopt their new roles and grow in virtue.

The key virtue in this inner transformation of the whole human person is humility, which is the correct understanding of our self-worth. The vice of pride might say that we are greater than we are: the original sin was that Adam and Eve thought they could be "as gods." But we must recognize that we come from dust and are completely dependent on God for our very existence.

The flip side of the vice of pride is believing that we are less than we are. The Protestant reformer Martin Luther described man as a pile of dung. Calvin followed this up with the doctrine of total depravity. It is true that we have a fallen nature and an inclination toward sin, but as image bearers of God, we have unfathomable dignity. In order to be truly humble, we need to hold at once this amazing paradox.

We don't become prideful as we discover our inherent dignity; we become more grateful. We are in awe at the way we have been given dignity from dust! Every human being is indeed precious in the sight of God, and when we understand just how much dignity God has given us, our attitude is one of awe. We are so overwhelmed by grace and love that we are more than happy to be out of the spotlight.

Humility allows us to accept who we are. The Cistercian (Trappist) monk Thomas Merton says, "In great saints you find that perfect humility and perfect integrity coincide. The two turn out to be practically the same thing. The saint is unlike everybody else precisely because he is humble.... Humility consists in being precisely the person you actually are before God."[112] We become down-to-earth and comfortable in our own skins. We no longer try to compete with everyone else, and we no longer need to be affirmed by everyone else. We realize we have many gifts and talents as well as limitations and weaknesses. We don't try to be more or less than who we are. There is a tremendous amount of relief that comes with being humble.

True humility is not Calvin's doctrine of total depravity. Sometimes some members of the Church have overemphasized man's sinfulness, but a proper understanding does not lead to a debasement; it leads to an interior quality or disposition of gratitude. We recognize our dependence on God, our weaknesses, and the way in which God loves us and upholds us. When we understand just how much dignity He has given us, our attitude is one of awe. We are so overwhelmed by grace and love that we are more than happy to be out of the spotlight.

St. John Cassian identified ten signs of humility: giving up control, vulnerability, willingness to change, obedience, patience, simplicity or detachment, a nonjudgmental attitude toward others, self-control, gentleness, and compassion for others.[113] These are all qualities of the inmost self, and when they are present, we know we are "in self" — that is, the inmost self is present and engaged. When there is an agenda, a condemnation, a need for control, or a lack of empathy, we know we are engaged with a burdened part. The inmost self is most identifiable by his or her humility. True humility brings about a powerful transformation of the human person.

True humility respects our individuality. As we become Christlike, as we are sanctified and transformed into His likeness,[114] our individual personhood is not erased. We never lose ourselves in a divine sea of sameness. We never become "one with the universe." When we talk of losing the self, we mean that we lose our unhealthy attachments and burdens. There is something beautiful

[112] Thomas Merton, *New Seeds of Contemplation*, 99.

[113] For a fuller treatment, see Michael Casey's *Living in the Truth: Saint Benedict's Teaching on Humility*.

[114] This is referred to in Eastern Christianity as *theosis*.

about each and every person created by God. Our uniqueness is to be valued and appreciated. Our own ultimate transformation in Christ will reveal this beauty, and the light of Christ will fully shine in and through us. A Trappist monk once shared this simple but profound prayer with me:

> Lord, lift me up in the cloud of unknowing
> That I might rest in You;
> Alone in the cloud of forgetting,
> That I might sit here and be with You;
> In the deepest cave of my heart,
> In that one pure, immaculate spot in the center of my being
> That You created,
> That I might rest in You.

Humility is the virtue that best characterizes the inmost self and that best describes his or her leadership style. Humility speaks to the true dignity of the human person. On one hand, we are fully and completely dependent on God's love and mercy. We are often lost, broken, and in need of rescuing. On the other hand, we are created in His image as the very pinnacle of creation. With the grace of God, the inmost self can lead each and every part into a deeper understanding of one's true dignity. As each part feels safe and begins to operate from his or her true purpose, adopting healthy and functioning roles within the self-system, the human person experiences a beautiful inner harmony.

SCRIPTURE STUDY: HUMILITY AND INNER HARMONY

If St. John Cassian's signs of humility — giving up control, vulnerability, willingness to change, obedience, patience, simplicity or detachment, a nonjudgmental attitude toward others, self-control, gentleness, and compassion for others — reflect the humility of the inmost self, then the opposite characteristics reflect pride. These would be a controlling mindset, closing off our hearts, refusing to change, disobedience, impatience, attachment to things, harshly judging others, lack of self-control, brutality, and indifference or heartlessness. A study of the Gospels reveals that the greatest sin, even greater than impurity, is pride. In the following passage, we see how Jesus is most critical of the Pharisees:

> A Pharisee invited [Jesus] to dine with him; so he went in and took his place at the table. The Pharisee was amazed to see that he did not first wash before dinner. Then the Lord said to him, "Now you Pharisees clean the outside of the cup and of the dish, but inside you are full of greed and wickedness. You fools! Did not the one who made the outside make the inside also? So give for alms those things that are within; and see, everything will be clean for you.
>
> "But woe to you Pharisees! For you tithe mint and rue and herbs of all kinds, and neglect justice and the love of God; it is these you ought to have practiced, without neglecting the others. Woe to you Pharisees! For you love to have the seat of honor in the synagogues and to be greeted with respect in the marketplaces. Woe to you! For you are like unmarked graves, and people walk over them without realizing it." (Luke 11:37–44)

In this passage, we see how the Pharisees judge others without mercy or true compassion. They are more concerned with rules than with people. They do not understand true justice and how God's love works. They are more concerned about their own power and prestige than about the needs of people.

If true humility involves loving ourselves properly — that is, seeing our true value as children of God, made in His image — then we must also recognize this dignity in others. In the parable of the Good Samaritan, Jesus shows us the true path, which involves humility:

> Just then a lawyer stood up to test Jesus. "Teacher," he said, "what must I do to inherit eternal life?" He said to him, "What is written in the law? What do you read there?" He answered, "You shall love the Lord your God with all your heart, and with all your soul, and with all your strength, and with all your mind; and your neighbor as yourself." And he said to him, "You have given the right answer; do this, and you will live."
>
> But wanting to justify himself, he asked Jesus, "And who is my neighbor?" Jesus replied, "A man was going down from Jerusalem to Jericho, and fell into the hands of robbers, who stripped him, beat him, and went away, leaving him half dead. Now by chance a priest was going down that road; and when he saw him, he passed by on the other side.

> So likewise a Levite, when he came to the place and saw him, passed by on the other side. But a Samaritan while travelling came near him; and when he saw him, he was moved with pity. He went to him and bandaged his wounds, having poured oil and wine on them. Then he put him on his own animal, brought him to an inn, and took care of him. The next day he took out two denarii, gave them to the innkeeper, and said, 'Take care of him; and when I come back, I will repay you whatever more you spend.' Which of these three, do you think, was a neighbour to the man who fell into the hands of the robbers?" He said, "The one who showed him mercy." Jesus said to him, "Go and do likewise." (Luke 10:25–37)

We do not know whether it was pride, indifference, heartlessness, or strict adherence to the law that caused the Levite and the priest to walk past the suffering man. Their inaction may have been due to a misguided or obsessive desire to maintain ritual purity. In any case, it was the Samaritan who expressed compassion and gentleness as he generously offered assistance to the wounded man.

We can understand the inmost self as the Good Samaritan within the interior world. The inmost self finds the wounded parts and cares for them, even when other parts of the self-system are too busy with their own agenda to take notice. The humble example of the inmost self, however, sends a message to all of the parts and calls them to repentance and change. One's various "priest" parts, "Levite" parts, and "Pharisee" parts are called to true humility. As all the parts of the self-system respond to this call to humility, and as their roles change in such a way as to embody more and more the qualities of compassion, gentleness, and patience (among others), then the whole self-system — ultimately the whole human person — is radically transformed. In this way, the person is called to proper self-love or self-friendship.[115]

[115] Philosopher Anthony Flood discusses his use of the term *proper self-love* for the somewhat disputed but interesting term *self-friendship*. *The Metaphysical Foundations of Love,* 16. Flood is inspired by St. Thomas Aquinas, who says, "Since charity is a kind of friendship, as stated above (q. 23, art. 1), we may consider charity from two standpoints: first, under the general notion of friendship, and in this way we must hold that, properly speaking, a man is not a friend to himself, but something more than a friend, since friendship implies union, for Dionysius says (*Div. Nom.* iv) that love is *a unitive force,* whereas a man is one

And as these parts, now in sync with the inmost self, respond to the call to be Christlike, there is a powerful inner harmony. It is as if one's internal orchestra in unity plays the most beautiful symphony. The inner temple sings in one accord as all the worshippers pray joyfully from their hearts. The inner kingdom operates in harmony when everyone of every station works for the good of all and for peace in the realm.

Humility is the key to being liberated from the sins and burdens that our parts carry. St. James says, "He gives all the more grace; therefore it says, 'God opposes the proud, but gives grace to the humble.' ... Humble yourselves before the Lord, and he will exalt you" (4:6, 10). Dietrich von Hildebrand notes that the man who cultivates humility is primarily concerned with pleasing God, not his own ego. He expresses this powerfully in the following statement: "The inward nobility of good, its intrinsic beauty, touches his heart and delights him. In his devotion to the good he participates in the harmony of values; his soul is bright and serene, free from the corrosive poison that eats the heart of the proud."[116]

LIFE APPLICATIONS FOR INNER TRANSFORMATION

Meditation — Loving God with Your Whole Heart and with All Your Parts[117]

Let us begin: "In the name of the Father, and of the Son, and of the Holy Spirit. Amen."

Let us slow down and notice what's happening inside. What's prominent in your experience right now? As we discuss loving God with our whole heart and with all our parts, notice body sensations, memories, images, desires, and impulses.

with himself, which is more than being united to another. Hence, just as unity is the principle of union, so the love with which a man loves himself is the form and root of friendship. *Summa Theologica*, II-II q. 25, art. 4; 17:239.

[116] Von Hildebrand, *Transformation in Christ*, 155.

[117] This meditation has been adapted from an exercise developed by Dr. Peter Malinoski for the Resilient Catholics community.

What do you feel or sense inside as you consider bringing all your parts into relationship with God? How do your parts feel about the idea that God wants to be in relationship with all your parts, your body, your mind, your soul — all of you. God invites you — your entire being — to be in relationship with Him, and He loves you in your entirety, every part of you.

I invite you to notice what happens inside with the idea that God wants to be in relationship with all of you.

Notice any protectors who have concerns. They may have doubts that God really wants to be in relationship with this part or that part.

Is it interesting to your protectors that God might love all of you, love all your parts — that God doesn't pick and choose parts based on their acceptability or presentability? Our God looks for the lost sheep, connects with the tax collectors, the outcasts, the prostitutes, and the lepers.

Can your parts give you a little more space so that, with a big, open heart, you can lead and guide your internal system? When you're "in self," when you're recollected, there's clarity, confidence, courage, and creativity about how to connect your parts with God. And God helps you on this journey. He's not passively watching, but He's also not going to intrude, invade, or take you over. He respects your dignity and freedom of choice; you have to let Him in. God really and truly loves you with an unconditional love.

Can your parts connect with your faith, your confidence in God?

What do your parts need to allow you, as the inmost self, to more freely mediate between your parts and God? What are the concerns? What might be in the way for any parts?

I invite you to connect your parts with God as it seems good and right with your protectors. If your protectors are not open to it, don't force it. If there's an impulse to force it, then it's coming from a part and not from the inmost self. You want to bring a lot of patience to this process. It can be scary for some parts to connect with God because of the distorted God images they may have.

Would a part like the inmost self to speak for him to God? If so, let God know what that part would like to communicate.

If there is an identifiable message back from God to that part, then you can share it with that part as well.

Take as much time as you need to connect with God, your inmost self, and all your parts. As the parts are more connected with the inmost self, who is mediating with

God, the whole person — the self and all the parts — experiences greater measures of harmony, peace, serenity, calm, and connection.

End with a prayer:

> Dear God, thank You for being present with me today as I explored my inner world and connected with my parts. Thank You for the love that You have for every part of my self-system. Thank You for the love I can offer back to You. I am grateful for the gift of being in communion with You. And so I sing with the psalmist:
>
> Praise the Lord!
> Praise the Lord, O my soul!
> I will praise the Lord as long as I live;
> I will sing praises to my God all my life long. (Ps. 146:1–2)

Reflection Questions

1. As we recollect and access the inmost self, what qualities of the Holy Spirit can we find within? How is humility expressed? What happens when we extend those qualities to our parts?

2. When the inmost self is fully engaged and expresses compassion toward our parts, what is that like for our parts? What is it like for a part to absorb, or "bask" in, the compassion from the inmost self? What emotions can you feel now? As compassion is received, what do you notice in your physical body as a result?

3. As your protectors and exiles take on new beliefs and new roles, what does that feel like for those parts? What is it like for a part to exercise a new role in the self-system? How do your other parts react to a part's exercising a new role?

4. What is it like to love yourself in a healthy and appropriate way? How can you allow your inmost self to lead you to be able to love others more fully? How will this improve your prayer life and your relationship with God?

EPILOGUE

If you are a survivor of trauma, I hope that this book has provided you with a new way to experience your inner world and enrich your healing journey. In my way of thinking, we are all survivors of original trauma, and we all need to heal, evangelize, and renew our burdened parts. It is my hope that as you experience greater levels of inner harmony and true consciousness, you will thrive and flourish.

I began writing this book with the goal of writing an introduction to "parts work," especially in relation to Internal Family Systems[118] and Ego State Therapy[119] for Christians. My own curious inner researcher and inner treasure hunter happily got lost in acquiring knowledge, grasping difficult concepts, and cataloguing psychological and philosophical theories. I have a natural inclination to do a deep dive into how this theory works and how it is and isn't compatible with orthodox Christian theology. I also know that real healing happens every single day in my work with clients, using the fundamental principles of parts work, as they experience powerful moments of relief, inner calm, healing, and greater levels of inner harmony. My challenge was to *show* how working with one's parts is life-changing and to provide a way for my readers to *experience*

[118] For a good outline of Internal Family Systems (IFS), see Richard Schwartz and Martha Sweezy's book, *Internal Family Systems,* 2nd edition.

[119] John and Helen Watkins's book *Ego States: Theory and Therapy* (1997) is foundational, but Maggie Phillips and Claire Frederick's *Healing the Divided Self: Clinical and Ericksonian Hypnotherapy for Post-traumatic and Dissociative Conditions* (1995) is also brilliant. Both books are written primarily for clinicians.

this on their own, all the while providing just enough psychological theory and theology to show how the whole approach hangs together.

I had to decide whom this book could best serve. I sense that therapists and counselor educators, pastors, life coaches, and spiritual directors would all benefit from gaining an understanding of IFS from a Christian perspective. This book might even propel them to seek further training in IFS. But my real audience is *the survivor of trauma* because this parts approach has the greatest impact on those who have experienced the most pain. All of us have experienced trauma — it's a part of life — and all of us can improve wellness by using this approach, but the examples and experiential exercises in this book were chosen to promote greater levels of calm, reduction of anxiety, and perhaps the beginning of the healing process. Although not by any means a replacement to therapy,[120] this book might serve as a helpful adjunct to your therapeutic and healing journey.

I describe myself as a wounded healer because I have experienced significant complex trauma,[121] engaged my own journey of healing, and helped others overcome anxiety disorders and post-traumatic stress. My life's work as a professional counselor and a marriage and family therapist is dedicated to working with trauma survivors in clinical and retreat settings. I wrote this book because my heart goes out to survivors of abuse — whether physical, sexual, verbal, emotional, spiritual, or all of the above. I understand the feelings of shame, loneliness, fear, and hopelessness that we carry every single day. This book was written for you if you grew up believing you were unlovable or unworthy; if you have been hurt by family members, clergy, or close friends; if you have stayed in unhealthy relationships; if you have engaged in self-sabotaging, self-destructive, or addictive behaviors.

I drew from my own personal experience as a wounded healer as well as almost two decades of treating trauma and anxiety disorders. The greatest clinical success that I have witnessed as a therapist includes the integration of trauma-informed approaches (e.g., EMDR), parts work (e.g., IFS and EST), and Christian spiritual interventions (e.g., biblical, Ignatian, and contemplative

[120] If you have experienced trauma and are experiencing psychological distress, seek out a mental health professional, such as a licensed psychologist, a professional counselor, a clinical social worker, or a marriage and family therapist.

[121] Complex trauma involves multiple traumatic events of an interpersonal nature over a period of time.

approaches). Most people do not have the time, training, or resources to explore all these topics. My goal in writing this book was to bring the wisdom of my knowledge and experiences into a readable, digestible, practical format.

There are five important and perhaps radical teachings that I hope became clear as you read this book. I see them as life-changing, as they have transformed both my clinical practice and my own life. Here they are in summary:

1. The human psyche has multiplicity and is made up of an inmost self and many parts of the self-system.

2. Our exiled parts carry burdens as they learn to cope with the pain, fear, and shame caused by trauma. Our manager and firefighter parts carry burdens based on the roles they take on to protect exiled parts.

3. True self-love occurs when the inmost self, with God's grace, exercises the role of secure inner attachment figure, loves the parts, and helps them let go of their burdens.

4. With a fuller, more authentic self-love, we can more fully love God and others. We seek an inner harmony between the inmost self and our parts.

5. The inmost self serves as the mediator between God and the parts. The inmost self invites the parts of the self, once unburdened, into a deeper communion with God.

As we come to know our parts, especially the parts that, at first glance, appear troubled or even self-destructive, we need to account for the reality of sin and evil in the world and in ourselves. The multiplicity of our self-system is not caused by sin, but sin and other wounds cause our parts to carry burdens that fill our rich inner lives with reactivity, defensiveness, avoidance, anger, fear, shame, and self-hatred. Our negative reactions are generally ways that we have learned to cope. Our unhealthy behaviors are often the ways we have learned to avoid pain or find comfort that numbs pain.

The answer to the problems of trauma, sin, suffering, self-hatred, avoidance, reactivity, and all sorts of emotional, psychological, and spiritual distress is simple but profound — we are to be transformed by supernatural love. We are saved by Christ's salvific work on the Cross. A parts-work approach can only provide healing on the natural level that can make natural pathways for grace to enter.

A Christian parts-work approach is a profound paradigm shift in which we relate to our hurting, avoidant, and even reactive and aggressive parts in a profoundly new way. We bring unconditional love to every part in our inner world. Christ is the perfect role model and exemplar for how the inmost self, in communion with the Holy Spirit, can love and heal all the parts of the self and, in so doing, can transform the whole human person. Christ teaches us how to love, protect, nurture, and heal all our parts, whether they are hurting, defensive, avoidant, anxious, or angry. We grow in humility as the parts of the self-system are unburdened and we experience true freedom. Our inner temple is sanctified as we grow in authentic love of God, self, and neighbor, and our inner kingdom glorifies God in gratitude as we experience what it means to be in true, loving communion with ourselves.

Of course, we are always works in progress, but when we are led by our inmost selves, in communion with God, and working with all the parts of our self-systems, we can experience greater love for others. We see their avoidance and reactivity for what it is — protective parts of their self-systems — and we are free to love without being ruled by our sometimes disordered emotions. St. Francis de Sales and St. Ignatius of Loyola called this "holy indifference," and it indicates that our identity, our very self-worth, is truly grounded in God's love. Another related term is the Greek word *apatheia*, which implies a detachment from disordered passions. Here we experience a sense of security, peace, contentment, and joy. It is in this state of inner harmony that we can experience recollection, awareness of the presence of God within the soul. It is from this place of holy indifference that we can purely love others and desire their ultimate good. The psalms, the letters of St. John, the letters of St. Paul, and the Gospels show us how to cultivate this way of relating internally, with others, and with God.

I pray that this book represents the beginning of a journey to discover how the riches of the Christian faith and an understanding of the inmost self and our parts can lead to inner calm, improved personal relationships, and a deeper union with God. May God bless you as you continue your journey of healing and sanctification.

APPENDICES

Appendix A

THE LITANIES OF THE HEART

THE LITANIES AND ATTACHMENT THEORY

The litanies in this book were informed, in part, by attachment theory, a psychological approach first developed by John Bowlby, who studied the relationship between adults and infants and identified their developmental and attachment patterns. Mary Ainsworth further developed this research and introduced the idea of a "secure base." She also identified various insecure attachment styles. Later research explored how these insecure attachment styles expressed themselves in adult relationships. Sue Johnson and Les Greenberg's emotionally focused therapy (EFT), for example, uses the principles of attachment theory in working with couples. The research of Daniel Brown and David Elliott was also influential in understanding how to repair and resolve attachment disturbances in adults.

I based the three original Litanies of the Heart on the three insecure attachment styles in attachment theory. The Litany of the Closed Heart is for the person with a dismissing-avoidant style. This type tends to be independent and has difficulty being vulnerable and sharing emotions. The Litany of the Wounded Heart is for the person with an anxious-preoccupied style. Those with this style want approval and intimacy and often become dependent. They often worry and are prone to emotional outbursts. The Litany of the Fearful Heart is for the fearful-avoidant style. Those of this type want close relationships but do not trust others. They also tend to believe they are not worthy of love. Although most people have a primary insecure attachment style, we all exhibit characteristics of all three styles at one time or another. As you pray the Litanies of the Heart, you may find that one is your preferred prayer, but you may benefit from the other two from time to time as well.

These healing litanies are rooted in a long tradition of Christian prayer, established psychological science, my observations in working with clients, and my own spiritual journey. The goal of all three Litanies of the Heart is to gently work through one's insecurities to enter a safe, loving, secure relationship with Jesus. He is the secure attachment figure par excellence.

PRAYING THE LITANIES

An intentional flow exists in each of the litanies of the heart. An opening prayer is followed by an initial offering of our hearts, with all their troubles, to Jesus. Here we are admitting to God that we have sufferings, doubts, hurts, fears, and burdens. We are also offering our hope, joy, and love as well as, and perhaps more importantly, our lack of hope, lack of joy, and lack of love. In each opening, we are admitting that we are broken and that we need help.

In the next section of the litany, the petition-and-response portion begins. Here, the petitioner brings to Christ the specific negative feelings and thoughts that are burdening the heart. These are different in all three litanies because each attachment style has different concerns. The response here is "Lord, have mercy." This is the most ancient and traditional of Jewish and Christian responses. We find it in multiple psalms in the Old Testament. In the New Testament, we hear the Canaanite woman cry out, "Have mercy on me, Lord, Son of David" when she asks Jesus to cure her daughter of a demon (Matt. 15:22). It can also be found in the parable of the Pharisee and the tax collector (or publican), in which the Pharisee is self-righteous and the tax collector says, "God, be merciful to me, a sinner!" (Luke 18:13). Jesus says that the tax collector's humility is what justifies him. Saying, "Lord, have mercy" can surely be an act of repentance, but it is also an act of surrender and trust in God. As we offer Him the burdens of our hearts in the litany, and we exclaim, "Lord, have mercy," we are, in effect, saying, "I give You this burden. I trust You with this pain. I can't do it on my own."

The next section is shorter, but here we identify *who Jesus is in relation to ourselves*. Jesus is a consoler; He is tender; He is our dignity; He is our hope. And in response to this, we exclaim, "Open my heart." Here, we are opening our hearts to Him because the litany is revealing to us exactly who He is. We may know these truths about Jesus intellectually, but we are asking Him to open our hearts to receive these truths at a deeper level.

In the next section, we identify *what Jesus does for us*. He created us, sees us, knows us, comforts us, values us, and encourages us. These are all the actions of a secure attachment figure, a good and loving parent, a God who is love.

Occasionally someone will ask, "Is Jesus our Creator? I thought God the Father is the Creator." Theologically, all three Persons of the Trinity are involved in the creation of the world and everything in it. The Gospel of John identifies Jesus Christ as the "Word" and says that "all things came into being through him, and without him not one thing came into being" (John 1:1, 3). *The Catechism* states that "everything that belongs to the Father, *except being Father*, the Son has also eternally from the Father, from whom he is eternally born" (246, emphasis mine). Jesus, with God the Father and God the Holy Spirit, is indeed our loving Creator.

In this section of the litany, we turn to Christ, who is our God, and we acknowledge what He does for us out of love. He created us in love, for love, and to be loved. He meets all our intimacy needs, and we respond, "Hold me in Your arms." This is where we allow ourselves to be held by the One who loves us so deeply. We acknowledge that we are His beloved.

I love the response "Hold me in Your arms," as it evokes a warm embrace. But, in composing the litany, I contemplated simply saying "Hold me." I want to encourage you to adapt the prayer to your needs. If a line doesn't apply to you, feel free to delete or change it. If you would prefer to say "Hold me" instead of "Hold me in Your arms," that is perfectly acceptable. I hope you'll make the Litanies of the Heart your own; after all, other than God, you know your heart better than anyone!

In the final section of the litany, before the closing prayer, we offer a series of petitions. Here we *ask Jesus to act in our lives*. As Jesus is invited to hear, draw near, help, and soothe, we respond with "I trust in You." Now our surrender is complete, as we are truly open to receiving His healing mercy and comfort. For me, this evokes the Divine Mercy devotion of St. Faustina. In it, we find the message of God's great compassion.

In the closing prayer, we acknowledge Jesus' work as Healer of both soul and heart. We ask Him to help us become more like Him. As our hearts are transformed, we find renewed fervor in spreading God's love and mercy to others. We are perhaps inspired to acts of charity, works of mercy, and more meaningful relationships based on intimacy and trust.

Guidance for Praying the Litanies

You can pray the litanies on a bus, on a park bench, on a walk, on an airplane — anywhere! Jesus is happy to meet with us whenever and wherever we can make time for Him. But if you are able to be intentional about when and where you pray, here are a few suggestions that can help enhance the experience.

- Prepare a time and a place to pray.
- If you are praying with others, send them the prayers in advance or print out copies of the prayer for them to read aloud.[122]
- Find a comfortable and private place to pray. Some of us have the luxury of a dedicated prayer space in our homes. For others, it might be a comfy chair in a corner or a spot outside under a favorite tree. It's nice to have a place away from the hustle and bustle of regular life. A church or an adoration chapel is also a great option.
- Set an icon, image, or prayer card of Jesus before you. Select an image that means something to you and helps you remember Jesus in a positive way.
- Light a candle or burn incense, or both. A candle represents the light of Christ. Incense is a sign that our prayers are ascending to Heaven. The scent can also be soothing.
- No matter what setting you have chosen, before you pray, spend a few moments taking a few deep breaths and gently inviting all your muscles to relax. This prepares your body to be receptive and relaxed.

As you are praying the litanies, you may have distracting thoughts. Sometimes the cares of the world intrude and your mind might wander. That is perfectly normal. If that happens, just notice that it happens and redirect your attention to

[122] Printable PDF copies of the litanies are downloadable from the Souls and Hearts website, and you can stream audio versions as well: https://www.soulsandhearts.com/lit.

the words of the litanies and the imagery they produce. If you are praying alone, you can even pause and repeat a line or a whole section, but it is also perfectly fine to continue from where you are when you notice the distraction.

Litanies have a repetitive component like waves of the sea. As we develop a deeper, more secure relationship with Christ, we may find meaning in revisiting the litanies many times as we allow the words of the prayers to flow into our souls.

Going Deeper with the Litanies

Once you have prayed the litanies enough times to be comfortable with the experience, you may want to open your heart more consciously, more intentionally, during this prayer and this time of intimacy with Jesus. Here are some suggestions for how to become more aware of and further cooperate with the movements of your heart and the healing presence of Jesus while praying the litanies and to adjust them where needed.

Take time to notice and consciously reflect on your experience.

- Consider using a journal — or just a paper and pen — to take a few notes when you are praying a litany.
- You may notice that a particular line catches your attention. This can be a good line to hold on to. You can gently repeat it later at various times during the day in order to renew that grace in your heart.
- You may have been struck by a strong idea or impression to reflect on, or it may require some reflection to generate awareness of your experience in prayer. It might be helpful to consider the following questions and write down any observations, for further reflection:

  What did you notice happening in your body as you prayed the litanies?
  Did you notice a movement in your heart? What feelings or emotions did you notice?
  What thoughts or beliefs came to the surface as you prayed the litanies?
  Which lines moved you the most? Why?
  Which litany spoke to you the most? Why?

- Use the notes to reflect on and pray about what you experience in prayer. Take time to review them and consider what you have learned.

Acknowledge and respect negative reactions.

- You may have negative feelings while praying a litany. Perhaps you have difficulty relating to some of the lines in the prayer. It is normal and perfectly acceptable to have a variety of responses. Some lines may affect us, and some may not. When you are praying the litanies alone, you can skip over any lines that don't speak to you.

- If a line produces a negative reaction, this likely represents a part of you that needs attention. It is good to pause for a moment and listen to your "reacting" or "resisting" parts. Give yourself time to attend to and care for any parts that have negative thoughts or feelings. It's normal to have inner conflicts of some kind. Perhaps part of you loves a line and another part of you is angry, upset, sad, or concerned over that line. See these conflicts as opportunities to explore and attend to your inner self at a deeper level. Christ wants you to know, hear, and care for *all* the parts of you.

- It is also possible that as you pray the litanies, negative feelings about Jesus may show up. Although we *know* about Jesus — He is good, loving, merciful, and so forth — we may have negative beliefs about Him because of our past hurts. If this is the case, the litanies are an opportunity to develop a new relationship with Jesus at a heart level. We want to acknowledge our wounded parts that were hurt and allow them to experience Jesus as He is. This will likely take time, but the litanies are an opportunity to work with our wounded parts rather than hide them, exile them, or invalidate them.

Bring your insights back to your next prayer time. If you took notes from the prior litanies, reflect on them briefly before you pray them again.

- Take additional time to prepare for and enter into your time of prayer. Invite your body into a safe and more comfortable place with Jesus. Bring to Him any distracted thoughts, worries, and anxieties as you feel more peace and a sense of relief. Invite all of you to be present, even your inner conflicts, and if any part of you is carrying a burden, allow yourself the opportunity to give that burden to Jesus. Notice your emotions as you pray; these emotions sometimes tell us about our needs and unhealed wounds. Take your pain to Jesus as needed.

LITANY OF THE WOUNDED HEART

In the name of the Father, and of the Son, and of the Holy Spirit. Amen.

Lord Jesus, You created me in love and for love. Bring me to a place of vulnerability within the safety of Your loving arms. Help me today by transforming my wounded heart into a heart that can love You, myself, and my neighbor as You intend.

Jesus, I offer You my heart with all its sufferings.
Jesus, I offer You my heart with all its doubts.
Jesus, I offer You my heart with all its hurts.
Jesus, I offer You my heart with all its fears.
Jesus, I offer You my heart with all its burdens.
Jesus, I offer You my heart with all its hope and all its lack of hope.
Jesus, I offer You my heart with all its joy and all its lack of joy.
Jesus, I offer You my heart with all its love and all its lack of love.
Jesus, Son of God, *have mercy on me.*

When I feel unseen, *Lord, have mercy.*
When I feel unheard, *Lord, have mercy.*
When I believe I'm not good enough, *Lord, have mercy.*
When I feel inferior, *Lord, have mercy.*
When I doubt my worth, *Lord, have mercy.*
When I feel devalued, *Lord, have mercy.*
When I feel exposed, *Lord, have mercy.*
When I feel humiliated, *Lord, have mercy.*
When I feel discouraged, *Lord, have mercy.*
When I feel lonely, *Lord, have mercy.*
When my feelings overwhelm me, *Lord, have mercy.*
When I feel I'm too much, *Lord, have mercy.*
When I feel unlovable, *Lord, have mercy.*
When I feel despair, *Lord, have mercy.*
Jesus, I know You love me in all my wounds; *Lord, have mercy.*

Jesus, consoler of my sorrow, *open my heart.*
Jesus, most tender, *open my heart.*
Jesus, my dignity, *open my heart.*
Jesus, my hope, *open my heart.*

Jesus, You created me in love; *hold me in Your arms.*
Jesus, You created me for love; *hold me in Your arms.*
Jesus, You created me to be loved; *hold me in Your arms.*
Jesus, You created my heart; *hold me in Your arms.*
Jesus, You see my heart; *hold me in Your arms.*
Jesus, You know my true heart; *hold me in Your arms.*
Jesus, You comfort my heart; *hold me in Your arms.*
Jesus, You treasure my heart; *hold me in Your arms.*
Jesus, You encourage my heart; *hold me in Your arms.*
Jesus, You created me as Your beloved; *hold me in Your arms.*

Jesus, soothe and comfort my weary heart; *I trust in You.*
Jesus, see my pain; *I trust in You.*
Jesus, dispel my despondency; *I trust in You.*
Jesus, hear my cries; *I trust in You.*
Jesus, draw close to me; *I trust in You.*
Jesus, calm my fears; *I trust in You..*
Jesus, help me see my true worth as a child of God; *I trust in You.*
Jesus, shine Your radiant light on me; *I trust in You.*
Jesus, hold me in Your loving arms; *I trust in You.*
Jesus, help me love with my whole heart; *I trust in You.*
Jesus, You created me to love and to be loved; *I trust in You.*
Jesus, I offer You my heart with all its love; *I trust in You.*

Lord, You are the healer of my soul and my heart. I ask that, through this prayer, You would transform me more and more into the likeness of Your precious and Sacred Heart. Let Your kindness and compassion transform my heart and bring me always into the security of Your loving embrace.

In the name of the Father, and of the Son, and of the Holy Spirit. Amen.

LITANY OF THE CLOSED HEART

In the name of the Father, and of the Son, and of the Holy Spirit. Amen.

Lord Jesus, You created me in love and for love. Bring me to a place of vulnerability within the safety of Your loving arms. Help me today by transforming my closed heart into a heart that can love You, myself, and my neighbor as You intend.

Jesus, I offer You my heart with all its sufferings.
Jesus, I offer You my heart with all its doubts.
Jesus, I offer You my heart with all its hurts.
Jesus, I offer You my heart with all its fears.
Jesus, I offer You my heart with all its burdens.
Jesus, I offer You my heart with all its hope and all its lack of hope.
Jesus, I offer You my heart with all its joy and all its lack of joy.
Jesus, I offer You my heart with all its love and all its lack of love.
Jesus, Son of God, *have mercy on me.*

When I'm withdrawn, *Lord, have mercy.*
When I'm consumed with worry, *Lord, have mercy.*
When I numb out, *Lord, have mercy.*
When I feel cynical, *Lord, have mercy.*
When I lose trust, *Lord, have mercy.*
When I'm distracted, *Lord, have mercy.*
When I try to escape my feelings, *Lord, have mercy.*
When my body holds my stress, *Lord, have mercy.*
When I'm under pressure, *Lord, have mercy.*
When I'm filled with anger, *Lord, have mercy.*
When I become obsessed with tasks, *Lord, have mercy.*
When I feel the urge to act out, *Lord, have mercy.*
When I feel ashamed, *Lord, have mercy.*
When I feel unforgiven, *Lord, have mercy.*
Jesus, I know You love me in all my wounds. *Lord, have mercy.*

Jesus, my helper, *open my heart.*
Jesus, light of my mind, *open my heart.*
Jesus, my guide, *open my heart.*
Jesus, my teacher, *open my heart.*
Jesus, Bread of Life, *open my heart.*
Jesus, face of mercy, *open my heart.*
Jesus, my Redeemer, *open my heart.*
Jesus, my life, *open my heart.*
Jesus, my desire, *open my heart.*
Jesus, my comforter, *open my heart.*
Jesus, my trust, *open my heart.*
Jesus, my safe haven, *open my heart.*

Jesus, You created me in love; *hold me in Your arms.*
Jesus, You created me for love; *hold me in Your arms.*
Jesus, You created me to be loved; *hold me in Your arms.*
Jesus, You created my heart; *hold me in Your arms.*
Jesus, You see my heart; *hold me in Your arms.*
Jesus, You know my true heart; *hold me in Your arms.*
Jesus, You comfort my heart; *hold me in Your arms.*
Jesus, You treasure my heart; *hold me in Your arms.*
Jesus, You encourage my heart; *hold me in Your arms.*
Jesus, You created me as Your beloved; *hold me in Your arms.*

Jesus, awaken and restore my stony heart; *I trust in You.*
Jesus, receive my new heart; *I trust in You.*
Jesus, draw close to me in my struggles; *I trust in You.*
Jesus, forgive me; *I trust in You.*
Jesus, give me new life; *I trust in You.*
Jesus, hold me; *I trust in You.*
Jesus, contain my stress; *I trust in You.*
Jesus, relieve the pressure; *I trust in You.*
Jesus, comfort my pain; *I trust in You.*

Jesus, help me see that I'm not defined by what I do; *I trust in You.*
Jesus, let all my actions flow from Your love for me; *I trust in You.*
Jesus, You give meaning to my life; *I trust in You.*
Jesus, help me love and forgive others; *I trust in You.*
Jesus, help me embrace my vulnerability; *I trust in You.*

Lord, You are the healer of my soul and my heart. I ask that through this prayer, You will transform me more and more into the likeness of Your precious and Sacred Heart. Let Your kindness and compassion transform my heart and bring me always into the security of Your loving embrace.

In the name of the Father, and of the Son, and of the Holy Spirit. Amen.

LITANY OF THE FEARFUL HEART

In the name of the Father, and of the Son, and of the Holy Spirit. Amen.

Lord Jesus, You created me in love and for love. Bring me to a place of vulnerability within the safety of Your loving arms. Help me today by transforming my fearful heart into a heart that can love You, myself, and my neighbor as You intend.

Jesus, I offer You my heart with all its sufferings.
Jesus, I offer You my heart with all its doubts.
Jesus, I offer You my heart with all its hurts.
Jesus, I offer You my heart with all its fears.
Jesus, I offer You my heart with all its burdens.
Jesus, I offer You my heart with all its hope and all its lack of hope.
Jesus, I offer You my heart with all its joy and all its lack of joy.
Jesus, I offer You my heart with all its love and all its lack of love.
Jesus, Son of God, *have mercy on me.*

When I feel afraid, *Lord, have mercy.*
When I don't know how to feel safe, *Lord, have mercy.*
When life feels chaotic, *Lord, have mercy.*
When I'm confused, *Lord, have mercy.*
When I don't know how to trust, *Lord, have mercy.*
When I feel hurt, *Lord, have mercy.*
When I feel unloved, *Lord, have mercy.*
When I feel disappointed, *Lord, have mercy.*
When others fail me, *Lord, have mercy.*
When I feel let down, *Lord, have mercy.*
When I feel all alone, *Lord, have mercy.*
When I feel rejected, *Lord, have mercy.*
When I feel I don't belong, *Lord, have mercy.*
When I feel hopeless, *Lord, have mercy.*
When I'm afraid of being hurt, *Lord, have mercy.*
Jesus, help me love others when it is difficult; *Lord, have mercy.*

Jesus, help me pray for those who have hurt me; *Lord, have mercy.*
Jesus, I know You love me in all my wounds; *Lord, have mercy.*

Jesus, most compassionate, *open my heart.*
Jesus, healer of my wounds, *open my heart.*
Jesus, my shepherd, *open my heart.*
Jesus, my protector, *open my heart.*
Jesus, unspeakable love, *open my heart.*

Jesus, You created me in love; *hold me in Your arms.*
Jesus, You created me for love; *hold me in Your arms.*
Jesus, You created me to be loved; *hold me in Your arms.*
Jesus, You created my heart; *hold me in Your arms.*
Jesus, You see my heart; *hold me in Your arms.*
Jesus, You know my true heart; *hold me in Your arms.*
Jesus, You comfort my heart; *hold me in Your arms.*
Jesus, You treasure my heart; *hold me in Your arms.*
Jesus, You encourage my heart; *hold me in Your arms.*
Jesus, You created me as Your beloved; *hold me in Your arms.*

Jesus, You are present with me; *I trust in You.*
Jesus, You bring me close to You; *I trust in You.*
Jesus, You walk with me; *I trust in You.*
Jesus, You accept me; *I trust in You.*
Jesus, You calm all my fears; *I trust in You.*
Jesus, You protect me from threats; *I trust in You.*
Jesus, You delight in me; *I trust in You.*
Jesus, help me trust You; *I trust in You.*

Lord, You are the healer of my soul and my heart. I ask that through this prayer, You would transform me more and more into the likeness of Your precious and Sacred Heart. Let Your kindness and compassion transform my heart and bring me always into the safety and security of Your loving embrace.

In the name of the Father, and of the Son, and of the Holy Spirit. Amen.

Appendix B

A CHRISTIAN PARTS-WORK-MODEL GLOSSARY

For most people, the challenge of understanding parts work is that we are dealing with complex psychological, philosophical, theological, and spiritual concepts. This glossary provides definitions as a reference to help make sense of these sometimes difficult and confusing terms. Another challenge is that some terms are used differently in different languages, cultures, time periods, disciplines, and contexts. This section represents an attempt at theoretical and faith integration. Some IFS terms may be defined differently to accommodate this integration; I have made every effort to identify these differences when they occur.

Activation: This occurs when negative thoughts and emotions emerge because a part is triggered. This can happen when a current experience or person reminds the part in some way of a past trauma.

Alliance: The working together of two parts to accomplish a goal in harmony with the inmost self. An alliance can also include two protectors who are polarized against one or more other protectors; this blocks the inmost self and creates disharmony in the self-system.

Apatheia: See *holy indifference*; *recollection*. The state of spiritual peace, joy, or well-being that comes with detachment from disordered passions and overthinking. The state of the soul in which the inmost self (nous) is unblended from the parts and the parts are unburdened. In this state, the soul can reconnect with God through the prayer of the heart or contemplation.

Attachment theory: A psychological theory developed by John Bowlby, Mary Ainsworth, and others that recognizes the human need for secure attachment and identifies different kinds of insecure attachment (anxious, avoidant, and fearful). As described by Dr. Peter Martin, the term *attachment* communicates that human persons form strong emotional bonds with others who provide "protection, comfort, and support." The attachment system itself is a mechanism of emotional regulation with a set goal of establishing sustained care and protection to bring about felt safety and security. In *Attachment Disturbances in Adults*, Daniel Brown and David Elliott identify five pillars of attachment: a sense of felt safety, of being seen and known, of felt comfort, of being valued, and of support for being one's best self.

Blending and unblending: In IFS, blending occurs when the core or inmost self is sidelined, eclipsed, or taken over by a burdened part or parts. When this happens, the person experiences the feelings, attitudes, and impulses of that part. When a part is fully blended, the person is likely to act on those impulses. A part can be partially blended with the self so that the self still has some presence. One of the goals of IFS is unblending so that one can achieve "self-leadership." Unblending allows the parts to experience self-energy.

Body: The physical human body is complex and is made up of cells, tissues, organs, and organ systems — circulatory, digestive, endocrine, immune, integumentary, lymphatic, musculoskeletal, nervous, reproductive, respiratory, and urinary. The Christian view is that the body and the soul are integrated. Trauma-informed therapies recognize that the body and the mind are deeply connected. *Somatization* refers to the way physical symptoms can occur due to psychological distress. In parts work, we can often identify a part of the self-system through sensations in the body. We can also identify how burdens impact the body and the physical relief that occurs when psychological burdens are lifted.

Burdens: In IFS, these are extreme ideas and feelings or states usually caused by traumatic experiences.

Capital virtues: These virtues are considered remedies for the seven deadly sins. There are several lists of these virtues from the early Church. Pope St. Gregory I lists the following: chastity, temperance, charity, diligence, kindness, patience, and humility. These virtues oppose the following corresponding vices: lust, gluttony, greed, sloth, envy, wrath, and pride.

Cardinal virtues: The basic virtues required for a virtuous life include prudence (the ability to discern appropriate actions), justice (fairness and righteousness), fortitude (courage and endurance), and temperance (self-control and restraint). They are found in classical philosophy and are mentioned in Wisdom 8:7.

Concupiscence: Man's inclination to sin — a consequence of the Fall. Concupiscence can be understood psychologically as a negative and unhealthy self-protective coping response. See *Catechism of the Catholic Church* 405–406, 2514–2515.

Contemplation: The inmost self in communion with God. Contemplation or prayer of the heart is lovingly and attentively focusing on God with vulnerability. Natural contemplation occurs when we commune with God through created nature. Active contemplation occurs when we seek God through our own initiative. Pure or infused contemplation is a mystical experience of God without passion, senses, concepts, or imagination. It is an act of God's love in which He makes Himself known to a receptive and passive soul.

Darkened nous: As a consequence of original sin, the inmost self needs redemption and conversion (see *metanoia*). When the inmost self is regenerated, it connects with God as a child of God and experiences illumination, which allows it to "see" all the parts of the self-system and bring them into communion with God.

Dissociation: See *dissociative identity disorder*. A protective mechanism of the mind in which threatening internal experiences (e.g., emotions, desires, beliefs, thoughts, and conflicts) are disconnected and kept from conscious awareness. Examples range from mild (e.g., missing cues from a romantic partner that clearly indicate a loss of interest in the relationship) to more severe (e.g., finding oneself in a strange city and not knowing how one arrived there). During the initial traumatic experience, a person may dissociate and experience numbing, disengagement, and even amnesia. Post-traumatic stress disorder (PTSD) is a dissociative subtype that often has symptoms such as depersonalization, derealization, flashbacks, and hypervigilance of the self-system.

Dissociative identity disorder: Formerly known as multiple personality disorder or split personality, this is a serious mental disorder in which parts of the self-system are not aware of or do not remember the behavior of other parts. It is often comorbid with other disorders, such as post-traumatic stress disorder (PTSD), borderline personality disorder, and obsessive-compulsive disorder.

Divine Liturgy: The Eucharistic or Communion service of the Byzantine Rite, used by the Eastern Orthodox and Eastern Catholic churches. This corresponds with the Mass, which is the name for the celebration of the Eucharist in the Western Latin Church.

Dreams: These are images, ideas, emotions, and sensations that occur during certain stages of sleep, especially during rapid-eye movement (REM). Dreams can be understood as representations of the unconscious mind in which a natural kind of therapy happens. Waking up from a nightmare may represent the mind's inability to process material. With EMDR, disturbing unprocessed memories are processed using bilateral stimulation. In parts work, we can identify and work with the parts of the self-system that represent the unconscious defenses that drive our dreams.

Ego cathexis: See *self-energy*.

Ego state: In Ego State Therapy, this refers to a "part" of the self or a "subpersonality" with its own thoughts and feelings.

Ego State Therapy (EST): A parts-work approach that was developed by John and Helen Watkins from the psychodynamic tradition and was influenced by clinical hypnosis and family therapy.

Emotions: Core emotions include fear, shame, sadness, joy, disgust, contempt, anger, and surprise. Emotions can lead to virtuous or sinful actions, but they are morally neutral and a natural part of being human. They are not the same as the passions but can be permeated by them.

Exiles: In IFS, these are parts that represent trauma and carry burdens of pain, fear, and shame. Exiles are phenomenologically very young parts. Managers often attempt to banish these parts and block their access to the inmost self, and so they often operate outside of conscious awareness. Firefighters distract the attention from the exiles when the exiles threaten to break into conscious awareness.

False beliefs: Trauma often creates in us generalized false beliefs, such as "All others are untrustworthy" or "I am unlovable"; those beliefs then inform our thinking and emotions. We have parts that hold to these false beliefs, and these become burdens that they carry. We help our parts to let go of false beliefs and accept truths such as "I can trust people who show themselves to be trustworthy" or "I am worthy of God's love."

Firefighter part: In IFS, this is a part that quickly appears and works to calm or divert attention away from the exiled part. Firefighters distract us by excessively focusing on behaviors such as work, exercise, sex, media consumption, and overconsumption of substances.

Gnomic will: In contrast with the natural will, which is a movement that fulfills its being (telos) or purpose, the gnomic will is a spontaneous deliberation between a variety of options when one doesn't know what one wants. This concept was developed by St. Maximus the Confessor, who claimed that Jesus Christ did not have a gnomic will and that His divine and human wills were in perfect harmony.

God concept: One's conscious, cognitive, and rational understanding of God. A God concept is usually developed from reading sacred texts and learning from parents, teachers, and religious leaders.

God image: One's often unconscious, emotional, and experiential understanding of God. A God image may refer to how a person feels about God and how he believes God feels about him.

Heart: See *inmost self.* The "unique, interior core of personal existence."[123] "The desire for God is written in the human heart" (*CCC* 27). In this sense, the human heart can be understood as the inmost self or the nous. Unlike the IFS "Self," however, the human heart can be "hardened" or "restless" or "darkened." Despite this, the natural law is written in our hearts, and grace enlightens the "eyes of the heart" (Eph. 1:18). Jesus reminds us to love God with all our heart, soul, mind, and strength" (Mark 12:30); the heart is so included because it involves three things: affections, depth, and centrality. The heart is the deepest part of the person, in which a person experiences most acutely his thoughts, desires, and affections, particularly consolation and joy. Clearly, it is an important aspect, if not the most central aspect, of personal identity for St. Thomas Aquinas. It represents the core of who a person is — a core encountered in love of God and that which is loved in others through intimate friendship.[124]

Hesychia: A Greek word used to describe a state of calm, peace, rest, and inner silence. In this state, the psyche is free of inner disturbance and agitation.

[123] Flood, *The Metaphysical Foundations of Love*, 7.

[124] Ibid., 114.

The soul experiences union with God and a lack of worries or anxiety. This also leads to the practice of virtues, repentance, purity of heart, and *nepsis* (sobriety or watchfulness of the heart).

Holy indifference: See *apatheia*; *recollection*. A state of being in which one recognizes one's true identity as a child of God and one's parts are in harmony with the inmost self. With holy indifference, one experiences detachment from internal and external burdens and is capable of loving others in a selfless manner. Holy indifference is the opposite of the psychological concept "codependence," in which one relies on others to define one's sense of worth.

Human formation: Dr. Peter Malinoski defines *human formation* as "the lifelong process of natural development, aided by grace, by which a person integrates all aspects of his interior emotional, cognitive, relational, and bodily life, all of his natural faculties in an ordered way, conformed with right reason and natural law, so that he is freed from natural impediments to trust God as His beloved child and to embrace God's love. Then, in return, because he possesses himself, he can love God, neighbor, and himself with all of his natural being in an ordered, intimate, personal, and mature way."[125] The Program of Priestly Formation defines *human formation* as "education in the human virtues perfected by charity."[126]

Humility: A natural virtue and precondition for growth in virtue. Dietrich von Hildebrand calls humility the highest of human virtues. It refers to having an accurate understanding of one's true self-worth, neither arrogant and boastful nor overly self-effacing and self-critical. Humility is the primary virtue in achieving purity of heart, in which we realize our complete dependence on God.

Inner harmony: This occurs when the inmost self and all the parts of the self-system collaborate and communicate in positive and productive ways. There is a sense of connection while respecting the individual qualities of all the parts.

Inmost self: See *nous*; *heart*. The conscious center of the soul, which can connect with God in an intimate way. By virtue of sanctifying grace, the inmost

[125] *Interior Integration for Catholics*, podcast, episode 63.

[126] United States Conference of Catholic Bishops, *Program of Priestly Formation in the United States of America*, 6th ed. (Washington, DC: United States Conference of Catholic Bishops, 2022), 88.

self, in a state of holiness, reveals a person's true beauty as a child of God and experiences friendship with God. This is sometimes referred to as the core self, the higher self, or the regenerated self. The inmost self is the agent of healing for all the parts of the self-system. Even for those who are not baptized, the inmost self is characterized by IFS's eight Cs and five Ps: confidence, calm, compassion, courage, creativity, clarity, curiosity, and connectedness; patience, persistence, perspective, playfulness, and presence. The inmost self can receive sanctifying and infused grace and therefore experiences the theological virtues: faith, hope, and love. The inmost self also exercises and extends the cardinal and capital virtues to the parts of the self-system. In this way, the inmost self is a unifying presence within the self-system and can express the "unity of the virtues."

Inner conflict: This occurs when two parts or two camps of parts internally battle each other for dominance, typically in reaction to a perceived extreme position or behavior in the other part or parts, and in so doing, they obscure the inmost self. In IFS, this is referred to as a *polarization*.

Insecure attachment: In response to relational trauma, neglect, or inconsistent and nonresponsive care, we may respond with anxiety and become preoccupied, clingy, or reactive and amplify negative emotions, such as anger. Alternatively, we may respond with avoidance and suppress emotions, disconnect from others, and become obsessed with tasks. We may also respond with fear and by alternating between or simultaneously experiencing anxiety and avoidance.

Integration: Daniel Siegel writes: "Integration is defined as the linkage of differentiated elements. The mind's process of linking differentiated parts (distinct modes of information processing) into a functional whole is postulated to be the fundamental mechanism of both. Without integration, chaos, rigidity, or both ensue. Integration is both a process and a structural dimension, and can be examined, for example, in the functional and anatomic studies of the nervous system."[127]

Internal Family Systems (IFS): A parts-work approach developed by Richard Schwartz.

[127] Daniel Siegel, *The Developing Mind: How Relationships and the Brain Interact to Shape Who We Are*, 2nd ed. (New York: Guilford Press, 2012), 506.

Lectio Divina: Often referred to as "divine reading," *Lectio Divina* involves reading, meditating, praying, and contemplating using a passage from the Bible.

Litany: A form of prayer and worship that typically includes a series of petitions and responses. The earliest identified litany in the Judeo-Christian tradition is Psalm 136. The Litany of the Saints became popular in the sixth century. In the Catholic Church, the recitation of the litanies of the Holy Name of Jesus, the Sacred Heart of Jesus, the Precious Blood of Jesus, the Blessed Virgin Mary, and St. Joseph grew in popularity in the later Middle Ages. Litanies are also popular in the Eastern Orthodox, Anglican, Lutheran, and Methodist traditions.

Liturgy of the Hours: Sometimes referred to as the Divine Office or Divine Services, the Liturgy of the Hours is a set of daily prayers found in a breviary and recited throughout the day. St. Benedict of Nursia developed an early liturgy for the recitation of the psalms that was used in Christian monasteries.

Love: An act of the will and a sincere gift of self for the good of another. When we love, we choose to be vulnerable.

Manager part: In IFS, this part influences interactions with the external world. Manager parts can be very functional in that they help us complete tasks and interact with others. Their goal is to minimize the negative feelings or distress of the exiles. They often take on protector roles by preventing the system from being overwhelmed by disturbing thoughts and strong emotions.

Meditation: A practice in which one focuses one's mind to become emotionally calm and achieve a spiritual goal. Christian meditation is not about self-emptying but about reflecting on divine revelation and being open to the movement of the Holy Spirit within. It is more structured than contemplation and may precede contemplative prayer. Two popular types of Western Christian meditation are the Rosary and *Lectio Divina*. A popular meditation prayer in Eastern Christianity is the Jesus Prayer.

Metanoia: A transformation or conversion of the heart. The word *metanoia* is formed from the Greek word *meta* (beyond) and the root word *nous* (heart or mind). It involves a kind of new "seeing" that illuminates the inmost self. This is often followed by repentance and a change in behavior. In Jungian psychology, it can refer to a change in personality following a crisis, healing, and rebirth. In transactional analysis, it can involve a change from an old script (narrative or internal story) of the false self to a new one connected with the true self.

Mind: According to Plato, the mind is the reasoning part of the soul that loves wisdom. The mind is associated with consciousness and is identified with the faculties of cognition, imagination, emotion, memory, will, perception, and sensation.

Multiplicity: The belief that the human mind is naturally made up of many subpersonalities, ego states, or parts.

Natural virtues: See *capital virtues*. Despite being fallen, we can all exercise positive virtues because we are created in the image of God. According to Catholic theology, we acquire natural virtues through repeated good choices and actions. According to IFS, these qualities are naturally present in the self and are blocked by blended parts. Examples of these qualities in IFS include the eight Cs (confidence, calm, compassion, courage, creativity, clarity, curiosity, and connectedness) and the five Ps (patience, persistence, perspective, playfulness, and presence).

Negative cognitions: These are lies that we believe in our hearts, even if our rational minds know they are not true. They are informed by false beliefs and may be triggered by memories.

Nous: See *inmost self*; *heart*. This is a Greek term often translated as "mind" or "heart of the mind." It is the faculty whereby man enters into communion with God; it is the "eye" or "heart" or "essence" of the soul. The nous can perceive God and can receive visions. It is naturally intuitive. It has the power of wisdom and can move toward God (Matt. 5:8; Luke 11:41; 24:45; Rom. 12:2; 1 Cor. 14:14–15; 2 Cor. 4:6; Eph. 1:17–18). A darkened nous (unregenerated or without sanctifying grace) can be "captured" by negative thoughts and images when blended with burdened parts of the self.

Original sin: Due to the Fall of man, we no longer have God's sanctifying grace within us; we are alienated from God and distrust Him, and we have a tendency to take on burdens and act in harmful ways. We also have a darkened nous, which creates a disconnection between us and God. Through Baptism, conversion, and lifelong sanctification, the parts are unblended from the inmost self, and the soul is renewed and sanctified, allowing us to connect with God and receive graces.

Original trauma: See *insecure attachment*. A term coined by the author of the present work. The Fall of man and its consequences mean that trauma is a universal experience, and so we all experience a measure of insecurity.

Part or part of the self-system: This refers to a subpersonality or an ego state that has its own perspective, thoughts, feelings, beliefs, and memories. Parts are sometimes referred to as neural networks or clusters, modes of experience, self-states, states of mind, schema states, inner selves, sides of a person, aspects of a person, internal voices, or facets of a person. In IFS, they are understood as internal people, which diverges from an orthodox Christian understanding of the human person. From a Christian perspective, parts have a phenomenological existence but not an ontological existence; they are not separate entities. Perhaps one could say they "flow" from being an embodied human person.

Passions: The passions are morally neutral and represent a movement of the sensitive appetite toward a perceived good or away from a perceived evil. Many of the Christian Fathers refer to the passions as unrestrained or excessive emotions, and these may perhaps be best understood as disordered emotions that can potentially lead to unhealthy attachments, addictions, or even compulsions. Examples of disordered passions include vices or deadly sins, such as gluttony, lust, avarice, envy, anger, acedia, vainglory, and pride. Parts of the self-system may be burdened by disordered emotions or passions. Evagrius Ponticus believed we must eradicate the passions, whereas St. Maximus the Confessor claimed they could be transformed not only by repentance, humility, and communion and dialogue with God but by contemplating the inner essence of sensible things. St. Gregory the Great suggested that natural or capital virtues were remedies for vices such as the seven deadly sins.

Pathology: In this context, pathology occurs when the inmost self is blended with burdened parts, and there is insufficient self-leadership or self-energy in the self-system. The inmost self or nous is darkened by unhealthy attachments and subjugated to disordered passions. Others become objects of the person's pleasure, and creatures are idolized. The inmost self or nous is separated from God, and the burdened parts of the self are consumed by false beliefs and cognitive distortions.

Person: The human person is made up of a body and a soul with a rational nature. In secular terms, personhood is associated with human and legal rights.

Personalism: A phenomenological philosophy and theological approach developed within Catholicism by Servant of God Dorothy Day and Pope St.

John Paul II. Personalism emphasizes that a person should be approached with an attitude of love and is not to be used as an object or a means to an end.

Personality: The inmost self and all the parts express personality through patterns of behaviors, thoughts, and emotions. Personality can change over time, especially as one lives more consistently "in self" and unburdens the parts of the self-system. Personality disorders tend to be understood in IFS as manifestations of burdened and blended dominant protector parts.

Prayer: A conversation with God as a person develops an intimate relationship of love with Him.

Pride: Aristotle understood pride as the virtue of thinking oneself worthy of great things and connected it to good character, whereas the vice of hubris involved considering oneself superior to others. The Church has identified pride as an excessive love of oneself, whereas humility is realizing one's complete dependence on God. St. John Cassian identifies pride as the vice that can attack the whole person and destroys all virtue.

Purity of heart: Divine union can take place when purity of heart has been achieved — that is, when the inmost self has been illuminated and all the parts of the self have been purified of vices and relieved of burdens.

Protector part: See *manager part*; *firefighter part*. In IFS, protector parts can be manager parts or firefighter parts. Before a therapist can work with an exiled part, it is important to ally with the protector.

Psalmody: A type of prayer that involves the recitation of and meditation on the biblical psalms. The Christian monastic tradition emphasizes the praying of the psalms throughout the day, especially in the Liturgy of the Hours. A book containing the psalms is called a psalter.

Psychoanalysis: A therapeutic approach developed by Sigmund Freud and others in the psychodynamic tradition; it is focused on uncovering the unconscious meaning behind conscious behavior. Freud identified the id, the ego, and the superego as components of the personality within the psyche.

Recollection: See *apatheia*; *holy indifference*. The act of bringing one's attention and all the parts of the self-system away from the external world into the presence of God. It is a process of integration and unification of the parts of the self-system. The inmost self unblends from the parts and refocuses on higher truths and purposes. Recollection is also a state of inner solitude in which the inmost self and all the parts enter into communion with God.

Reparenting: By reparenting, the inmost self takes on the role of an ideal and compassionate parent to provide a part, usually a wounded child part, with what he needs. As a result, the part can develop a secure attachment to the ideal internal attachment figure known as the inmost self; this leads to overall self-leadership, self-energy, and internal harmony.

Role: This is a job or an identity that a protector (a manager or a firefighter) part adopts that usually comes with expectations and social scripts. Extreme roles represent dysfunctional ways that parts adapt in response to trauma and not having their needs met. Parts can adopt relaxed and healthy roles when they release their burdens.

Sanctification: The process of growing in holiness and virtue. This is facilitated by unburdening the parts.

Schema modes: In schema therapy, a schema is a framework or organized pattern of thoughts, beliefs, and behaviors. A schema mode is a "mind state" made up of schemas and coping styles. Examples of schema modes include the vulnerable child, the angry child, the impulsive child, the detached protector, the punitive parent, and the healthy adult.

Secure attachment: In attachment theory, secure attachment occurs when a child feels safe, protected, and comforted by a stronger, wiser caregiver who reliably and consistently meets his needs. With secure attachment, a person can better regulate his emotions and experience joy. Persons who experience secure attachment have the felt sense that they are seen, known, comforted, and encouraged. Adult relationships characterized by secure attachment have a greater capacity to self-disclose and exhibit empathic responsiveness.

Self: see *inmost self*. IFS refers to this as the seat of consciousness and the spiritual center of the person.

Self-system: The psychological structure that organizes and gives meaning to human existence. It is sometimes defined as the whole person, both body and soul. In the context of this book, the self-system refers to the inmost self and all the parts.

Self-energy: Paul Federn referred to this as ego cathexis — the investing of mental and emotional energy into a person or thing. In IFS, it refers to the natural qualities of presence when we access the inmost self. When we are "in self," we can access the qualities of confidence, calm, compassion, courage, creativity, clarity, curiosity, and connectedness (the eight Cs) and extend them to our parts.

Self-leadership: This occurs when the parts trust the inmost self to make decisions and guide the self-system.

Self-worth: Although this concept is similar to the secular notion of self-esteem, a Christian understanding of self-worth focuses on the inherent value of the human person, created in God's image and redeemed by Jesus Christ. Self-worth does not depend on achievements, but achievements may emerge from a positive sense of self-worth. Self-worth is tied to the virtue of humility, which is an accurate understanding of one's value, and it avoids excessive self-love (narcissism) and self-abasement.

Silence (inner): See *hesychia*.

Sin: An orthodox Christian parts-work approach accepts the doctrine of original sin and asserts that the whole human person, including the inmost self, needs redemption. Sinful acts may be influenced by burdened parts, but it is the human person who commits sin. The Catholic Church teaches that "sin is an offense against reason, truth, and right conscience; it is failure in genuine love for God and neighbor caused by a perverse attachment to certain goods. It wounds the nature of man and injures human solidarity. It has been defined as "an utterance, a deed, or a desire contrary to the eternal law"[128] (*CCC* 1849).

Soul: The human soul is the unifying spiritual principle and innermost aspect of a person, created by God in His image. God is said to "breathe" into Adam, thus giving him a soul and making him a whole living creature. The soul (in Greek, *psyche*) can be understood to include the conscious mind, the unconscious mind, the inmost self, and all the parts of the self. In Christianity, the soul is said to be immortal, and it is referred to as the "form of the body."

System: A structure or organization made up of subsystems, hierarchies, and boundaries. This can include families, communities, churches, corporations, cities, and nations. In IFS and other parts-work approaches, the system is internal, so there is a recognition of the individual's internal family or world.

[128] St. Augustine, *Contra Faustum* 22:*PL* 42, 418; St. Thomas Aquinas, *Summa Theologica* I-II, q. 71, art. 6.

System theory: An approach in marriage and family therapy in which interactional patterns are tracked and mapped. Strategies are designed to change patterns of behavior with an understanding of the larger dynamics and relationships between individuals. Family systems have a structure that includes rules and responsibilities. The internal family system also includes a structure with rules and responsibilities.

Theological virtues: These are faith, hope, and love (see 1 Cor. 13). St. Thomas Aquinas explains that the theological virtues are infused into our souls by God and have God as their object. We can know them only by divine revelation (the Bible). According to the *Catechism*, the theological virtues dispose Christians to live in relationship with the Trinity.

Theosis: The goal of becoming one with God through purification (sanctification), leading to glorification and deification. It is a work or action of the Holy Spirit that restores the lost likeness to God. One retains one's personal identity but is in perfect communion with God. One attains theosis through *nepsis* (watchfulness), *ascesis* (practice), and *hesychia* (stillness).

Trailhead: An inner voice, feeling, image, sensation, or thought that can lead one to engage with a part.

Trance: A state of dissociation or semiconsciousness that can be induced with clinical hypnosis. The Christian mystical tradition has many examples of saints entering what appears to be a trance state, such as the ecstasies of St. Teresa of Ávila. A mild trance is often described as focused attention and therefore can include experiences of deep prayer, contemplation, and meditation.

True consciousness: See *recollection*. A term used by Dietrich von Hildebrand to describe a state in which the inmost self is alert and aware of its relationship with God. The self is in touch with the true meaning and purpose of his life.

Unblending: See *blending and unblending*.

Unburdening: The process of identifying and then releasing the extreme beliefs, cognitive distortions, and disordered emotions that a part is carrying.

Unconscious mind: Sometimes referred to as the subconscious mind, this is the area of the soul or psyche that contains memories, desires, emotional conflicts, and urges that are unavailable to conscious awareness. Exiles generally exist in the unconscious mind.

Unity of the virtues: See *inmost self*. The belief that the virtues are not separate from each other but are interconnected. The inmost self (heart or nous) is the unifying agent for receiving, exercising, sharing, and acting upon the virtues. When the parts are self-led, they participate in these virtues as well.

Vice: These are habitual dispositions to do evil, such as gluttony, lust, avarice, anger, envy, sloth and pride. Vices can be associated with burdens carried by parts of the self-system and maladaptations that create habitual patterns of behavior.

Virtues: See *capital virtues; cardinal virtues.*

Vulnerability: This involves having the courage and love to be honest, authentic, and emotionally exposed. When we are vulnerable with others, we allow them to "see" us at a deeper level, and we risk being hurt, shamed, or rejected. The inmost self embraces vulnerability as one aspires to more intimate and meaningful relationships with loved ones. The parts of the self-system, especially the exiles, are more willing to become vulnerable when they are befriended and loved by the inmost self.

Will: A faculty of the mind that enables us to make free moral choices.

Witnessing: The act of the inmost self seeing the origin of the wounded part's burden.

Appendix C

A BRIEF HISTORY OF PARTS WORK

WILLIAM JAMES AND THE VARIOUS SELVES

William James (1842–1910), often credited as the father of American psychology, described "various selves" as part of "me"; these include the social self, the material self, and the spiritual self. He depicted these "selves" as separate from the "I" or the "pure ego," which is perhaps best described as the soul.

SIGMUND FREUD—ID, EGO, AND SUPEREGO

In identifying the id, the ego, and the superego, Sigmund Freud (1856–1939), the founder of psychoanalysis, and others popularized the concept of multiplicity. The id represents a part of the psyche that is dominated by instinctual desires, while the superego represents a part of the psyche that is critical and moralistic. The ego is the conscious part that acts as a kind of referee, organizing and managing life in a realistic manner. The ego informs the "persona," which is the way a person presents or expresses himself outwardly to others.

CARL JUNG, THE TRUE SELF, ARCHETYPES, AND COMPLEXES

Carl Jung (1875–1961) was a Swiss psychologist mentored by Sigmund Freud. Jung suggested that the "true self" is often disconnected from the ego because the ego is concerned with self-esteem and maintaining an acceptable image.

As a result, aspects of selfhood are repressed and move to the unconscious domain. Self-realization requires honesty and a radical acceptance of the true self, which, in Jung's understanding, includes the "shadow." The shadow has both masculine and feminine aspects (*anima* and *animus*) and must be integrated rather than denied.

Jung and the other psychodynamic psychologists of the time believed that humans had an unconscious mind in which deeper issues reside and that human behavior was influenced by these unconscious or subliminal thoughts and feelings. They believed that healing could happen when we bring the unconscious into awareness and integrate it with the conscious mind. For Jung, the whole person includes a conscious ego, a personal unconscious, and a collective unconscious. The collective unconscious is an aspect of the psyche shared in common with all of humanity. This universal psyche can be perceived in motifs, symbols, and themes. Jung identified a variety of human archetypes that many of us adopt and that influence our thoughts, feelings, and perceptions. These archetypes, which appear differently in individuals but follow common patterns, show up in myths and stories in all cultures; examples include the hero, the mother, the mentor, the warrior, and the lover.

Jung also discussed the existence of complexes in the unconscious mind. A complex is a subpersonality or collection of thoughts and concerns that influences a person's thoughts, emotions, and behaviors. Freud saw these complexes as coming from childhood trauma, whereas Jung saw them as connected to the collective unconscious and the instincts of the archetypes.

The goal of Jung's therapy was to bring about individuation, whereby the person becomes a "whole" individual. There is an appreciation here for the uniqueness of the true self, in whom all complexes and unconscious elements are harmoniously integrated. Problems arise when these elements operate outside of conscious awareness. This integration of the unconscious and the conscious involves a great deal of self-acceptance and reconciliation within the self.

The psychodynamic tradition and Carl Jung deserve a great deal of credit for identifying unique internal parts operating within our internal system. The idea of archetypes and complexes introduces the idea of parts with their own thoughts and feelings. The conflict between the superego and the id represents a deeper understanding of inner conflicts and polarizations. From an IFS perspective, the notion of a true self, distinct from the id, the ego, and the superego, means that the ego and the superego are burdened manager parts, and the id is a kind of firefighter part. The idea of a collective unconscious is more in line with Richard Schwartz's concept of an overarching SELF that encompasses all of humanity or the whole planet.[129]

PAUL FEDERN AND EDOARDO WEISS

Paul Federn (1871–1950) was an Austrian psychologist who developed the field of ego psychology. He pioneered the concepts of "ego states" and "ego cathexis." Cathexis introduces the idea of bringing emotional energy to a part of the self-system. IFS often refers to this as gaining "self-energy."

Edoardo Weiss (1889–1970) was a student of Federn and completed Federn's manuscript *Ego Psychology and the Psychoses*.

JACOB MORENO AND PSYCHODRAMA

Jacob Moreno (1889–1974) was a contemporary of Freud and Jung, and he sought to bring the therapy couch into the real world. He had people act out their internal dynamics and inner conflict through theater-like role-plays. The interior world made up of multiple parts was represented in staged therapeutic events with others, often family members. Moreno believed that through play, people could access their unconscious mind and the various parts that inhabit it. Through role-playing and psychodrama, the patient could manipulate and correct internal conflicts and bring about resolution and healing. Moreno also worked with survivors of military trauma and was a pioneer of group therapy. His work was revolutionary as he introduced the idea that we could work out our internal issues through experiential activities with others.

[129] *SELF* is not well defined by Schwartz. It is described as a "field" or energy. All individual "Selves" are part of this greater SELF.

ERIC BERNE, TRANSACTIONAL ANALYSIS, AND THE KARPMAN DRAMA TRIANGLE

Eric Berne (1910–1970) was a Canadian psychologist who was influenced by Paul Federn and who analyzed people's social interactions and identified three "ego states" that people assumed: parent, child, and adult. He referred to the communication between two people's ego states as a transaction, and he referred to the patterns of communication as games.

I have found Berne's transactional analysis to be useful in strengthening the adult states when working with couples. For example, when a person acts like a child or assumes a child ego state with his or her spouse, it brings out the parent ego state in the person's spouse. Conversely, when a person acts like a parent with his or her spouse, it brings out the child ego state in that person's spouse. The goal for couples is to respond to each other from one adult ego state to another.

Although he identified only three parts, Berne's work introduced the dynamic between one's parts and others' parts.

Influenced by Eric Berne and developments in family therapy, Stephen Karpman introduced the "drama triangle" and identified three roles people play in dysfunctional relationships: victim, persecutor, and rescuer. Karpman was influenced by family therapy pioneer Murray Bowen's concept of triangulation.

VIRGINIA SATIR'S STANCES

Virginia Satir (1916–1988) was a brilliant pioneer in the field of marriage and family therapy. She identified negative "stances" that people adapt to handle challenges and stressors. They include a part that placates, a part that blames, a part that is super reasonable, and a part that says irrelevant things. These stances are ways to cope, and they represent the real problem. When we consider the situation or context and validate our own needs and the needs of others, we can resolve relational problems. Satir also believed in an internal drive interested in being more fully human and maintained that growth and change occur through relationships.

FRITZ PERLS, GESTALT, AND THE EMPTY CHAIR

Fritz Perls (1893–1970) developed Gestalt therapy, and its "empty chair" technique played an important role in the development of parts work and directly influenced Richard Schwartz's IFS. In this technique, the client role-plays speaking to someone from his past, an emotion, an attitude, or a part of himself. The client typically moves from one chair to the other as he takes on the role of the person or thing he is talking with.

ROBERTO ASSAGIOLI AND PSYCHOSYNTHESIS

Roberto Assagioli (1888–1974) was an Italian psychiatrist who helped develop the psychological movement known as psychosynthesis in the 1960s and 1970s. Although influenced by Freud's psychodynamic theories and understanding of the unconscious mind, he aligned best with Carl Jung, as he emphasized spiritual elements and the collective unconscious. Assagioli was a pioneer in modern parts work, identifying subpersonalities as different from the self. He saw these subpersonalities as existing within different layers of the unconscious mind. The lowest, most primitive level contains repressed memories, complexes, and dreams. This is where the most painful emotions, such as shame and fear, reside. The middle unconscious contains normal yet unconscious functioning, such as walking, dancing to a familiar jig, or exercising a routine skill. The higher unconscious refers to creative and inspired states of mind, full of insight. Assagioli developed a process to recognize, accept, coordinate, integrate, and synthesize these subpersonalities in order to discover the "transpersonal self." He was the first to develop a therapeutic approach to work with parts.

In Assagioli's model, the "I" reflects the self and exercises awareness and will. This is different from "Self" in the IFS model. The self here is a source of wisdom, guidance, and perhaps enlightenment, as it can exist in any part of the personality while being different from it. Although it is sometimes difficult to follow what Assagioli means by "I" and "self," his concepts seem to align well with Schwartz's understanding of "self" and "SELF" in Schwartz's book *No Bad Parts.*

THE INNER CHILD—CHARLES WHITFIELD, JOHN BRADSHAW, AND OTHERS

Inner-child work introduced the idea that within all of us is a wounded part that must be attended to now. Carl Jung first identified the divine child archetype, and Arthur and Vivian Janov further explored this in primal therapy in the 1970s. In 1987, physician and psychotherapist Charles Whitfield set out to heal the "child within" with his groundbreaking book *Healing the Child Within: Discovery and Recovery for Adult Children of Dysfunctional Families*. In the late 1980s, Penny Parks created a methodology for accessing and helping the inner child and for healing adults sexually abused as children. In 1991, psychologist and art therapist Lucia Capacchione introduced the idea of reparenting one's inner child and recognized the existence of an inner "critical parent." Self-help guru John Bradshaw popularized the movement in the 1990s. IFS posits that there may be more than one inner child in the form of multiple exiles.

JOHN AND HELEN WATKINS AND EGO STATE THERAPY (EST)

John Watkins (1913–2012) and Helen Watkins (1921–2002), influenced primarily by Paul Federn and the clinical hypnosis tradition, developed Ego State Therapy (EST) in the 1970s as an intentional parts-work approach. The Watkinses pioneered research in the areas of dissociation and multiple personality disorder (now called dissociative identity disorder).[130] They were also influenced by Berne's transactional analysis, Assagioli's psychosynthesis, and various Gestalt concepts. The mind includes a "family of selves" made up of subpersonalities, parts, or ego states. These ego states are natural, and they represent integrated neural pathways with their own thoughts and emotions. They speak in the first person, have a unique identity, adopt their own roles in the system, and can evolve

[130] It is important to note here that although we all naturally have parts of the self-system or ego states, the self and all the parts are aware of one another or can gain awareness of one another. In dissociative identity disorder, there are parts so disconnected from the system that there is no conscious memory of them. This is a rare, complex disorder.

and change. They may have been formed in childhood, but they do not go away. At times, an ego state may take the "executive" role and be in the driver's seat, so to speak. At other times, an ego state may be in close conscious awareness but not active in the system until needed or motivated to respond. Some ego states choose to be hidden and remain in the unconscious mind. EST also identifies inner strength states and introjects, which have specific roles and functions.

The goal of EST is to locate and treat unhealthy ego states, resolve conflicts between parts, and encourage positive communication between them. The therapist works with the ego states as she would with a family, using family systems principles. The therapist begins by connecting with the ego state (part) and aligning with the purpose of that part, listening to understand, and responding in a developmentally appropriate way, especially if she is working with a child ego state. The goal here is to collaborate and empathize with the ego state, recognizing that it has an adaptive purpose. In other words, the ego state or part learned to behave and respond in a certain way in order to survive. It did the best it could at the time. One goal of EST is to help the parts adapt in new ways. Once the therapist earns trust and a working relationship with the parts, she can use a trauma treatment approach, such as EMDR (Eye Movement Desensitization and Reprocessing) or Peter Levine's Somatic Experiencing.

JEFFREY YOUNG AND SCHEMA THERAPY

Jeffrey Young (1950–) is an American psychologist who was trained by Aaron Beck, the father of cognitive behavior therapy. Schema therapy incorporates object relations theory, cognitive behavior therapy, Gestalt therapy, and attachment theory. Young identified schemas, which are organized belief systems, and schema modes, which are "ways of being" or "modes of experience." Schema modes include the vulnerable child, the angry child, the impulsive child, the detached protector, the punitive parent, and the healthy adult.

RON KURTZ, PAT OGDEN, AND THE HAKOMI METHOD

Ron Kurtz developed the Hakomi Method in the 1970s, founded the Hakomi Institute in 1981, and later founded the Hakomi Education Network.

The Hakomi Method is a mindfulness-centered somatic psychotherapy heavily influenced by Eastern philosophy. Pat Ogden founded the Sensorimotor Psychotherapy Institute and identified various character strategies. From the work of Kurtz and Ogden, EMDR trainer Deborah Kennard then developed a series of relatable and user-friendly character types.[131] Similar to parts, these character types adapt to their environment in both positive and negative ways. An early adaptive response, such as working independently when no support is available, can turn into a problem when later in life we fail to ask for help when needed.

SUBPERSONALITIES, THE DIALOGICAL SELF, AND VOICE DIALOGUES

During the 1970s and 1980s, a number of parts-work approaches appeared. John Rowan (1925-2018) was a British psychologist who conducted workshops on subpersonalities at that time. He helped popularize the idea that parts (subpersonalities) were a normal feature of everyday psychological life. He contributed to the concept of the "dialogical self," which posits that the mind can imagine different parts having an internal dialogue. This concept was further developed by Hubert Hermans in the 1990s. Psychologists Hal and Sidra Stone developed the voice dialogues process in the 1970s with updates into the 1980s. They developed the idea of an "inner family," including the critic, the pleaser, the protector, and the vulnerable child. They used guided imagery to connect with subpersonalities, which they sometimes called "energy patterns." They referred to primary selves and disowned selves, which likely correspond to IFS managers and exiles.

RICHARD SCHWARTZ AND INTERNAL FAMILY SYSTEMS

Richard Schwartz is a marriage and family therapist who applied family systems theory and the "empty chair" technique to his work with trauma survivors and discovered that when clients were "in self," they were able to work with their

[131] For more information, please see https://emdr-training.net/wp-content/uploads/2019/10/Character-Types.pdf.

various dysfunctional parts and bring about healing and change. In his 1987 article "Our Multiple Selves: Applying Systems Thinking to the Inner Family," he cites Assagioli's psychosynthesis, Hal Stone's voice dialogues, and Sandra Watanabe's cast of characters. In later IFS texts, he references the work of John and Helen Watkins on ego states. Schwartz introduced the idea of unblending parts from the self in order to gain perspective and objectivity and the idea of unburdening parts — a process essential to allowing parts to let go of past wounds and unhealthy patterns of coping and adopt new ways to function. He identified that parts take on the roles of manager, firefighter, and exile. His Internal Family Systems has made parts work accessible and user-friendly.

Appendix D

A CRITIQUE OF *NO BAD PARTS*

One reason I set out to write this book was that, although I admire Richard Schwartz and his tremendous achievement with Internal Family Systems (IFS), I had growing questions and concerns about how compatible it is with Christian anthropology, philosophy, and theology. On the surface, there is a great deal of compatibility. The process of unblending, for example, feels like an extension of the ministry of Christ, who understands people, heals their wounds, and relieves them of their sins and life burdens. But there were other unanswered questions. Does the Self[132] need redemption in Christ? What is the role of sin, and is evil real? Is the Self the same as the soul? Is the idea of parts in the Bible? When Schwartz's book *No Bad Parts* was released, it became clear that Schwartz saw IFS as a spiritual movement, with unmistakable elements of Eastern religion, as found in Hinduism and Buddhism. It was important, then, for me to explore this to understand, clarify, discern, reevaluate, and possibly redefine or even rework my approach to parts work.

Christianity has a history of discerning truths from secular sources and even pre-Christian sources and filtering, applying, and integrating those truths

[132] Schwartz capitalizes the word *Self,* so I have capitalized it here when referring specifically to his usage. Otherwise, I prefer to use the term *inmost self* (innermost self, core self, or nous), which is more than the seat of consciousness; it is also the heart of the soul and the means by which we enjoy friendship with God. Although we are created in the image of God and aspire to theosis, we are nevertheless creatures, so I do not capitalize the word *self,* even when referring to the inmost self.

with divine revelation. We know, for example, that St. Augustine was influenced by the pre-Christian philosopher Plato. St. Thomas Aquinas was influenced by Plato's esteemed pupil Aristotle, whom he called "the Philosopher." Even without divine supernatural revelation, these philosophers were able to discover important truths in the natural realm using reason. The Second Vatican Council affirmed that, to varying degrees, there is some measure of truth in the major world religions. I will show that IFS, especially as articulated in Richard Schwartz's *No Bad Parts,* has the characteristics and qualities of a spirituality and a religion. This IFS religion is perhaps best described as a secularized, pantheistic, Western-style Eastern religion in the tradition of Buddhism, with possible influences from Hinduism and transcendental meditation. I will take my cue from Popes Paul VI and Benedict XVI in approaching IFS with respect while pointing out important differences and concerns.

In the Second Vatican Council's Declaration on the Relation of the Church to Non-Christian Religions, we find the following (emphasis mine):

> From ancient times down to the present, there is found among various peoples a certain perception of that hidden power which hovers over the course of things and over the events of human history; at times some indeed have come to the recognition of a Supreme Being, or even of a Father. This perception and recognition penetrates their lives with a profound religious sense.
>
> Religions, however, that are bound up with an advanced culture have struggled to answer the same questions by means of more refined concepts and a more developed language. Thus in Hinduism, men contemplate the divine mystery and express it through an inexhaustible abundance of myths and through searching philosophical inquiry. They seek freedom from the anguish of our human condition either through ascetical practices or profound meditation or a flight to God with love and trust. Again, Buddhism, in its various forms, realizes the radical insufficiency of this changeable world; it teaches a way by which men, in a devout and confident spirit, may be able either to acquire the state of perfect liberation, or attain, by their own efforts or through higher help, supreme illumination. Likewise, other religions found everywhere try

> to counter the restlessness of the human heart, each in its own manner, by proposing "ways," comprising teachings, rules of life, and sacred rites. *The Catholic Church rejects nothing that is true and holy in these religions.* She regards with sincere reverence those ways of conduct and of life, those precepts and teachings which, though differing in many aspects from the ones she holds and sets forth, nonetheless often *reflect a ray of that Truth which enlightens all men*. Indeed, she proclaims, and ever must proclaim Christ "the way, the truth, and the life,"[133] in whom men may find the fullness of religious life, in whom God has reconciled all things to Himself.
>
> The Church, therefore, exhorts her sons, that through dialogue and collaboration with the followers of other religions, carried out with prudence and love and in witness to the Christian faith and life, they recognize, preserve and promote the good things, spiritual and moral, as well as the socio-cultural values found among these men.[134]

In Pope Benedict XVI's apostolic exhortation on the Word of God in the life and mission of the Church, we find the following:

> Here too I wish to voice the Church's respect for the ancient religions and spiritual traditions of the various continents. These contain values which can greatly advance understanding between individuals and peoples. Frequently we note a consonance with values expressed also in their religious books, such as, in Buddhism, respect for life, contemplation, silence, simplicity; in Hinduism, the sense of the sacred, sacrifice and fasting; and again, in Confucianism, family and social values. We are also gratified to find in other religious experiences a genuine concern for the transcendence of God, acknowledged as Creator, as well as respect for life, marriage and the family, and a strong sense of solidarity.[135]

[133] John 14:6.

[134] Second Vatican Council, Declaration on the Relation of the Church to Non-Christian Religions *Nostra Aetate* (October 28, 1965), no. 2.

[135] Pope Benedict XVI, Post-Synodal Apostolic Exhortation *Verbum Domini* (September 30, 2010), no. 119.

It is important to emphasize that parts work — and, in particular, IFS — is a tremendous gift to the clinical mental health field and to the world at large. It is an approach that is transformative, effective, insightful, and life-changing.

We know that treatment approaches such as cognitive behavior therapy and mindfulness are effective in treating depression because we have seen their effectiveness in clinical experience and because they have been evaluated in numerous peer-reviewed research studies. Scores of individual therapists claim positive results with their own clients. In addition to this, numerous studies have demonstrated the effectiveness of this or that treatment compared with placebos or with this or that other treatment approach. In various ways, we know the approach works.

The same can be said of parts-based therapies, such as Internal Family Systems and Ego State Therapy. So many therapists, myself included, say that it works because they have seen the results. In addition to this, a growing body of research supports its effectiveness. Richard Schwartz has also made a number of claims about the Self, the SELF,[136] flow, and field energy. These are less clear, less clinically obvious, and less researched. Nevertheless, I think Schwartz is onto something — even though he is likely to disagree with me about exactly what he is "onto." I might argue that his own interpretation of his experience is influenced by his secular humanist background and his experience with transcendental meditation. There are philosophical assumptions operative behind these traditions that influence the way he understands the data.

EASTERN NON-CHRISTIAN CONCEPTS OF THE SELF

Before we examine key spiritual assertions in *No Bad Parts*, I think it is important to outline the ways in which the self is generally understood in Eastern religions. We need to keep in mind that these brief descriptions represent a snapshot and not a comprehensive exploration of the nuances of these religions. I will endeavor to capture the key points in order to compare and contrast with Christianity and with the position of Richard Schwartz in *No Bad Parts*.

[136] As mentioned earlier, "SELF" is not well defined by Schwartz. It is described as a "field" or energy. All individual "Selves" are part of this greater SELF.

Buddhism

Although Buddhism is a world religion with a developmental history and a divergence of views and practices, there are some basic tenets worth mentioning. There is disagreement about the existence of the soul in Buddhism. The self is understood as imaginary and false and leads to selfish desires. The teaching of "anatta" or "anatman" or "non-self" means that there is no permanence or ultimate individuality. The goal is to transcend the "self" and escape from attachments. The "enlightened self" or "great self" has self-control and is emotionally detached as he moves through different stages and rebirths. In order for one to progress, one's behavior must be ethical. The final stage, called "arahant," involves being self-less and recognizing that the self is an illusion. Once this stage is achieved, the person escapes the cycle of reincarnation and reaches nirvana. Nirvana is the state of pure happiness, detachment, and release. There is disagreement among Buddhists about whether nirvana is the true self.

There is a minority and later tradition within Buddhism that teaches that the essential nature in all living things is equivalent to the self. As we will see, this position is possibly the closest to Richard Schwartz's view in *No Bad Parts*.

Hinduism

Hinduism teaches that the soul or self is "atman," which is pure consciousness, and this implies post-body continuity. The atman is different from the ego, which does change, has no permanent essence, and is temporarily tied to a body and a mind. Like Buddhism, Hinduism teaches that the soul experiences rebirths and that advancing toward higher states is based on one's personal actions. Unlike Buddhism, Hinduism teaches that self-knowledge is the way to achieve liberation from the self. Some branches of Hinduism teach that nirvana is the union of the true self (atman) with the universe or with ultimate reality (brahman) or that nirvana is the discovery that the true self is the same as ultimate reality. This notion that the true self or the soul is essentially the same as ultimate reality correlates well with what Schwartz says about the Self and the SELF in *No Bad Parts*.

Transcendental Meditation

Transcendental Meditation (TM) is a meditation technique influenced by Hindu Vedic texts and developed in the 1950s by the yogi Maharishi Mahesh. This form of meditation claims to help people relieve stress and access higher states of consciousness. There is a belief that within the self we have an inexhaustible source of energy and creative intelligence, and this can guide us in living our lives. Like psychologist Carl Jung, TM teaches that there is a personal transcendental consciousness, a union of the conscious and unconscious minds, as well as a cosmic consciousness.

SCHWARTZ AND THE INFLUENCE OF EASTERN RELIGIOUS CONCEPTS

The influence of TM in *No Bad Parts* is most obvious in chapter 8, when Schwartz describes a "unified flow state" or a "wave state," which he compares to the Buddhist concept of anatta (no-self). In this state, he claims, we are not aware of the Self, and we operate blissfully independent of it as our parts "meld" and "temporarily dissolve."[137] This lands in direct conflict with the experience of Christian mystics and contemplative prayer. The individual personhood is not lost in union with God but is fully realized. Contemplative prayer involves an intimate relationship that brings joy, peace, faith, hope, and love. But there is no dissolution of self or melding with other selves. It is the beauty of the unique individuality within relationship that is precious.

Schwartz cites transpersonal psychologist Steve Taylor, who claims that there are commonalities in the experiences of all people who achieve this "flow state." These include "a sense that all things are one," a connection to a "much more stable, deep-rooted, and expansive self," compassion for all people, clarity, wisdom, calm, and "a vibrating energy … accompanied by a feeling of intense joy" as well as "diminished fear."[138] There is, of course, a great deal of truth in this. My clinical hypnosis training would call this a deep trance, focused

[137] Richard C. Schwartz, *No Bad Parts: Healing Trauma and Restoring Wholeness with the Internal Family Systems Model* (Boulder: Sounds True, 2021), 143.
[138] Ibid., 144.

attention, or positive dissociation. My religious training would perhaps call the "pure wave state" contemplative prayer, or hesychasm. Again, the important difference between these higher-consciousness wave states and Christian meditation practices and experiences is that, in Christianity, we connect with a personal God. We never lose our individuality. We are never absorbed in a sea of emptiness and extinguished in a state of nirvana. As Christians, we are instead sanctified in this life, and we look forward to being uniquely resurrected.

Everything Is Ultimately "One"

Schwartz highlights the theme of "oneness" as he cites the work of Kate Diebels and Mark Leary, who assert that "everything is fundamentally one," and that "separation among individual things is an illusion."[139] At this point, there can be no doubt that Schwartz is advocating for pantheism, which is the belief that all of reality is identical with God or with the universe and that there is no distinction between creature and Creator.

Schwartz describes the Self as a "spiritual essence within us and around us, like a field, that can quiet that thinking part of the brain."[140] This definition poses several problems for orthodox Christians. The inmost self, as I have described it, is the heart or the center of the uniquely created human person's soul. It can never be reduced to an impersonal "field" or elevated to a spiritual essence that is equivalent to divinity. This is exactly why one of the themes of this book is humility, which, properly understood, is a correct understanding of one's true worth. The paradox here is that, on one hand, we risk dehumanization when our self is destined to merge with an all-encompassing larger "SELF," and on the other hand, we risk committing the greatest form of arrogance by equating ourselves with God.

Schwartz notes that "we are sacred beings — as are our parts, as is the Earth";[141] this expresses some truth. God created the earth and said it was good, and all humans are created in His image. We are meant to be image-bearing stewards of this good creation. In this way, we can say that we are sacred, and

[139] Ibid., 146.
[140] Ibid., 145.
[141] Ibid., 150.

the earth is sacred. But is it correct to identify our parts as beings? Is the earth a being? Our parts, as aspects, dimensions, modes of being, or ego states, cannot have a separate ontological existence apart from the inmost self or distinct from the human person. We can say that parts have a phenomenological reality in that we subjectively experience them, but they are not separate and distinct entities. Therefore, we say they are parts of the self-system. The earth is part of creation, but it does not have a separate existence as a person, and it does not have a consciousness of its own. This matters in two important ways. First, in *No Bad Parts*, there's a fundamental denial of the significance of evil and the reality of our fallen world. Second, Schwartz seems to be making a case that all of creation is divine and that we are all one nature.

Schwartz goes on to describe the Self as a "drop of the divine within" which is not frightened by "apparent" evil as it pursues its goal of healing the interior world.[142] If the Self is a "drop of the divine within," then the Self and whatever counts as divinity is the same substance. The distinction between Creator and creation is blurred. And since Schwartz claims that we are essentially divine, we need not be intimidated by evil. In fact, he says "apparent evil," as if to suggest it might not be real anyway. Healing and transforming the inner world are, of course, very good things. As Christians, we would call this sanctification. But there's no need to sanctify something that is already sacred and only apparently but not really evil. This is a denial of both the Fall of man and the reality of our fallen world. Once you deny the Fall, you no longer have any need for a Savior. The entire reason for Christ's being is wiped out.[143] And we don't really need God because we are, in fact, mini "God droplets." As Christians, however, we don't want to be so fearful of and obsessed with evil that we deny the triumph and glory of the work of Christ, nor do we want to be so naïve as to downplay the dreadful seriousness of evil in the world and in the hearts of men.[144]

[142] Ibid., 162.

[143] There are some Christian theologians who argue that Christ would still have become incarnate even without the Fall. Even if this speculation is accurate, Christ would not have come as a Savior. Since we did experience a Fall, we cannot deny the need for a Savior or deny the reality of evil.

[144] Genesis 6:5: "The LORD saw that the wickedness of humankind was great in the earth, and that every inclination of the thoughts of their hearts was only evil

SCHWARTZ AND THE BODY

It is good that Schwartz doesn't minimize or demonize the body. He implies that there are religious groups that do this, and he is right about that. The early Church heresies of Gnosticism and Manichaeism believed that the body was created by an evil god and that it was the goal of the human to escape the body and become a pure spirit. The Catholic Church formally affirms that the body and the soul make up the whole human person and that both will be glorified in the world to come. In affirming the two natures of Christ, human and divine, we affirm the inherent goodness of the body. In the account of God's creating the world, we read several times, "God saw that it was good." And we read of the creation of Adam and Eve: "So God created humankind in his image, in the image of God he created them; male and female he created them" (Gen. 1:27). One hopes that Schwartz is affirming Catholic teaching when he describes the body as a "sacred temple."[145] St. Paul reminds the Corinthians in his letter, "Do you not know that your body is a temple of the Holy Spirit?" (1 Cor. 6:19). It is perhaps worth noting that Schwartz uses the phrase "temple of spirit," which implies an indwelling "force" or "field," whereas the Christian phrase "temple of the Holy Spirit" refers to a divine Person, a personal God. Christians understand that God does indeed dwell within their inmost selves — not as a ball of benign energy but in a loving, intimate relationship. This love is difficult to define because it transcends the usual definitions of love, such as *storge,* or familial love; *eros,* or desire; *caritas,* or charity; and *philia,* or friendship. The New Testament often uses the word *agape,* which means unconditional love. It has the quality of two lovers, a bride and groom, in a deep mutual appreciation, but it also has the quality of complete self-donation, as manifested in the Cross.

THE SELF AND LOVE

Love, then, implies a desire for the good of the other, and we see this when Schwartz says, "When you can love all your parts, you can love all people." He

continually" (Gen. 6:5). "Jesus, perceiving their thoughts, said, 'Why do you think evil in your hearts?' " (Matt. 9:4).

[145] Schwartz, *No Bad Parts,* 171.

goes on to say that loving your parts helps you "feel connected to the Earth" as you combat exploitation by other parts. This, in turn, increases the "field of self," heals the planet, and connects one to SELF.[146] Schwartz once again accesses some essential elements of truth while missing the mark. I'm not sure about the truth of the logic that in loving all your parts, you can love all people. It resonates with Christ's command to love others as you love yourself (Mark 12:31). In my mind, however, there still needs to be an act of the will to love people and embrace others, especially those who may not be easy to love. The Christian understanding of love would say that it is self-giving and sacrificial. Schwartz says that if you lead your life from Self, you will feel connected to the earth and want to save it; your "field of self" will expand; and you will be connected to SELF. The only way I can think of "SELF" is to think of God, who is the Author of, and distinct and different from, the rest of creation. As I conceive of the inmost self, I see it as the core of my being, which is relational, connected, and compassionate. The SELF, which Schwartz leaves rather undefined, must at least be relational and loving. It cannot be an impersonal "force," like the one in *Star Wars*. And yet that is exactly what he makes it out to be.

Schwartz explains how each Self is part of the larger SELF and how, as the Self acts, it causes harmony among people and contributes to the growth and potency of the larger SELF.[147] So Schwartz identifies the SELF as a correlate to the person's Self, but he is not quite comfortable identifying it as a personal and loving God; instead, it is a kind of "field." According to Schwartz, our inner Selves are part of a bigger SELF which is a field (my inner *Star Wars* fan wants to say "force") that covers the earth and perhaps the universe itself.

Schwartz sees Self and parts as "contagious" and "aspects of fields." He describes the planet Earth as a "living, sentient organism" affected by the way we treat it and other people. He specifically mentions "right-wing nationalist leaders" as contributing to a "dark field" that in some way covers the planet.[148] And here we find several problematic conclusions for the Christian reader. Again, we find that the planet Earth is anthropomorphized into a "sentient" or

[146] Schwartz, *No Bad Parts*, 186.

[147] Ibid., 187–188.

[148] Ibid., 188.

conscious being, which it is not. But why does Schwartz want to suggest this? In this view, the earth is an innocent sacred "person" that we must fight for in the battle between good and evil. There is a political message thrown in about right-wing ideologies, identified with the "dark field" that is enveloping whole countries. It is the good and sacred unblended "Self," united with others, who is compelled to save the planet. I suppose there are elements of this position that might resonate with some Christians. There is a program of evil, oppressive leaders and ideologies, and inhumane treatment of people and destruction of the planet. As Christians, we are called to build the kingdom by freeing captives, being good stewards of the earth, and challenging evildoers. But the earth is not a sacred being equated with the divine. The earth is part of creation and is not sentient. And there isn't a "dark field" enveloping countries. According to Schwartz, we defeat evil by expanding our good energies into a positive network of love as we and others experience unburdening. This process allows for the negative field to decrease and the planet's positive field to increase.[149] Not only is this reworked Manichaeism,[150] but it is unscientific and unproven to suggest that there is a kind of planetary "energy level" that we influence when we unburden our parts.

Schwartz sees the importance of unburdening not only our individual parts but nations and cultures. He does emphasize the importance of individual unburdening of things such as racism and sexism in order to achieve greater goals. He then claims that our parts need to feel securely attached to the Self, to the planet, and to the SELF; otherwise, our protectors will continue to focus on power and materialism, and we will continue to abuse the earth.[151] I think this is fascinating, since I have long advocated that we need to develop a secure attachment with God and build trust among parts and increase inner harmony.

[149] Ibid., 188.

[150] Manichaeism is a complex, dualistic, Gnostic heresy that appeared in the third century AD. It saw the world as a struggle between the equal powers of good (light) and evil (darkness). Material things, including the body, were evil. The way to escape the material world was through secret knowledge. St. Augustine of Hippo describes his experience with Manichaeism in his autobiography (*The Confessions*).

[151] Ibid., 188–189.

The Litanies of the Heart were written with this in mind. I don't believe, however, that we can have secure attachment with the planet Earth, no matter how hard we try to anthropomorphize it. And I don't believe we can have secure attachment with an impersonal, nebulous "SELF" if by "SELF" we mean "the force" or some kind of "field." If we understand this "SELF" as a personal God who is distinct from us — namely, the Judeo-Christian God — then, yes, we can be securely attached once we come to know and love God and feel His love. But Schwartz's understanding of "SELF" doesn't allow for this.

Schwartz emphasizes that the Self is to feel connected to its parts, others, and the planet. He describes people as "sacred beings." As we receive direction from the SELF, we become less materialistic, and we "relax and slow down." In this way, "we increase the field of Self on the planet and work to reduce the fields of burdens that engulf it."[152] It is fascinating that Schwartz says that the SELF can give "wise guidance" and that it is a higher level of consciousness. Again, if we understand "SELF" as a personal and loving God, then this is possible. If this SELF, however, is just a larger extension of all of our "Selves," then Schwartz has equated us with the divine. If "SELF" and each individual expression of "Self" are the same substance, then we have a kind of pantheism. At a very basic level, Christianity distinguishes the Creator from creation. What Schwartz proposes here is the same sin described in Genesis that caused the Fall of humankind. "But the serpent said to the woman, 'You will not die; for God knows that when you eat of it your eyes will be opened, and you will be like God, knowing good and evil' " (Gen. 3:4–5). The intentions may be good, but equating Creator and creation is the very sin of pride. It also evokes a kind of Pelagianism, according to which we believe that by our own efforts alone we can transform and literally save ourselves and consequently the whole world.

But aren't we, as Christians created in His image, redeemed by His Son, and meant to transform the world and usher in His kingdom? Is the difference semantic and the project not the same? Here I will agree that some truths are contained in Schwartz's vision. I also believe it is possible for God to work in and through IFS and other approaches, even if they are philosophically or

[152] Ibid., 189.

theologically imprecise and contain error. So why is this important? Why is it necessary to mince words and point out difficulties if the project is sound overall?

I would argue that the project is a powerful therapeutic modality that overlaps with and can perhaps enhance some spiritual practices, but it is not sound overall. We cannot create a utopia out of our fallen world by our mere human efforts. As Christians, we recognize our complete dependence on God to save us from the evil in this world and from our own personal sin. Even though IFS and other parts-work approaches have the ability to improve lives, relationships, families, and communities and perhaps even have a positive effect in the geopolitical sphere, they do not have the ability to save souls or bring about the kingdom of God. We can, however, adapt IFS and other similar approaches, recognize what is good and useful in them, and reject what is problematic.

Appendix E

WHO'S WHO IN THE HISTORY OF THE CHRISTIAN PARTS-WORK MODEL

A Christian parts-work approach must be grounded in both the psychological sciences and the Christian tradition. This list includes key figures who have influenced the development of parts work in general as well as parts work from a Christian perspective.

Assagioli, Roberto (1888–1974): An Italian psychiatrist who developed psychosynthesis. He is a pioneer of modern parts work and identified subpersonalities. He identified a process to discover the "transpersonal self." The self is a source of wisdom, guidance, and enlightenment.

Anthony of the Desert (251–356): A Catholic saint and monk from Egypt and one of the founders of Christian monasticism. He left the safety of the city to live alone in the desert, where he battled both external and internal threats. The desert can be understood as an analogy for the unconscious mind and the interior world. Anthony was able to find a sense of peace and inner harmony through the ascetical life.

Aristotle (384–322 BC): A Greek philosopher and student of Plato. His teachings influenced Christian medieval philosophy and ethics, especially those of St. Thomas Aquinas, who called him "the Philosopher." Aristotle's writings on the virtues influenced later Christian writers.

Athanasius of Alexandria (296–373): A Catholic saint and Doctor of the Church who defended Christianity against the heresy Arianism. He described the soul as a mirror reflecting the image of God. St. Athanasius also suggested that the soul can be either brightened or clouded. When brightened, it beholds God the Father and the Word. When clouded, it cannot adequately access its divine intelligence and corresponding teaching. This corresponds well with the IFS notion of blending and unblending.

Augustine of Hippo (354–430): A Catholic saint and Doctor of the Church who was a bishop, theologian, and philosopher. He is well known for his conversion story, described in his autobiography, *The Confessions,* and for his book *The City of God.* St. Augustine affirms not only God's great love and mercy but also His love for the unrepentant sinner. Augustine recognized the existence of both "inward" and "higher" parts. He identified that we have a divided soul with "split hearts." Holiness involves unifying ourselves under God and seeing in Him our true selves. For St. Augustine, God does not just return us to Eden; He elevates us to Heaven.

Basil the Great (320–379): A Catholic saint, and one of the three great Cappadocian Fathers, who present a very positive view of humankind. He alluded to the idea of the soul as an "inner hospital." St. Basil makes a distinction between God's image and God's likeness in man. The idea here is that God's image is inherent in man's nature, whereas God's likeness is something that is not yet fully realized. There is a foundation, but it must be developed. The image is fulfilled in the likeness.

Benedict of Nursia (480–547): A Catholic saint who wrote the *Rule of Saint Benedict* and is considered the founder of Western Christian monasticism. He was a pioneer in the development of *Lectio Divina* (meditating on Scripture) and praying the Liturgy of the Hours. He taught the value of "being with oneself" and seeking inner integration primarily through cultivating virtue.

Berne, Eric (1910–1970): A Canadian psychologist influenced by Paul Federn. He identified three ego states: parent, child, and adult. He is the founder of transactional analysis.

Bowen, Murray (1913–1990): An American psychiatrist who was a pioneer in family therapy and systems theory. Family systems theory inspired Richard Schwartz and others to recognize an internal system made up of parts within each person.

Bowlby, John (1907–1990): A British psychiatrist and the originator of attachment theory. Attachment theory helps us understand how we can develop a secure relationship based on seeing, knowing, encouraging, and delighting in one another. The inmost self, like a loving parent, develops secure attachment with all the parts. In turn, the human person can love God and others more fully.

Bradshaw, John (1933–2016): An American educator and motivational speaker who popularized the concept of the "wounded inner child."

Capacchione, Lucia (1937–2022): An Italian American psychologist and art therapist who introduced the idea of reparenting one's inner child. She also identified a "critical parent" role.

Cassian, John (360–445): A Catholic saint, monk, and theologian. He identified ten signs of humility: giving up control, vulnerability, willingness to change, obedience, patience, simplicity or detachment, a nonjudgmental attitude toward others, self-control, gentleness, and compassion for others. He is credited with bringing the Eastern monastic tradition to Western Christianity. He was influenced by Evagrius Ponticus, but he emphasized the role of grace as well as prayer as a movement of the heart.

Cook, Alison (U/A): An American psychologist, podcaster, and author. She wrote *The Best of You* and *Boundaries for Your Soul* and incorporated a faith-based approach to IFS.

Crete, Gerry (1969–): A Catholic professional counselor and marriage and family therapist. He is an IFS-informed EMDR consultant and has received training in Ego State Therapy, clinical hypnosis, and emotionally focused therapy. He is a co-founder of Souls and Hearts and the author of the Litanies of the Heart. He coined the term "original trauma" and provided a comprehensive examination of parts work with the biblical and Christian tradition.

Dionysius the (Pseudo) Areopagite (sixth century): A Greek Christian mystical theologian of the sixth century who presented himself as St. Paul's convert Dionysius, mentioned in Acts 17:34. His writings influenced many medieval writers, including St. Maximus the Confessor, St. John of Damascus, and St. Gregory Palamas.

Evagrius Ponticus (345–399): A Christian monk and ascetic who developed the concepts of *logismoi* (overthinking, evil thoughts, temptations) and *apatheia* (detachment) and the importance of tears for being open to God. His writings influenced Pope Gregory the Great in forming his list of the seven deadly sins.

Federn, Paul (1871–1950): An Austrian psychologist who developed the field of ego psychology. He described an "ego state" as a subpersonality that assumes a part of normal functioning. He developed the idea of "ego cathexis," which can be equated with "self-energy." Federn also taught that the stronger the ego, the better the boundaries the person will have with others and with his own id.

Ferrucci, Piero (1946–): An Italian psychologist and student of Roberto Assagioli. He was a staff member at the Psychosynthesis Institute of Florence.

Fraser, George A. (1941–): A Canadian psychiatrist who developed the dissociative table technique. The dissociative table is an internal meeting place for the parts of the self. Fraser is the author of *The Dilemma of Ritual Abuse: Cautions and Guides for Therapists*.

Frederick, Claire (1932–2015): An American psychiatrist who integrated hypnoanalysis and Ego State Therapy. She and Maggie Phillips built on the work of the Watkinses and developed a foundational intervention model for Ego State Therapy.

Freud, Sigmund (1856–1939): The father of modern psychoanalysis. He identified the id, the ego, and the superego and described the existence of an unconscious mind.

Gregory the Great (540–604): A Catholic saint, pope, Doctor of the Church, and Latin Church Father who initiated many missions to convert pagans. He is associated with Gregorian chant and is credited with listing the seven capital virtues as remedies for the seven deadly sins.

Gregory of Nazianzus (329–389): A Catholic saint and one of the three great Cappadocian Fathers, who present a very positive view of humankind. We are created in God's image, and despite the Fall, we are destined to become like Christ. Our true human nature reflects God's divinity in that we have a rational soul, free will, and the capacity for compassion. St. Gregory posits that our pre-fallen state is naturally virtuous and that a restoration is possible in Christ.

Gregory of Nyssa (ca. 332–395): A Catholic saint and one of the three great Cappadocian Fathers. St. Gregory refers to the soul's "elements" or "impulses," which can correspond to parts of the self-system.

Hubert Hermans (1937–): A Dutch psychologist and developer of Dialogical Self Theory. He described the relationships between different I-positions within the dialogical self of the individual person in the landscape of the mind.

Honeycutt, Julie (1978–): A certified IFS therapist who specializes in counseling and teaching with a Christian approach to the IFS model of therapy.

Ignatius of Loyola (1491–1556): A Catholic saint and the founder of the Society of Jesus (the Jesuits). He developed the Spiritual Exercises — an experiential approach to developing secure attachment with God and cultivating holy indifference.

James, William (1842–1910): The father of American psychology. He described the "social self," "the material self," and the "spiritual self." He identified a "pure ego" as different from these "selves."

John of the Cross (1542–1591): A Catholic saint, Doctor of the Church, Carmelite priest, and medieval mystic. His poetry is considered a beautiful and profound exploration into the interior world of the soul.

Jung, Carl (1875–1961): A Swiss psychologist mentored by Sigmund Freud. He discussed a "true self" different from the ego. He developed concepts such as individuation, collective unconscious, the shadow, complexes, and archetypes.

Karpman, Stephen (1942–): A American psychiatrist influenced by Murray Bowen and Eric Berne. He developed the "drama triangle," which includes the roles of victim, persecutor, and rescuer.

Kempen, Harry (1937–2000): A Dutch cultural psychologist who helped develop Dialogical Self Theory. He and Hubert Hermans published *The Dialogical Self: Meaning as Movement*.

Kurtz, Ron (1934–2011): A psychologist who founded the Hakomi Method in 1981. This method was influenced by Ericksonian hypnosis, neuro-linguistic programming (NLP), Buddhism, and Taoism and focuses on body-centered psychotherapy and mindfulness. Kurtz and later researchers developed character types, which correspond to parts of the self-system.

LaCroix, Molly (U/A): A marriage and family therapist and speaker and the author of two books integrating the IFS model and aspects of Christianity: *Restoring Relationship: Transforming Fear into Love through Connection* and *Journey to Shalom: Finding Healing, Wholeness, and Freedom in Sacred Stories*.

Lemke, Wendy (U/A): A licensed psychologist and co-founder of Ego State Therapy International. She is a recognized global expert in clinical hypnosis, Ego State Therapy, and trauma-related disorders. She wrote and produced the DVD *You're Not Crazy and You're Not Alone: Inside the Inner World of Dissociative Identity Disorder* and has also produced self-hypnosis CDs.

Malinoski, Peter (1969–): A Catholic psychologist, founder of Secure Foundations, co-founder of Souls and Hearts, and host of the influential podcast *Interior Integration for Catholics*. He is a thought leader in the integration of Catholic spirituality and IFS.

Martin, Peter (1975–): A Catholic psychologist and therapist trained in IFS and EMDR. He is a thought leader in the integration of Catholic spirituality and attachment theory. He is the internship director of Integrated Training and Formation at Immaculate Heart of Mary Counseling Center in Lincoln, Nebraska — the only Catholic APA-accredited doctoral internship site in the United States.

Maximus the Confessor (580–662): A Catholic saint, monk, theologian, and scholar. He was born in Constantinople and lived at various times in Asia Minor, North Africa, and Rome. Against the Monothelite heresy, he defended the orthodox teaching on Jesus' two wills (divine and human). He was especially influenced by Evagrius Ponticus, Dionysius the Areopagite, and the Cappadocian Fathers. Maximus saw divine union as a union of love. He understood the human person to be a microcosm analogous to the larger universe. He also described man as a workshop and as a mediator and thought that man was to bring his divided extremes into a harmonious unity.

Merton, Thomas (1915–1968): A Cistercian monk, priest, writer, and mystic at the Abbey of Gethsemani. He is known for his conversion story in *The Seven Storey Mountain* (1948) as well as numerous books about contemplative prayer. His later works were influenced by his exploration of Eastern religions. He distinguished between a true self and a false self.

Miller, Kimberly (1974–): A licensed marriage and family therapist, speaker, and retreat leader who specializes in the integration of psychology and spirituality. She is the founder of Leading Wholeheartedly ministry and co-author of *Boundaries for Your Soul*.

Moreno, Jacob (1889–1974): Romanian American psychiatrist who used theater-style role-plays to enact client internal dynamics and inner conflicts. He is considered a father of group counseling.

Nouwen, Henri (1932–1996): A Dutch Catholic priest, writer, and theologian who wrote *Life of the Beloved*, which reaffirms the identity of the Christian as the beloved of God.

Ogden, Pat (1950–): An expert in trauma and the pioneer of sensorimotor psychotherapy, a body-centered approach. She co-founded the Hakomi Institute and developed character strategies.

Ornstein, Robert (1942–2018): An American psychologist who taught at Langley Porter Neuropsychiatric Institute and Stanford University. He was an expert in the study of the brain and consciousness.

Parks, Penny (1943–2020): An expert in the field of child abuse who developed a therapy for working with the inner child. Her book *Rescuing the "Inner Child"* was published in 1990.

Paul of Tarsus (5–65): A Catholic saint and author of multiple biblical letters. He was a Pharisee who converted to Christianity, became an evangelist, and founded multiple churches in Asia Minor and Europe. He is considered the Apostle to the Gentiles. St. Paul speaks of the "inmost self," which delights in the law of God, and he refers to inner "members" at war with the law of his mind.

Paulsen, Sandra (1952–): An American psychologist who specializes in the treatment of complex trauma and dissociation. She developed Neuroaffective Embodied Self-Therapy (N.E.S.T.) — which integrates EMDR, somatic and ego state therapies — and the early trauma approach. She is the author of *When There Are No Words: Repairing Early Trauma and Neglect in the Attachment Period* (2017) and *Looking Through the Eyes of Trauma and Dissociation: An Illustrated Guide for EMDR Therapists and Clients* (2009).

Perls, Fritz (1893–1970): The founder of Gestalt therapy. He developed the "empty chair" technique, which influenced Richard Schwartz's understanding of parts.

Phillips, Maggie (U/A–2021): An American psychologist and expert in Ego State Therapy. She was the director of the California Institute of Clinical Hypnosis and specialized in applying Ericksonian approaches to the treatment of trauma. She and Claire Frederick built on the work of the Watkinses and developed a foundational intervention model for Ego State Therapy.

Plato (428–347 BC): Greek philosopher who taught Aristotle. His understanding of the forms and the soul influenced the development of Christian philosophy. In the *Theaetetus,* he describes our thinking as an inner conversation between the soul and the self.

Riemersma, Jenna (U/A): A professional counselor and author of *Altogether You: Experiencing Personal and Spiritual Transformation with Internal Family Systems Therapy*. She integrates Christianity with IFS.

Rowan, John (1925–2018): An English psychologist who was an expert in humanistic and transpersonal psychology as well as integrative psychotherapy. He was a pioneer in the study of the dialogical self and subpersonalities.

Satir, Virginia (1916–1988): An American psychotherapist and pioneer in the field of marriage and family therapy. She developed conjoint family therapy and identified "stances" that people adopt to handle challenges and stressors.

Schwartz, Richard (1949–): A marriage and family therapist who developed Internal Family Systems in the 1980s. He founded the Center for Self Leadership in 2000. He was influenced by family systems theory and the Gestalt "empty chair" technique as well as by Roberto Assagioli, Robert Ornstein, Hal Stone, and Sandra Watanabe. He developed the therapeutic process of unblending and unburdening and the three types of parts: managers, firefighters, and exiles. Schwartz also developed the idea of a universal SELF.

Shapiro, Francine (1948–2019): An American psychologist and the originator of EMDR therapy.

Steege, Mary (1961–): A marriage and family therapist, certified IFS therapist, and a Presbyterian pastor. She wrote *The Spirit-Led Life: A Christian Encounter with Internal Family Systems,* which includes an interview with Richard Schwartz.

Stone, Hal (1927–2020), and Stone, Sidra (1937–): Psychologists Hal and Sidra Stone developed the voice dialogues process in the 1970s to work with subpersonalities and developed the system of psychology of selves. They identified an "inner family" that included protectors, critics, pleasers, and a vulnerable child.

Teresa of Ávila (1515–1582): A Catholic saint, Doctor of the Church, Carmelite nun, and medieval mystic. She is considered an expert in mental prayer, meditation, and contemplation. Her seminal work, *The Interior Castle,* describes the soul as a collection of mansions with Christ at the center. She experienced phenomena described as ecstasies, raptures, and levitation.

Thomas Aquinas (1225–1274): A Catholic saint, Doctor of the Church, and Dominican friar who is considered by some to be the greatest Catholic philosopher and theologian. He is known as the Angelic Doctor and attempted to synthesize Aristotelian philosophy with Christianity. His most famous work is the *Summa Theologica*.

Watanabe (Hammond), Sandra (1943–): Co-founder and faculty member of the Boston Family Institute. She describes the personality as including an internal system made up of characters with interrelationships.

Watkins, Helen (1921–2002): A psychotherapist and founder of the International Society for the Study of Dissociation. She co-founded Ego State Therapy with her husband, John Watkins.

Watkins, John (1913–2012): The founder of Ego State Therapy. Influenced by Paul Federn, he was a pioneer in understanding dissociation and multiple personality disorder (dissociative identity disorder). He was influenced by Berne's transactional analysis and Assagioli's psychosynthesis as well as many Gestalt concepts. He described a "family of selves" made up of subpersonalities, parts, or ego states.

Whitfield, Charles (1938–2021): A physician and psychotherapist who developed the concept of the "child within" in the book *Healing the Child Within: Discovery and Recovery for Adult Children of Dysfunctional Families*. He was an expert in the field of childhood trauma and addiction recovery.

Weiss, Edoardo (1889–1970): An Italian psychoanalyst and student of Paul Federn. He introduced the idea of "psychic presence," a mental awareness of an internalized image of another part or ego state, such as a parent.

Young, Jeffrey (1950–): An American cognitive psychologist who developed schema therapy, which integrates cognitive psychology, Gestalt therapy, and attachment theory and has been primarily used to treat personality disorders. Schema modes correspond in many ways to parts of the self-system.

Appendix F

A TIMELINE FOR THE PSYCHOLOGY OF THE SELF AND OUR PARTS

This timeline follows the history and development of the psychology of the inmost self and our parts (multiple selves, ego states, and subpersonalities), with consideration for biblical and theological contributions.

50s — St. Paul the Apostle describes his inner conflict and identifies the inmost self.

400 — St. Augustine of Hippo writes *The Confessions* and describes "split hearts."

640 — St. Maximus the Confessor understands the inner world of the human person to be a microcosm of the universal. He describes man as a mediator, created in God's image, to bring about internal and external unity in Christ. He describes inner "extremes" that are divided and need to be brought into unity.

1274 — St. Thomas Aquinas describes the connection between internal unity and self-love. He says that a man must be a friend to himself. St. Thomas draws on Aristotle and describes the "powers" of the human person as the sensitive soul, the intellectual soul, and the nutritive soul.

1577 — St. Teresa of Ávila writes *The Interior Castle*, which describes the soul as an interior world made up of many mansions. The inmost, seventh mansion, at the heart of the castle, is a place of union with God in a mystical marriage.

1890 — The founder of American psychology, William James, identifies the social, material, and spiritual "selves." He also identifies a "pure ego," which equates with the "self."

1911–1950s — Psychiatrist Carl Jung identifies complexes and archetypes as well as a "true self" different from the ego.

1923 — The founder of psychoanalysis, Sigmund Freud, identifies the id, the ego, and the superego.

1920 — Mikhail Bakhtin uses the metaphor of the polyphonic novel and the works of Dostoyevsky to describe characters who represent a multiplicity within a unified world. This would later inspire Hubert Hermans, Harry Kempen, and Rens van Loon to apply this to the inner world and develop the concept of the dialogical self.

1920s — Psychiatrist Paul Federn develops ego psychology and describes ego states as subpersonalities. He also identifies self-energy as ego cathexis.

1961 — Trappist monk Thomas Merton describes the conflict between the true self and the false self.

1964 — Psychoanalyst Edoardo Weiss further develops ego psychology and identifies a mental awareness of an internalized image of an ego state.

1950s, 1964, 1976 — Psychiatrist Eric Berne develops the theory of transactional analysis and identifies parent, child, and adult ego states.

1965 — Psychiatrist Roberto Assagioli develops psychosynthesis and identifies the transpersonal self and subpersonalities.

1976, 1979, 1997 — Psychologists John and Helen Watkins develop Ego State Therapy from psychodynamic theory and clinical hypnosis. They identify concepts such as the hidden observer (self), the executive state, protectors, child states, adult states, and other ego states as subpersonalities.

1972, 1978 — Marriage and family therapist Virginia Satir develops conjoint family therapy, identifies character "stances," and writes about having "many faces."

1970s, 1985 — Psychologists Hal and Sidra Stone develop voice dialogues and describe multiple "selves" that lived in an "inner family."

1976, 1990, 2002 — Ron Kurtz and Pat Ogden identify character types and strategies.

1986 — Occupational therapist Sandra Karen Watanabe describes a "cast of characters" as an internal system.

1986 — Neurologist Robert Ornstein describes the mind as diverse and including multiple "minds."

1987 — Psychologist Michael Gazzaniga identifies the brain as having "modules."

1987 — Medical doctor Charles Whitfield focuses on healing the inner child.

1987, 2001 — Marriage and family therapist Richard Schwartz develops Internal Family Systems as he applies family systems theory to the internal system and introduces concepts of unblending and unburdening.

1990 — Psychologist John Rowan describes the history of subpersonalities (parts work).

1990 — Psychologist Jeffrey Young develops schema therapy, which includes schema states.

1992 — Dutch psychologist Hubert Hermans, influenced by William James and Mikhail Bakhtin, develops dialogical self theory, which describes a "society of mind" and "self-positions" and focuses on the relationships between participants of an inner dialogue.

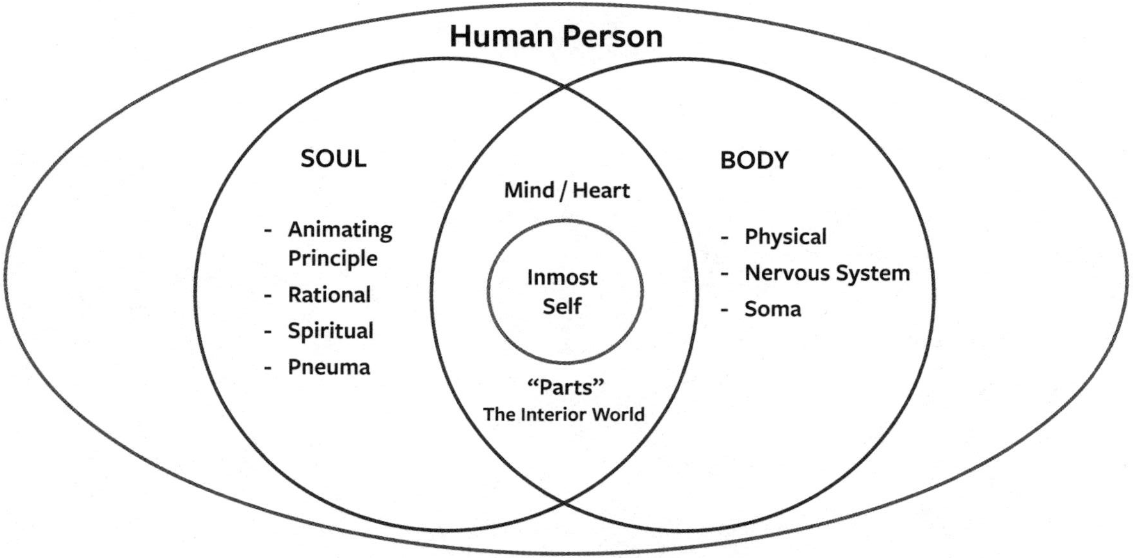

The "I" of "Self" is the subjective reality of the conscious person

Mind / Heart:

- Parts
- Cognitive Faculties
- Emotions (Affectivity)
- Desires
- Appetites
- Virtues and Vices
- Memories and Imagination
- Perception and Sensation
- Passions
- The Will

Inmost Self:

- Dwelling Place of Christ
- Mirror of the Soul/Eye of the Heart/Nous
- Recollection (Unites with God)
- Wisdom, Truth, Love/Compassion
- Conscience

BIBLIOGRAPHY

Acklin, Thomas, and Boniface Hicks. *Spiritual Direction: A Guide for Sharing the Father's Love*. Steubenville, OH: Emmaus Road Publishing, 2018.

Anderson, Gary. *Sin: A History*. New Haven, CT: Yale University Press, 2009.

Assagioli, Roberto. *The Act of Will*. New York: Penguin Books, 1973.

———. *Psychosynthesis*. New York: Penguin Books, 1965.

Benedict XVI, Pope. Post-Synodal Apostolic Exhortation *Verbum Domini* (September 20, 2010).

Berne, Eric. *Games People Play: The Basic Handbook of Transactional Analysis*. New York: Ballantine Books, 1964.

Blowers, Paul M. *Maximus the Confessor: Jesus Christ and the Transfiguration of the World*. Christian Theology in Context. Oxford, UK: Oxford University Press, 2018. Kindle.

Brady, Bernard V. *Christian Love: How Christians through the Ages Have Understood Love*. Washington, DC: Georgetown University Press, 2003.

Brown, Daniel P., and David S. Elliott. *Attachment Disturbances in Adults: Treatment for Comprehensive Repair*. New York: W. W. Norton, 2016.

Casey, Michael. *A Guide to Living in the Truth: Saint Benedict's Teaching on Humility*. Liguori, MO: Liguori Publications, 1999.

Catechism of the Catholic Church. 2nd ed. Washington, DC: United States Conference of Catholic Bishops, 2019. https://www.usccb.org/sites/default/files/flipbooks/catechism/II/.

Cook, Alison, and Kimberly Miller. *Boundaries for Your Soul: How to Turn Your Overwhelming Thoughts and Feelings into Your Greatest Allies*. Nashville: Thomas Nelson, 2018.

Cooper-White, Pamela. *Braided Selves: Collected Essays on Multiplicity, God, and Persons*. Eugene, OR: Cascade Books, 2011.

Earley, Jay. *Self-Therapy: A Step-By-Step Guide to Creating Wholeness and Healing Your Inner Child Using IFS, a New, Cutting-Edge Psychotherapy*. 2nd ed. Larkspur, CA: Pattern System Books, 2009.

Federn, Paul. *Ego Psychology and the Psychoses*. New York: Basic Books, 1952.

Flood, Anthony T. *The Metaphysical Foundations of Love: Aquinas on Participation, Unity, and Union*. Washington, DC: Catholic University of America Press, 2018.

Francis, Pope. Apostolic Exhortation *Evangelii Gaudium* (November 24, 2013). Vatican website. https://www.vatican.va/content/francesco/en/apost_exhortations/documents/papa-francesco_esortazione-ap_20131124_evangelii-gaudium.html.

Frankl, Viktor E. *Man's Search for Meaning*. Boston: Beacon Press, 1992. Kindle.

Fraser, George A. "The Dissociative Table Technique: A Strategy for Working with Ego States in Dissociative Disorders and Ego-State Therapy." *Dissociation* 4, no. 4 (December 1991): 205–213.

Graziano, Michael S. A. *Consciousness and the Social Brain*. New York: Oxford University Press, 2013.

Gregory the Great, Saint. *Dialogues*. Translated by Odo John Zimmerman. In *The Fathers of the Church: A New Translation*. Vol. 39. Washington, DC: Catholic University of America Press, 2002.

Herman, Judith. *Trauma and Recovery*. New York: Basic Books, 1992.

Hermans, Hubert. "The Dialogical Self: Toward a Theory of Personal and Cultural Positioning." *Culture and Psychology* 7, no. 3 (September 2001): 243–281.

Hermans, Hubert, and Agnieszka Hermans-Konopka. *Dialogical Self Theory: Positioning and Counter-Positioning in a Globalizing Society*. New York: Cambridge University Press, 2010.

Hildebrand, Dietrich von. *Transformation in Christ: On the Christian Attitude*. San Francisco: Ignatius Press, 2001.

Jung, Carl. *The Archetypes and the Collective Unconscious*. In *Collected Works of C. J. Jung*, vol. 9, pt. 1. Princeton: Princeton University Press, 1959.

Knabb, J., R. Pate, J. Lowell, T. De Leeuw, and S. Strickland. *Lectio Divina for Trauma-Related Negative Emotions: A Two-Part Study* (conference presentation). 2022. CAPS 2022 Virtual Conference. https://caps.net/2022-conference/.

Kurtz, Ron. *Body-Centered Psychotherapy: The Hakomi Method: The Integrated Use of Mindfulness, Nonviolence and the Body*. Mendocino, CA: LifeRhythm, 2015.

Kurtz, Ron, and Hector Prestera. *The Body Reveals: An Illustrated Guide to the Psychology of the Body*. New York: Harper and Row, 1976.

Leman, J., W. Hunter, T. Fergus, and W. Rowatt. "Secure Attachment to God Uniquely Linked to Psychological Health in a National, Random Sample of American Adults." *International Journal for the Psychology of Religion* 28, no. 3 (2018): 162–173.

Maximos, the Confessor. *On Difficulties in the Church Fathers: The Ambigua*. Vol. 1. Edited and translated by Nicholas Constas. Dumbarton Oaks Medieval Library. Cambridge, MA: Harvard University Press, 2014.

Merton, Thomas. *The Inner Experience. Notes on Contemplation*. Edited by William H. Shannon. San Francisco: HarperCollins, 2004.

———. *New Seeds of Contemplation*. New York: New Directions, 1961.

———. *The Seven Storey Mountain: An Autobiography of Faith*. New York: Harcourt, 1948.

Moriarty, Glendon L., and Louis Hoffman, Louis, eds. *God Image Handbook for Spiritual Counseling and Psychotherapy: Research, Theory, and Practice*. New York: Haworth Press, 2007.

Njus, David M., and Alexandra Scharmer. "Evidence That God Attachment Makes a Unique Contribution to Psychological Well-Being," *International Journal for the Psychology of Religion* 30, no. 3 (2020): 178–201.

Ogden, Pat, Kekuni Minton, and Clare Pain. *Trauma and the Body: A Sensorimotor Approach to Psychotherapy*. New York: W. W. Norton, 2006.

Ogden, Pat, and Janina Fisher. *Sensorimotor Psychotherapy: Interventions in Trauma and Attachment*. New York: W. W. Norton, 2015.

Ornstein, Robert. *Multimind: A New Way to Look at Human Behavior*. Boston: Houghton Mifflin, 1986.

———. *The Psychology of Consciousness*. 4th ed. San Jose: Malor Books, 2021.

Ott, Ludwig. *Fundamentals of Catholic Dogma*. Translated by Patrick Lynch. Rockford IL: TAN Books, 1974.

Parnell, Laurel. *Attachment-Focused EMDR: Healing Relational Trauma*. New York: W. W. Norton, 2013.

Paul VI, Pope. Declaration on the Relation of the Church to Non-Christian Religions *Nostra Aetate* (October 28, 1965).

Paulsen, Sandra, and Katie O'Shea. *When There Are No Words: Repairing Early Trauma and Neglect from the Attachment Period with EMDR*. Self-published, CreateSpace, 2017.

Phillips, Maggie, and Claire Frederick. *Healing the Divided Self: Clinical and Ericksonian Hypnotherapy for Post-Traumatic and Dissociative Conditions*. New York: W. W. Norton, 1995.

Rowan, John. *Subpersonalities: The People Inside Us*. New York: Routledge, 1990.

Rowe, Angela C., Emily R. Gold, and Katherine B. Carnelley. "The Effectiveness of Attachment Security Priming in Improving Positive Affect and Reducing Negative Affect: A Systematic Review." *International Journal of Environmental Research and Public Health* 17, no. 3 (2020).

Satir, Virginia. *The New Peoplemaking*. 2nd ed. Palo Alto, CA: Science and Behavior Books, 1988.

Schwartz, Richard. "Our Multiple Selves: Applying Systems Thinking to the Inner Family." *Networker* (March/April 1987): 25–31.

Schwartz, Richard C. *Introduction to the Internal Family Systems Model*. Oak Park, IL: Trailheads Publications, 2001.

———. *No Bad Parts: Healing Trauma and Restoring Wholeness with the Internal Family Systems Model*. Boulder: Sounds True, 2021.

Schwartz, Richard C., and Robert R. Falconer. *Many Minds, One Self*. Oak Park, IL: Trailheads Publications, 2017.

Schwartz, Richard C., and Martha Sweezy. *Internal Family Systems*. 2nd ed. New York: Guilford Press, 2020.

Siegel, Daniel. *The Developing Mind: How Relationships and the Brain Interact to Shape Who We Are*. 2nd ed. New York: Guilford Press, 2012.

Steege, Mary K. *The Spirit-Led Life: A Christian Encounter with Internal Family Systems*. Self-published, CreateSpace, 2010.

Stone, Hal, and Sidra L. Stone,. *Embracing Our Inner Critic*. San Francisco: HarperCollins, 1993.

———. *Embracing Our Selves: The Voice Dialogue Manual*. Novato, CA: New World Library, 1989. First published 1985, De Vorss.

Teresa of Ávila. *The Interior Castle*. Translated by P. Silverio de Santa Teresa. New York: Image, 1961.

Van der Kolk, Bessel. *The Body Keeps the Score: Brain, Mind, and Body in the Healing of Trauma*. New York: Viking, 2014.

Watanabe, S. K. "Cast of Characters Work: Systematically Exploring the Naturally Organized Personality." *Contemporary Family Therapy* 8 (1986): 75–83.

Watkins, John. G., and Rhonda J. Johnson. *We, the Divided Self*. New York: Irvington, 1982.

Watkins, John G., and Helen H. Watkins. "Ego States and Hidden Observers." *Journal of Altered States of Consciousness* 5 (1979): 3–18.

———. *Ego States: Theory and Therapy*. New York: W. W. Norton, 1997.

Weiss, Bonnie J. *Self-Therapy Workbook: An Exercise Book for the IFS Process*. Larkspur, CA: Pattern System Books, 2013.

Whitfield, Charles L. *Healing the Child Within: Discovery and Recovery for Adult Children of Dysfunctional Families*. Deerfield Beach, FL: Health Communications, 1987.

Young, Jeffrey E., Janet S. Klosko, and Marjorie E. Weishaar. *Schema Therapy: A Practitioner's Guide*. New York: Guilford Press, 2003.

ABOUT THE AUTHOR

Dr. Gerry Crete has worked as an educator and mental health professional for more than thirty years. He has long been passionate about integrating principles of the Christian faith with effective mental health treatment and general wellness. Dr. Crete completed a bachelor's degree in history at Queen's University in Kingston, Canada, and a doctorate in counselor education with a cognate in marriage and family therapy at the University of Georgia.

Dr. Crete founded Transfiguration Counseling and Coaching (www.transfigurationcounseling.com), and his clinical specialties include the treatment of trauma, addictions, and anxiety disorders. He is a licensed professional counselor, a licensed marriage and family therapist, and an EMDRIA-approved EMDR consultant. He has received training in emotionally focused therapy, Internal Family Systems, Ego State Therapy, and clinical hypnosis.

Dr. Crete is also a former president of the Catholic Psychotherapy Association (https://catholicpsychotherapy.org), where he has often presented on the integration of faith and psychology.

With Dr. Peter Malinoski, Dr. Crete is a co-founder of an online mental health resource called Souls and Hearts (www.soulsandhearts.com), which provides mental health resources, such as online communities, courses, podcasts, and blogs for Catholics. Souls and Hearts specializes in developing psychologically informed human-formation programs and integrating the Christian faith with Internal Family Systems. Resilient Catholics Community and the Interior Therapist Community are two human formation programs informed by Internal Family Systems and grounded in a Catholic worldview.

Dr. Crete has hosted his own podcast, *Be with the Word,* and has been a recurring guest on Matt Fradd's podcast *Pints with Aquinas*. Dr. Crete has facilitated numerous retreats and workshops for various Catholic dioceses; and he has provided consultation for the Jesuit Conference of Canada and the United States and the Order of Cistercians of the Strict Observance (Trappists). He is a regular writer for Exodus 90 and has provided mental health meditations for the *Hallow* app.

Dr. Crete has been married for more than thirty years and has three grown children. He was born in Ottawa, Canada, and lives in Atlanta, Georgia.

SOPHIA INSTITUTE

Sophia Institute is a nonprofit institution that seeks to nurture the spiritual, moral, and cultural life of souls and to spread the gospel of Christ in conformity with the authentic teachings of the Roman Catholic Church.

Sophia Institute Press fulfills this mission by offering translations, reprints, and new publications that afford readers a rich source of the enduring wisdom of mankind.

Sophia Institute also operates the popular online resource CatholicExchange.com. *Catholic Exchange* provides world news from a Catholic perspective as well as daily devotionals and articles that will help readers to grow in holiness and live a life consistent with the teachings of the Church.

In 2013, Sophia Institute launched Sophia Institute for Teachers to renew and rebuild Catholic culture through service to Catholic education. With the goal of nurturing the spiritual, moral, and cultural life of souls, and an abiding respect for the role and work of teachers, we strive to provide materials and programs that are at once enlightening to the mind and ennobling to the heart; faithful and complete, as well as useful and practical.

Sophia Institute gratefully recognizes the Solidarity Association for preserving and encouraging the growth of our apostolate over the course of many years. Without their generous and timely support, this book would not be in your hands.

www.SophiaInstitute.com
www.CatholicExchange.com
www.SophiaInstituteforTeachers.org

Sophia Institute Press is a registered trademark of Sophia Institute.
Sophia Institute is a tax-exempt institution as defined by the Internal Revenue Code, Section 501(c)(3). Tax ID 22-2548708.